THE BEST
SPIRITUAL
WRITING
1998

Dog: multi-flex

THE BEST
SPIRITUAL
WRITING
1998

EDITED BY
PHILIP ZALESKI

INTRODUCED BY
PATRICIA HAMPL

HarperSanFrancisco
A Division of HarperCollins*Publishers*

flying
Car Hood Hwy   Convenience St - Car Mis-
Car - Durango Cliff   Security   functio
  Hairpin   former
  Turn   Drug manufacturer

Page 323 constitutes a continuation of this copyright page.

Grateful acknowledgment is made for permission to reprint lines from "Zurich, the Stork Inn" from *Poems of Paul Celan,* translated by Michael Hamburger (Persea Books, 1995; Anvil Press Books, 1995). Copyright © 1995 by Michael Hamburger. Reprinted by permission of Persea Books and Anvil Press.

Designed by Elina D. Nudelman

FIRST EDITION

Library of Congress Cataloging-in-Publication Data

The best spiritual writing 1998 / edited by Philip Zaleski; introduced by Patricia Hampl.—1st ed.

p. cm.

Includes bibliographical references.

ISBN 0–06–251566–7 (pbk.)

1. Spiritual life—Literary collections. 2. American literature—20th century. I. Zaleski, Philip.

PS509.S62B47 1998   98–12368

810.8'038—dc21

99 00 01 02 03 RRD(H) 10 9 8 7 6 5 4 3

Contents

PHILIP ZALESKI

Preface

Why an anthology of the year's best spiritual writing? Why such an anthology now? By way of an answer, I'd like to describe a recent walk that I took with a dear friend of mine, a Benedictine priest and monk, the superior of a cloistered monastery in northern Massachusetts. Like most of his brethren, my friend takes pleasure in his monastic dress, and his long black robes swirled around him as we ambled, on this windy autumn day, down the main street in the small New England town that I call home. To our surprise, it soon became apparent that his clothes were gathering considerable attention. "Looking good!" shouted a tattooed biker from a sidewalk cafe; "Wild outfit!" offered a teenage girl. By the time we had gone three blocks—the entire length of town—my friend had basked in a symphony of approbation. Then it dawned on me why his robes had drawn so much comment: it was October 31—Halloween—and his monastic habit had been mistaken for a splendidly conceived and executed costume.

Now this little anecdote tells us two things. The first is that our culture feels comfortable about religion and spirituality, relaxed enough to take religious garb as appropriate Halloween gear. This would have been unthinkable just one generation ago. The second hinges on the astonishment that my friend felt at the chorus of praise—for ordinarily he saunters down Main Street with nary a glance from the passers-by. He expects nonchalance, and for a clear and significant reason: religious dress, in a dizzying variety of styles reflecting the pluralism of contemporary faith, is commonplace in America again.

Last month I spent a few hours stationed at the corner of Main and Pleasant Streets, cataloging the religious wear that floated past. I saw crucifixes and yarmulkes, clerical collars and monastic robes, veils and prayer beads, spanning a globe of traditions— Jewish, Christian, Hindu, Muslim, Buddhist, Sikh. This colorful promenade shows just how pervasive spiritual symbol and practice have become in the contemporary American landscape. Gregorian chant tops the hit parade, angels soar up the best-seller list. Many mainstream faiths, especially those that call for intense commitment—Roman Catholicism, evangelical Protestantism, orthodox Judaism—are growing at an explosive rate. Islam, Hinduism, and Buddhism have become permanent parts of our nation's religious mix, while eclectic forms of spiritual life abound. This luxuriant flowering reflects the situation in the larger world. A few years ago, the greatest gathering of human beings in recorded history—upwards of four million people—assembled in the Philippines, not for a rock concert or a sporting event, but for a mass celebrated by Pope John Paul II. The Dalai Lama and other beloved spiritual figures are instantly recognized from New York to New Delhi. The conclusion is inescapable: we no longer live in a monolithically secular age. The crack-up of modernism is under way, and Enlightenment nay-saying seems curiously passe, an intellectual fad that, like Marxism, for a time hypnotized the world soul but now seems no more than a bad dream. The ghosts of three centuries of doubt still haunt high culture—one sees them flitting around in deconstruction, for example—but this too shall pass. Increasingly, the post-modern world is a religious world.

As one might imagine, this volte-face has been mirrored by a tremendous upsurge in religious publishing. Books on prayer, meditation, and mindfulness cram the shelves; armfuls of new religious journals appear each year; mainstream periodicals devote more and more pages to memoirs and confessions about the search for faith. Spiritual writing, at least in quantity, is entering its glory days.

But what about quality? Can spiritual writing ever be great writing? The phrase "best spiritual writing"—emblazoned on the cover of this book—strikes some as an oxymoron and others as redundant. Those in the first camp insist that such writing, no matter how skilled, can never be classed with high literature, that it falls under the same general laws that govern such shadowy genres as propaganda, pornography, or ghost stories: that is, the primary intent is extra-literary, to produce a jolt of erotic bliss, a frisson of supernatural dread—or, in the case of spiritual writing, veiled theology or arguments for conversion. How can one speak of literature, when the quality of writing is so irrelevant to the end desired? Those in the second camp agree that the phrase "best spiritual writing" is unacceptable, but for the opposite reason: all spiritual writing, they say, deserves the accolade "best," for it deals with the only thing that matters, the relationship between human beings and God.

This collection steers a middle course. I take the best spiritual writing to be prose or poetry that addresses, in a manner both profound and beautiful, the workings of the soul. Tilling this middle way, one needs to be on the lookout for exceptional gardeners. One learns quickly that some people speak with authority on the inner life, while others compose with flair; but to find the writer who combines both skills is akin to locating a ballerina who plays the horses or, rarer still, a horse that dances ballet. Yet persistence—and the incessant culling of scores of periodicals—pays off. Every piece of writing that appears in this anthology meets the twin criteria of literary merit and spiritual insight. After all, we are hardly at a loss for past masters to emulate. In every epoch and tradition, great spiritual writers abound, from St. Paul to Jalaluddin Rumi to Basho. Such writers almost never win literary prizes (as Thoreau put it, they address not the times, but the eternities), but they do win the hearts of those who love God and the life of the soul.

Our current cultural situation puts us, I believe, at an advantage in the production of good spiritual writing. As I said above, the post-modern age is proving to be much more open to religion than anticipated (one is reminded of Andre Malraux's dictum that the twenty-first century will be religious or it will be nothing at all). Yet much of post-modern culture, especially those aspects of it driven by mass media, remains under the influence of forces—materialism, consumerism, hedonism, moral and intellectual relativism—unfriendly to spiritual values. The upshot is a fierce tension between our highest aspirations and our cultural norms. This tension should produce some outstanding spiritual writing, for all great writing is born in struggle. This anthology, I believe, contains some of the fruits won in this battle.

The contemporary ferment in religion and culture pays a second dividend: the boundaries of spiritual writing have expanded greatly in recent years. Subjects that once seemed barren have become fertile ground for religious inquiry, giving rise to some of the best writing of the age: I am thinking in particular of nature writing, science writing, travel writing, and similar disciplines. In addition, writers who work within the canvas of orthodox traditions—and certainly this constitutes the great majority of spiritual writing today, as it has in the past—are demonstrating renewed intensity and vision. It may be too early to say that we are entering a new golden age of spiritual writing, akin to the sixteenth century or the Patristic era—our age has yet to produce an Augustine or a Shankara—but the signs are auspicious.

This inaugural volume of the year's best spiritual writing includes selections from twenty-three different periodicals. These range from long-established magazines like *Parabola* to new journals like *Image*, from well-known sources of spiritual writing like *Yoga Journal* or *Christianity Today* to unexpected well-springs like *Esquire* or *The New York Times Magazine*. In addition, several unpublished works make their first appearance here. Along with twenty-nine prose essays, the volume includes nine poems, for poetry, from the time of the Vedas, has ever been at the heart of spiritual writing. Very little journalism is included, for this is a volume of spiritual writing, not of reporting about spiritual subjects. Nor is there much in the way of spiritual advice; in theory such writing could be included, but most of the available material proved too saccharine or too inaccessible to readers outside a specific tradition. One hopes that this situation will improve in the future. On the other hand, memoirs abound. Spiritual writing, as Augustine reminds us, is almost always a form of confession. The definition of spirituality has been left deliberately broad, to encompass both an essay about Princess Diana and Mother Teresa and a report of sojourning into the darkness of the months-long Greenland night.

Submissions are encouraged for subsequent volumes of *Best Spiritual Writing*. Entries must be published in English, in an American or Canadian periodical in the calendar year preceding our publication. Please send writings to Philip Zaleski, Smith College, 138 Elm Street, Northampton MA 01063. The easiest way for a periodical to submit material is to add the Best Spiritual Writing series, at the above address, to their complimentary subscription list.

I wish to extend heartfelt thanks to the many people who have helped me to assemble this volume: to my wife, Carol, whose advice always delights and improves; to Patricia Hampl for her splendid introduction; to the many editors and authors who sent along so much good material; to my editor John Loudon and his assistant Karen Levine for their friendship and support; to my agent Kim Witherspoon and her assistants Josh Greenhut and Gideon Weil for help too plentiful to recount.

Introduction

We live, for good or for ill, in an autobiographical age. The memoir practically nudges the novel off the book review pages. All around us, the first-person voice murmurs its troubles and truths, punctuated inevitably by self-serving deceits. Blame Saint Augustine—he started it. His *Confessions* scandalized many of his first readers, but how could it be otherwise, given his intention: "Truth it is," he wrote, "that I want to do in my heart by confession in your presence, and with my pen before many witnesses."[1] And, in a discovery all spiritual writers must make, he found this truth could not be God's. It had to be his own.

When Augustine wrote his *Confessions* sixteen centuries ago, in 397, he bonded the personal narrative voice not simply to the story of an individual life but to the human search for transcendence. Autobiography, that literary form our famously cool secular age has claimed as its own, was born of a religious ache, and to the life of the spirit it ever returns, haunted and hungry for the bread that is not bread alone.

This passionate magnetism between personal voice and spiritual quest was consummated in the West's literature long before Augustine taught us to write autobiography. The Psalms, the West's great treasury of praise and fury, do not form a story, as an autobiography must. Yet the exaltations and complaints of the Psalmist bear in lyric form the same telltale voice of the bedeviled consciousness trying to claw its way out of the cell of the self:

Hide not thy face from me in the day when I am in trouble;
   incline thine ear unto me; in the day when I call answer me
   speedily.
For my days are consumed like smoke, and my bones are burned
   as an hearth.
My heart is smitten, and withered like grass; so that I forget to eat
   my bread.
By reason of the voice of my groaning my bones cleave to my
   skin.
I am like a pelican of the wilderness: I am like an owl of the
   desert.
I watch, and am as a sparrow alone upon the house top.
Mine enemies reproach me all the day; and they that are mad
   against me are sworn against me.
For I have eaten ashes like bread, and mingled my drink with
   weeping.
Because of thine indignation and thy wrath: for thou hast lifted
   me up, and cast me down.
My days are like a shadow that declineth; and I am withered like
   grass.

        —Psalm 102, KJV

The moodiness of the Psalms and the dizzy emotional compass
they describe call out with an uncanny contemporary voice we
instantly recognize. We may not have a c.v. note for the Psalmist,
but we know him. This is not the omniscient voice of the divine
speaking from his perch above us. This is our voice, the sometimes
elated, sometimes panicked call of the individual caught between
the glory of creation and the anguish of existence. On the one
hand, the Psalmist is overwhelmed with joy, bursting his lungs in
praise—"I will bless the Lord at all times." Then in a sharp rever-
sal, the soul which had been singing freely its sunny "new song" is

suddenly held captive in the dank prison of paranoid accusations, crying out against its "lying enemies," accosting God for His indifference: "Lord, how long will you thou look on? Rescue my soul from their destructions, my darlings from the lions" (Psalm 35, KJV).

This ancient lyric impulse, to praise and to lament, to exalt and to blame, is the schizophrenic, but protean, seed of Western spiritual writing. Even Augustine, when he turned in his middle years to the deep task of his *confessio*, opened the Psalmist's mouth, not his own, to begin his book: "Great art Thou, O Lord, and greatly to be praised; great is Thy power, and of Thy wisdom there is no number."

Though he was a man of faith, Augustine did not have the luxury of being a man of certainty. The opposite, in fact. When he wrote the West's first autobiography, he did not write a story that was an edifying reminiscence, nor are the *Confessions* a testament of triumphal conversion. Augustine was already ten years a baptized Catholic when, at age forty-three, he paused in the midst of a pressured, exhausting life, to write his book as an act of renewal. Like any midlife memoirist, he was using memory not to look back, simply. He had to look back in order to go forward.

Augustine was pausing to find himself in the mode of Dante's later midlife declaration that "in the middle of the journey of our life, I came to myself within a dark wood where the straight way was lost." Augustine's story reveals how strenuous the real spiritual life is, how often absurd. The spiritual story is the one in which the soul, finally aware of its existence, must bushwhack its way to its true home against perilous odds. "For," as Augustine says early in the *Confessions,* "Thou hast made us for Thyself and our hearts are restless till they rest in Thee."

This raw autobiographical urge may explain why strong spiritual writing (or perhaps simply *real* spiritual writing) is allergic to pietism. Thomas Merton came to know this when he looked back ruefully on the book that made him famous, *The Seven Storey Mountain*. In a letter he wrote in 1967 to a young student named Suzanne Butorovich ("one of your fans," as she described herself), he admitted that if he were to rewrite *The Seven Storey Mountain* he would "cut a lot of the sermons I guess . . . the sales pitch."[2] Merton recognized, as a more mature man and monk, that pietism is to spiritual writing what sentimentality is to poetry. His later work—*Conjectures of a Guilty Bystander*, for instance, and the sketchbook-like *Asian Journals*—are more sinewy, unpredictable, mysterious. They belong to the voice of uncertainty and search. The rigors and joys of monastic life had burned away the fat of his romantic religiosity.

The comforting absolutes and the complacent preening of the saved have nothing to do with the autobiographical business Augustine and his literary descendants accept as their task as spiritual writers. "My desire . . . ," Augustine says to God in Book VIII of the *Confessions*, "was not to be more sure of You, but more steadfast in You."

A telling distinction. The burden of proof is not God's, but the human soul's. For it is the soul in its life, not God in His eternity, who has a story it must tell.

As moderns, we are born into a tradition of disbelief. It is part of the ether we breathe, along with materialism, scientific method, consumerism, and an increasingly global network that makes it difficult for any religion to lay a universal claim on truth. No matter what our allegiance—to the religion of our ancestors, to a personal belief system, to nothing at all—the life of the spirit is not an assumption. It is a struggle. And the proof of its existence for a modern is not faith, but longing.

The legendary lament of the Psalmist (and of Jesus)—"My God, my God, why have you forsaken me?"—morphs in our own age into the cover of *Time* magazine, announcing GOD IS DEAD. Never mind that the statement was originally Nietzsche's, written in the nineteenth century. The cold emptiness of the words, over a century old, still feels modern. We are heirs to this uneasy atheism.

Emily Dickinson, whose poetry was written with the rhythms of New England hymns beating in her mind, expressed the chill of this disbelief early:

My period had come for Prayer—
No other Art—would do—
My Tactics missed a rudiment—
Creator—Was it you?

Our culture doesn't worry, as the Psalmist did, that God doesn't listen. We suspect He doesn't exist. Or rather we feel we can *decide* if God exists. For two people to begin talking about religion in America, in fact, often means quizzing one another on this point: So, do you believe in God? H-m-m. Well, *I* think . . .

It is a strange preoccupation, this voting for or against the divine. It may be entirely off the mark in purely spiritual terms. "Discussing God," Thich Nhat Hanh has written with the deceptive mildness of Buddhism, "is not the best use of our energy."

Easy for a Buddhist not to waste time wondering about the existence of God, the heirs of Western monotheism might say. But even Jesus was impatient with this question: "Why does this generation demand a sign?" he asks snappishly in Mark. Spiritual life "is not a matter of faith," as Thich Nhat Hanh says, "it is a matter of practice."

We live, in fact, in a startling paradox. While it is true that we moderns do not enjoy the spiritual security we see (or think we see) in the ages of faith that preceded our own, it is precisely our deep sense of not knowing that makes ours an age of great spiritual inquiry and links us to the enduring voices of mystical experience of all times, orthodox or otherwise. When Emily Dickinson admits she lacks a "rudiment"—God himself—for her prayer, she has kicked out the side of the pristine white frame chapel in Amherst where everyone else is sitting with folded hands. She has entered the "Vast Prairies of Air" that lead to the "Infinitude" that has "no Face." It is here, finally, she says simply, without embarrassment, "I worshipped." Perhaps the greatest spiritual poem in American literature, Wallace Steven's "Sunday Morning," is about *not* going to church.

There is much beauty—and horror—in the world. It keeps us busy. Why seek beyond it? Because we can't help it, of course. It may be that, at least in the modern context, only an irreverent age can produce authentic spiritual writing. Only a woman drinking coffee in her nightgown on Sunday morning, avoiding church, can talk to us convincingly, passionately, of "the tomb in Palestine."

The author of the medieval mystical treatise, *The Cloud of Unknowing,* says the heart has "a naked intent toward God." That nakedness cannot be articulated by an institutional voice, nor by one upholding an orthodoxy. Even if the writer is in fact an orthodox practitioner of a faith, the voice must be individual, must be personal and inevitably autobiographical—though it reaches out for what will subsume it and render it impersonal and anonymous, absorbed by the oneness it longs to become.

It would be hard to find an age more populated with such individual voices than our own. The very absence of faith has exposed the raw longing at the heart of life. We are a people who cannot get enough of self-help books (the sermon literature of our day), of meditation guides, accounts of spiritual journeys, and spiritual autobiographies. The very term "spiritual journey" has become a cliché precisely because it is so apt. This is travel writing about a foreign land we long to reach ourselves because we know it to be home.

The Psalmist's great caution, clanging down the millennia, says that "the fool says in his heart there is no God." Presumably even the Psalmist (and certainly the modern rationalist) can imagine someone claiming, "There is no God." Such a statement gleams with the bold surface evidence of the mind. But when a person says "in his heart" that there is no God, he does not simply deny God. He refuses the evidence of his own capacity for wonder. That seemingly modest phrase—*in his heart*—is the fulcrum of the Psalmist's insight. The heart is the intersection of reality and consciousness, the spark point of awe.

Even Augustine, bishop though he was, knew the ache of uncertainty we consider so modern, so our own. Early in the *Confessions* he poses a problem that has a familiar ring: "It would seem clear," he says delicately, "that no one can call upon Thee without knowing Thee." He is touching the sore point of God's invisibility and distance, His none-ness.

Then Augustine makes a bold move: "May it be," he asks, "that a man must implore Thee before he can know Thee?" With this daring question, he sets the tone for Western spiritual writing from his time to our own. His brilliance, which is also his humility, was to understand he could seek his faith *with* his doubt, not in opposition to it.

For Augustine, prayer is not ritual or pious gesture. Prayer is a way of thinking; indeed, the most immediate and nuanced way of thinking. His address to God in the *Confessions* has lived through the centuries because of the extraordinary intimacy of its voice, the palpable sense of a man thinking his most private thoughts on the page in the form of a prayer. Augustine's prayer is the acute focus of his entire self on the truest longing he recognizes in his heart. Prayer is his articulation of wholeness and his acknowledgment of brokenness. It is what he said he would seek at all costs: truth. There is no question of waiting for proof of God or proof of a spiritual realm. He must respond to the instinct thrumming within: he must acknowledge the life of the spirit. He must pray.

Evil, too, has proved to be an engine of spirituality—another paradox of the spiritual life, a cruel one. The Holocaust, the Gulag, the killing fields—the numberless ways we have found to humiliate and massacre one another in the twentieth century. And still, out of impossible circumstances and radical suffering, the testimony comes, rising up past the smoke and ashes. It would be too crude to call such writings—the diaries and memoirs, the fragmentary poems from the camps and transports—"triumphs of the human spirit." They constitute appalling evidence of smashed lives. But it is also true that they are documents that advance the meaning of spiritual writing in our times.

It goes without saying that spiritual writing is not about God. It is about the human longing for all that God can mean. It may be possible to be an atheist, but it is probably impossible, once alive, not to respond to the presence of something—soul, spirit, life-force, you name it—that is the human core from which the cry of anguish and the whoop of joy emanate. The sheer instinct to record these experiences of extremity is, in itself, a spiritual act. It may account for the reason that a little girl's diary is the single most eloquent voice of the Holocaust. Anne Frank did not only say that, in spite of everything, she believed people were good at heart. She also wrote—this child—"I hear the approaching thunder that, one day, will destroy us too, I feel the suffering of millions." The gravity and clarity of this writing moves well beyond the spiritual into the prophetic.

Another Jewish girl was writing a diary in Amsterdam at the same time. Her name was Etty Hillesum. She was older than Anne Frank, a bright, sophisticated graduate student in her mid-twenties, living on her own, carrying on two love affairs, watching with growing alarm as the world destroyed itself all around her. Her diary has been published under the title *An Interrupted Life.*[3]

In the midst of the political horror and her personal chaos, Etty Hillesum underwent, apparently to her surprise, what can only be called a conversion experience. It was a modern conversion: not "to" something specific, but into a frame of consciousness that changed all experience utterly and made her see the abyss she and Anne Frank were being thrown into with eyes fully open. "When I pray," she writes, "I hold a silly, naive or deadly serious dialogue with what is deepest inside me, which for convenience' sake I call God."

She knew her life had turned upside down. "The girl who could not kneel but learned to do so" is how Etty Hillesum describes this conversion experience. "Such things," she writes of this "kneeling," "are often more intimate than sex. The story of the girl who gradually learned to kneel is something I would love to write in the fullest possible way."

She began to pray and wrote about praying, this modern girl who had first sought out a therapist, turning to psychology before the life of the spirit found her. (She went to bed with her therapist—of course: her passion was immense.) The more she prayed, the more her life turned to the life of her times. "I feel like a small battlefield," she wrote, "in which the problems, or some of the problems, of our time are being fought out. All one can hope to do is to keep oneself humbly available, to allow oneself to be a battlefield."

Her diary became more and more a place for her to ponder her spiritual life. "Ultimately," she wrote, "we have just one moral duty: to reclaim large areas of peace in ourselves, more and more peace and to reflect it towards others. And the more peace there is in us, the more peace there will also be in our troubled world."

Like Anne Frank, whom of course she never knew, Etty Hillesum met the fate of her people—as she came to expect. She died in Auschwitz in November 1943. Her luminous writing does not reveal some secret radiance in suffering, some magic act of the murdered. It does not suggest that "after all" good triumphed. She, irreplaceable as all the others were irreplaceable, died. Paper—her diary—happened to survive. The survival of such documents of the human spirit must be read first as indictments, not as triumphs. But for a girl's diary to be read as a political and moral indictment does not deny its spiritual power. Such testimonies—the poems of the great Jewish poets of the Holocaust Nelly Sachs and Paul Celan, the memoirs of Primo Levi—extend the meaning of the spiritual. They remind us that the journey is to history's hell as well as to our imagined heaven. And that the voice of the spirit is always a singular human being, a beloved creature lost forever, consigned by blind hatred to oblivion. The voice is personal, interior. This most intimate voice ("more intimate than sex," as Etty Hillesum wrote) only proves the inevitability of spiritual meaning even in the hideous cauldrons of history.

There is no end to the human habit of finding meaning. As Paul Celan wrote in a poem to Nelly Sachs:

Of your God was our talk, I spoke
against him. . . .

Your eye looked on, looked away,
your mouth
spoke its way to the eye, and I heard:

We
don't know, you know,
we
don't know, do we?,
what
counts.[4]

And not knowing, there is only one thing for the spirit to do:
write it.

ENDNOTES

1. Passages from Augustine are from *The Confessions,* translated by
   Maria Boulding, O.S.B. (Hyde Park, NY: New City Press, 1997).

2. Quoted in Michael Mott, *The Seven Mountains of Thomas Merton*
   (Boston: Houghton Mifflin, 1984).

3. Etty Hillesum, *An Interrupted Life: The Diaries of Etty Hillesum,
   1941–1943,* introduced by J. G. Gaarlandt, translated from the Dutch
   by Arno Pomerans (New York: Pantheon Books, 1983).

4. From "Zurich, the Stork Inn," in *Poems of Paul Celan,* translated by
   Michael Hamburger (New York: Persea Books, 1995; Anvil Press
   Poetry, 1995).

DICK ALLEN

The Canonical Hours
from Image

MATINS

Risen at this most ungodly hour, God,
When stars evaporate, grayness takes the form
Of mountain ridge and forest, small bats swarm
Into the eaves above our empty beds,
We who follow you, who have withstood
The self's preclusion in the reptile's dream,
Seam ourselves to you, seam unto seam,
And praise you and adore you, our wayfaring Lord.

Now as the young lamb knock-knees toward the light,
The infant wakes beneath smudged windowpanes,
When hidden colors of the woods and fields
Call back your strokings, to emerge as bright
Twists of flowers tousling dark lanes,
We hallow and hosanna all your sun anneals.

PRIME

We hallow and hosanna all your sun anneals.
Our faces touched, our bodies warmed, we sing
As shepherds to the hills, as fishermen who fling
Their nets upon the oceans when the light reveals
Vast schools beneath small boats that lift and heel
Before the wind. Lord, with your sun you bring

Such grace upon our world, such happenings
Of glory, were minds dancers, minds would reel!

We praise you who have given us this day.
The light itself is beauty, is eternal life.
No matter what shall happen, who shall fail,
Which prayers are answered and which fall away,
The darkness is dispelled, and on the Earth,
Grass, tree and mountain lie within your will.

Terce

Grass, tree and mountain lie within your will,
Lord whom we thank. We thank you for this chance
To once again bear witness, for the dance
Of light on water, for the hawk's high trill,
Roads in yellow woods, breeze or gale
That blows the pine and poplar east or west
Depending on your whim. Praying, we confess
We live within your grace by your avail.

But most we thank you, Lord, for giving us
Ability to love, to love each other, and
By practicing this love, to reach for you.
When lover and beloved reach across
Barbed wire or table and touch hand to hand,
A touch delivers what the heart holds true.

Sext

A touch delivers what the heart holds true
And we are penitent. Forgive us, while the sun

Stands at its highest and no shadows run
Before us or behind. The soldier now renews
His plea that you might blunt the sword he drew
And raised above his land. Forgive each man
Who could not follow what he could not understand
So followed others who professed they knew.

Forgive us, give us solace. We have sinned,
Who have not cared enough, who left
Too many tasks undone, who disobeyed
Your highest biddings, who would win and win
When you would bid us lose. Give us belief.
Escort us, in your kindness, to the weeping glade.

NONES

Escort us, in your kindness, to the weeping glade.
There, let your justice be dispersed as evenly
As we would wish dispersion of your mercy
On those lives brightening and those which fade.
We love and labor for you, Lord, who robed
Our world in light and darkness. Tenderly,
Treat us, Lord, that we may come to be
More than those who spend their lives in trade.

For your purposes, so far beyond our dreams,
We offer you ourselves. The only price
We'd ask you pay is let our teeming world
Continue balancing between the great extremes
Of roar and silence. Curse or bless
You Lord, we still shall call you Lord.

VESPERS

You, Lord, we still shall call you Lord
Though this might be the final setting of the sun
Into the hills. The work of daylight done,
Fields deserted and the tools all stored,
We gather now to listen to your word.
For others, for the others whose lives spin
Downwards more than ours, who may have sinned
Yet seek repentance, we would now be heard.

Comfort the old whose bodies are infirm,
Who thought by now that they might understand
More than they do, and yet are left
More puzzled than when crooked in parents' arms.
Help and heal and care. Reach out your hand
For those who can't reach back. Be Thou their gift.

COMPLINE

For those who can't reach back, be Thou their gift.
But for ourselves, Lord, for ourselves we ask
Light mercies, also. Show us truer tasks
Than those yet known to us. Although night drifts
Across our portion of the planet, you will lift
The darkness up again, and we shall bask
In sunlight when it ends—your cold death mask
Broken by re-dawning of belief.

We are as children now, who ask you guide
Us safely into sleep, and lead us through

The valley to still waters, pasture land
Green with the tall grass where brown spiders hide.
When hope seems ended, let us be with you,
Risen at this most ungodly hour, God.

MARVIN BARRETT

Climbing to Christmas

from Parabola

It is December 25, and I am in the chapel of St. Luke's Hospital in Manhattan. There, on the balcony, a handful of us are weakly singing the Christmas hymns: "Hark the Herald Angels," "*Adeste Fideles,*" "O Little Town of Bethlehem," "Silent Night."

Then the service is over, the chaplain and organist are gone, and we wait in our hospital gowns and paper slippers for our caretakers to come and wheel or lead us away: an old lady, another old gentleman besides myself, two worn-looking younger women, and a couple in street clothes waiting for news, good or bad. Someone begins to sing "The First Noel." We all join in a cappella, thin and wobbly, but on key and maybe just a bit defiant. For me there is a sort of cumulative miracle, unexpected yet emphatic, a shining package with the words embedded in it.

This was the same hymn that, three months ago, I was singing in the manger at Bethlehem. There were sixteen of us, students enrolled in the long course, "The Bible and the Holy Land, Home of Three Great Faiths," at St. George's College in Jerusalem. Fifteen were hale, strong-lunged, young Third World clergymen of many denominations from many places: Taiwan, Brazil, Hong Kong, India, Tahiti, Cebu, Zimbabwe. And then there was me, the ringer, recently retired from the Columbia School of Journalism and pushing seventy, who was barely an Episcopalian. With the manger all to ourselves, and although Christmas was still a season away, we sang.

Here is the sort of thing that had been going on all fall in a land where miracles were commonplace: a climb up Tabor, the Mount of Transfiguration; Masada (the funicular down, not up); up both ends of Carmel; Scopus, many times; Ein Gedi; the Herodium; a thousand steps up the Mount of Temptation (with my defective heart what was I thinking); up the slow slope of the Mount of the Beatitudes, looking the heartbreaking, miracle-strewn distance down over Capernaum, over Tabgha to the Sea of Galilee. Up to Belvoir, up the Mount of Olives—not, however, the seven thousand steps up Sinai, but instead looking up in awe from St. Catherine's, the site of the Burning Bush, to the red stone heap above.

Still, a lot of climbing. A pilgrim (I was after all a pilgrim) is expected to climb and to visit—a lot of visits, to caves, to tunnels and tombs, to churches and palaces, tels and crypts, Joshua's Jericho, John's Jordan, digs and open fields, Megiddo where (at the moment it seems quite likely) the final battle is to be fought, Nazareth, Cana (water into wine), Acco, Nebi Samwil, Lod, Safed, San Saaba, Gamala, Gadara (the maddened swine), Emmaus (the resurrection confirmed). The Judaean wilderness, pink and mauve, spread out before me with Bethany, the raising of Lazarus, Gethsemane, the Mosque of Omar, the Temple Wall, Calvary, and the Sepulcher somewhere at my back. Spots holy and not so— Sodom to the right as we rattle south past Qumran to Akaba—and everywhere a conviction of authenticity, that this is certainly where it all happened: the history, the prodigies, the miracles.

Now, the Holy Land behind me, it is as if the nurse's aide had put me in my chair with wheels, a blanket across my lap, and intentionally pushed me through all those bleak hospital corridors to a final bright eminence.

Those men in their green dusters with their masks, their bakers' hats, their knives and saws—I have survived them. It is a miracle reinforced, realized, riding on top of our thin, wispy patients' voices.

Nor is it so dire as all this obliquity would seem to suggest, to be back in the hospital, recovering, they assured me (and I don't doubt it, as they have been right before with two heart attacks and one excised cancer) from a quintuple bypass. Not dire at all, but quite homey. There was a long wait for surgery from Friday noon to early evening, the last Friday but one of Advent, and the last bypass of the week, with my wife, Mary Ellin, and youngest daughter, Katherine, filling the time singing, not the appropriate carols, but all the songs we sang on the long drive to the beach, from the country into the city, or to Des Moines—the six of us, four children and two grown-ups, in our tarnished gold Chrysler station wagon with the defective shock absorbers, singing "Blue Skies," "Don't Bring Lulu," "Let's Have Another Cup of Coffee," "Mean to Me"—until they finally wheeled me away on a gurney with creaking wheels and a thin blanket up to my chin, not all that scared, a molehill being pushed to Muhammad.

Later, Mary Ellin and the three clergymen given the right to visit in the recovery room would say I looked appalling, that I had as many tubes and wires hanging from me as a cuttlefish has tentacles, not a particularly pretty picture. And when they asked me how I, how *it*, felt, I gave them all a very cold look and said, so Mary Ellin reports, "Disagreeable," answering both questions at once.

Now, for the moment, they are gone—the tubes and wires, the clergymen, my wife and daughter—and across my chest is a kind of grate, as if, were it not there, my heart might escape, swell, and flap away. Yesterday at chapel and a little later it seemed it must do just that, swell and break through. But it was contained.

My breath is shallow. I shuffle like the old man I have recently been claiming to be: not pretending now, but the real thing. Tubeless and wireless, I look in my lavatory mirror, and the face is gray almost as death—but death departing, not homing in.

Sometime during the eleven weeks I was in Israel, Mary Ellin had her sixtieth birthday. Katherine and Benjy gave the party, their first in their new apartment on Washington Heights, and read my greetings from the Holy Land. I celebrated our thirty-fifth anniversary in a sleeping bag on the cooling sands of the Sinai, and when I was back in Jerusalem Mary Ellin phoned to tell me that Elizabeth, our eldest, was expecting a baby, our first grandchild, next May.

Coming up from walking Molly, our dog, in Riverside Park, I had felt a little odd, short of breath, slightly dizzy: not much to go on, a ghost of older symptoms. After climbing every mountain in the Holy Land, to succumb to a few steps up from Riverside Drive to Claremont Avenue, which was what I was doing, seemed ludicrous.

So I am back where I have been many times before. They have, I am told, split me open like a chicken, rearranged things, and sewed me back up, as good as new, or at least a lot better than I was.

Mary Ellin reports that her father called, asking, before she could tell him the latest development, to talk to me. He had just got the card I sent him from Jerusalem, and with that curiosity which at ninety-eight is still not satisfied, demanded an accounting of what was going on in the land of his forefathers. Mary Ellin gave him my current address. "Oh, my God," he said, which was, in my opinion, an appropriate response. The in-laws' flowers are conspicuous on the windowsill along with a handmade Christmas card from our artist son, and the animals from the Christmas stocking our middle daughter put together for me: a papier-mâché zebra, a glass frog, a stuffed seal. Beyond the pane, past the largest Gothic church in Christendom, a mountain in gray stone, are the pigeons, the peacocks, and the chickens, in the sun of the cathedral yard.

Temper the wind to the shorn lamb—where do the old enter into that prescription? Are the old shorn, or are they covered by the wool of experience? Are the bright-eyed and bushy-tailed young (certainly not a shorn image) the truly shorn, having not yet grown their winter coats? It is another of those sayings that flips under examination, and then flips again. Did this latest sickness, did my sojourn in the Holy Land, shear me or furnish me with another, thicker blanket? And is it more desirable, after all, to be shorn—better to be exposed than protected?

Indeed, at sixty-six should I have been camping out in the Sinai, in the sand in a sleeping bag, celebrating a distant anniversary with questionable food and drink? Should I have been staring sleepless across a dry, stony valley to a soaring cliff that could be, under an almost full moon, a sleeping city, a deserted monastery, or a derelict temple? Experience would seem to answer yes.

As the group elder I had been allowed to carry the cross into the Church of the Holy Sepulcher and read the meditation before the tomb. I had been the first to read the Scripture and designate the hymns to be sung in the red wastes of the Sinai alongside the beehive huts—"the tombs of the damned." "A jolly desert," T. E. Lawrence told Robert Graves. The Jews thought otherwise.

At St. George's College, I was not only the oldest but also the only one unordained. But no one among that group of young clergymen was likely to take back to their congregations on five continents more than I, speechless, took to an unwitting congregation on that chapel balcony at St. Luke's Hospital. And it seemed to me a fair and appropriate distribution.

The list for my last day in Jerusalem:
The Dome of the Rock
The Fountain of Sultan Qa'it Bay

St. Anne's
The Marmaluke Houses
The Abyssinian Chapel
The Church of St. John the Baptist
The Church of St. Mary Magdalene
The Tomb of the Kings
The Bethesda Pool

I got as far as the Damascus Gate, where I met a classmate, a worldly Australian destined for a lifetime in a monastery in England, who said that four Arab students had been shot by Israeli soldiers up north and the army was pouring into the Old City by the Dung Gate in expectation of bad trouble. I turned back.

In the Holy Land everyone has fertile ground for anger. The old. The young. The Jews. The Arabs. When I heard the grievances of the Jews, I felt sorry for the Arabs. When I heard the Arabs, it was the Jews I felt sorry for. Facing the young, I did not know what to think.

So approaching three score and ten I have managed a peak experience. Does a pilgrimage to Jerusalem and back make me a little short of being old? Pilgrims are of no particular age. But perhaps pilgrims who come back are not yet quite old. And now with my quintuple bypass I am back yet again.

As you move through life your hope in miracles, in luck, in happy accidents, in immunity, disappears, along with your dread of the opposite. The miracle is not something that happens to you—it is all around you, and you are embedded in it, moving through it, part of it.

Accustomed to limits, to guidelines, to markers, I stand here stunned, amazed. I haven't had such a sense of space since I was twenty—the splendor, and the terror of it. All that out there ahead of me, around me, to be explored, to be prospected, mapped, traversed.

The Holy Land and the operating theater are out of sight. For the moment the space is clear, and it is up to me to cross it.

The Heart of a Forest

from Audubon Magazine

This holy place—a core of the Heiltsuk nation, who live here on the mainland coast of British Columbia, at the edge of the world's largest remaining temperate rain forest—is being destroyed, and we have come from a long way away to try to help. We have also come with curiosity to see one of the most spectacularly beautiful places on earth before it is lost.

It is a place so beautiful that when it is gone, if it is gone, people will not be able to believe, if they happen across a stray photo or a yellowing book or magazine, that it ever existed—not on this earth, and certainly not in this century. The whites named it Ellerslie Lake more than one hundred years ago; to the people who lived here the previous ten thousand years, the Heiltsuk, it had been known as Quskas. We've come to help the Heiltsuk, but we've also come to be helped—to have our spirits and imaginations, our desire for beauty, stunned back into us.

If Quskas is lost—and from here on I will call it Ellerslie, the name that the provincial government knows it by, for that government's officials are the ones who can still protect it—then it will be a brutal blow to the Heiltsuk nation, taking away a core place of spiritual healing. Already, the salmon by which the Heiltsuk once lived are almost gone; unemployment is about 80 percent in the Heiltsuk town of Bella Bella; 50 percent of Heiltsuk children do not finish high school; alcoholism is epidemic. . . . The story of the West, the story of North America.

The Heiltsuk have made it clear that they have not really invited us here. We—the writers, biologists, and students of Round River

Conservation Studies, a Utah-based research organization and ecological field school—have gathered at Ellerslie to inventory it, to conduct a biological survey that may help save this forest from the timber companies and assist the Heiltsuk in their efforts to reclaim this place from the British Columbia government, which now controls the Heiltsuk's ancestral lands. The Heiltsuk are only letting us know what's going on, tolerating our presence in their place of healing during a time of sickness. We're here on our own, uninvited.

I do not want to understate the puniness one feels, coming as a guest into a land and a culture to "fight" for a place that got along pretty damn well on its own for the first eon. I do not mean to presume to have any fraction of power comparable to that gained by the living upon of a place or the blood ancestry of those who live here. I cannot speak for the Heiltsuk. I am not a Heiltsuk. I can speak only for what I see and hear.

We spend the first night in the only hotel in Bella Bella, a coastal town with a population of 1,500. The hotel is old and perched right over the bay; you can look out the window and see blue water and evergreen forests. You can stare for hours at that calm scene, watching the occasional fishing boat or floatplane come sputtering into the dock. Giant Sitka spruce trees tower along the granite shores, and bald eagles circle continually, screeching with that beautiful clacking sound—as if they were running their talons down a slate.

Dennis Sizemore, the founder of Round River Conservation Studies, and the writer Terry Tempest Williams and I take lunch at the rec room in Bella Bella—cheeseburger, milk shake, and fries—and we watch the eagles and marvel at the depth of the beauty. It is raining: water the color of the gray sky, mist shrouding the myriad humped islands, which look like whales out in the bay. As we head out of Bella Bella we drive past the town dump, where bald eagles are feeding.

Our guide, Larry Jorgenson, married into the Heiltsuk nation. His wife, Marge, feeds us some salmon before we head out to the lake—we'll ride several hours through frigid July rain. She and Larry show me the jars of salmon they keep in the garage for when it is their turn to host a potlatch—essentially a cycle of cleansing and nurturing, in which one family feeds and makes gifts to the whole community. The jars are labeled by date, locale, and species. Marge tells us that she can sometimes tell what river a salmon came from by its taste. The salmon runs are dying in the Pacific Northwest, and logging is killing them up here, though the logging industry protests that it is not to blame. At any rate, the salmon is delicious, and it troubles me, as a writer, to have to figure out how to describe in words the taste of something that will not be here in a hundred years. All the old nouns, such as *rain* and *ocean salt* and *sun* and *clean river* and even *meat,* fall away. How do you describe the way that the flesh absorbs so readily the smoke from the type of forest wood with which it is cooked?

We eat the salmon with our fingers—it is light and oily—and stare out at the rain. Eating it makes you feel as if you have at least one more day.

I don't see how Larry can pilot his little boat inland through the islands in the fog and slashing rain, but he does so eagerly. Our packs are lashed down beneath canvas tarps, sheets of water pouring off them. Larry's wearing a yellow slicker, and the water is pouring off him, too. Dennis, whose students are out there somewhere, measuring wild things before they are gone, sips coffee from a thermos. Terry lowers her head as if in prayer.

This is the place where the phone books come from: the northern hemisphere's greatest old-growth forest—spruce trees as tall as two hundred fifty feet, ten feet in diameter at chest height—some of it being pulped as filler for telephone directories. We've seen aerial photos of this country, and we know the big cuts are out there, behind the buffers. And even from the boat we can see the clear-cuts here and there—the soil thrashed and slumping, barren. I've seen this kind of devastation before; my little valley in north-west Montana, the Yaak, also produces big timber. But to see it done in a new land—right next to the ocean, with steep clear-cuts plunging straight into the water—breaks one's heart further.

Larry's not wild about bringing us here. He offered to do it, but so deep is his bond to the hidden lake that for another's eyes to gaze upon its beauty represents an encroachment, and he is honest in explaining his ambivalence. He's grateful we've come so far to try to help, but he's also painfully aware that for the situation to have gotten this dire—for him to show us one of the most beloved things in his life, to bare his soul—might indicate that the final damage has already been done.

Larry knows we're going to fall in love with this place, once we see it and spend some time with it, and that this place will become, in some way, ours, too, by our loving it. In a sense Larry is inviting us into the Heiltsuk nation—an act almost as significant as, at the other end of the spectrum, declaring war against the Heiltsuk and Ellerslie, which, in effect, is what the British Columbia government and the big timber companies did six years ago, when Ellerslie and the surrounding pristine watersheds were opened to logging. So far, Western Forest Products, the Vancouver-based company that holds most of the logging rights in this region, has held off on cutting Ellerslie. But the company is now poised to start logging in the adjacent Ingram-Mooto watershed, and the fear is that Ellerslie will soon be surrounded by a wasteland of clear-cuts.

We continue on, and Terry points out the marbled murrelets, shaped like little footballs, that are skimming across the waves.

Down in our country, where we've already clear-cut to hell and back, they are as endangered as northern spotted owls. But here the murrelets nest in the tops of the towering spruces at ocean's edge—and now their homes are in danger of being swept out from beneath them. An occasional salmon surfaces alongside our puttering boat: elegant, sleek, heading the same direction as we are.

Larry takes his time cruising the straits—passing beneath the dripping, moss-shrouded cedars, the Sitka spruce and western hemlock, the occasional twisted shore pine. We cut the motor and drift alongside the cliffs. The water is so dark, so clean. There is the sound of the heavy rain striking the water—the rain is streaming down our faces, and we can taste it every time we open our mouths to speak. But there is another sound, too—a stronger, more resonant sound—and as we stare at the cliffs at the edge of the dark forest, we realize it is the sound of water riding in sheets and waves down out of the forest, water flowing in trickles and rivulets from out of the mosses and from beneath the roots of the giant trees. And above that, more lightly, there is a third sound, a harmony of water dripping from the overhanging branches— water dripping steadily from the different stages of the canopy. Finally, we hear the hiss of creeks cutting their way down through the granite, back to the ocean, to the source. And we sit there in Larry's boat, rocking gently in the waves, and listen to the clamor: a thousand different instruments of water.

It was not so long ago—ten or twenty years—that these straits were filled with salmon, and the creeks and tidal inlets that ran down from these stony, forested mountains were stuffed so thick with fish that it was like a magic trick for a month or two each year, with the water turned to solid matter—as if the salmon were not *in* the river but had *become* the river.

We cruise on. Larry steers the boat into a secluded little bay, wipes the rain from his glasses, and stares into the forest intently, as if checking to see if someone's home, though no one's lived here for hundreds of years. Still, he shouts, nearly startling us out of the boat, to let the spirits or echoes of those who once were here know we are coming in, and coming not with greed or hunger but with respect.

We drift in as close as we can, drop anchor, and wade to shore. Right away we can feel the presence of those who were here before. Long carved poles that were once part of log lodges, the chiseled features obscured by moss and algae, by rain and snow, lie on the ground; here and there we find faint traces of carved logs, adze and ax work, but we have to stare long and hard at a log before we realize that it's been human-touched, probably hundreds of years ago. Some of the logs and poles are all but buried by the detritus of forest life—leaves, needles, branches, slow silt, moss—and very soon, in our own lifetime, almost surely, they will all be invisible; even now, it is only Larry's practiced eye that can point out these ghosts to us.

Round River has been working to help protect Ellerslie and its associated lakes and drainages—Ingram, Mooto, Polallie—for three years now. In the mid-1980s the Heiltsuk tribal council filed a legal claim to six thousand square miles of traditional lands, including territory that adjoins the Ellerslie watershed; that claim is now part of ongoing negotiations between the Heiltsuk and the provincial and federal governments. But the Heiltsuk are divided over the issue of logging; with unemployment so high, many Heiltsuk, especially the younger people, are far more interested in hearing about potential logging jobs than about the damage that industrial-scale clear-cutting can inflict on their ancestral lands.

As we head farther up the strait, we pass through a bottleneck between high cliffs, below the spot where an ancient chief once buried his daughter. The deeper we go into the heart of this wild place, the more we feel the stories rolling down out of the forest, like currents of cooling air. The forest is seething with them, as the rivers once seethed with salmon. And Larry does his best to accommodate us, to share the stories with us.

The shore to our left is where dozens of deer appeared one New Year's Day, during a blizzard. They'd been forced down out of the mountains by the rare snow—usually it just rains—and the villagers went out in their boats and shot them until they had enough meat for their people for a whole year; and then they returned home, with deer loaded on their boats and antlers piled up on the bows like the mastheads of old Viking ships.

Here is the beach, Larry tells us, where he once saw a single white wolf standing at water's edge in the falling snow. The wolf studied Larry as he rode past, and then, as Larry watched, six more white wolves, previously invisible in the snow, rose up and also stared back.

We stop for a moment beneath a giant cone of a mountain. There is a lake up there, Larry says, at the top of the five-thousand-foot cliff, where young Heiltsuk men would once go to dive for rock crystals that could heal the sick. It was rumored the crystals resting on the bottom had healing powers; and the young men would make pilgrimages to the lake and pick up the largest boulder they could lift, and then leap into the water, sinking quickly—plummeting, as their ancestors had for thousands of years. Finally, when they reached the bottom, they would spend a moment or two blinking wild-eyed, groping in the darkness, trying to touch one of those potent crystals, before having to abandon their ballast stone and kick hard for the shining surface above.

I know there are still people—a lot of people—who believe we can live in a world without stories and without salmon, but I have yet to meet anyone who believes we can survive without clean water.

The forest is "like a giant sponge," writes David Parker, a Canadian environmentalist and professional engineer. "Even a single old-growth tree can hold thousands of gallons [of water] in its roots and trunk, branches and needles." Numerous studies have shown that water flows have increased as much as 200 percent downstream from clear-cuts, resulting in floods; road construction on steep-sloped mountains, such as those in coastal British Columbia, has been shown to cause dramatic increases in the frequency of landslides. And the herbicides that are sprayed on the clear-cuts after the spruce and cedar are scraped away—herbicides designed to give the replacement species a head start over the forbs that some wildlife might eat—wash into the watershed.

The provincial governments in Canada have worked with international timber corporations to lock up most of Canada's forests in Forest Management Agreements, legal contracts that allow the companies to proceed with logging on public lands. And the cutting is proceeding at a frightening pace. The forests in the southern section of British Columbia have already been devastated by industrial-scale clear-cutting, and in the past few years the timber companies have moved into the temperate rain forest of the central coast, which encompasses twenty-six million acres of old-growth wilderness, including Ellerslie. Approximately one thousand square miles of British Columbia are being logged annually; at this rate, according to a report by the Canadian government, in as few as twelve years, all the commercial coastal old growth in British Columbia will be gone, except the minuscule amount that is protected in parks. That could jeopardize an estimated 120,000 forestry jobs, if something isn't done quickly to restructure the forest industry.

Actually, the provincial governments in Canada are already helping industry restructure, but with the aim of increasing stockholder profits, not the number of jobs. They have provided millions of dollars in loans and subsidies to the timber industry, enabling it to expand and blanket Canada with pulp mills. "The pulp industry is termed 'capital intensive' rather than labor intensive, meaning that machines and computers can replace the work of many men and women," writes Ann Sherrod, director of the British Columbia–based Valhalla Wilderness Society. "These new mills are high tech. Minimum education for employees is often grade twelve, which leaves out almost all native people."

Across Canada, much of the northern forest is being clear-cut. Many of the cuts fail to regenerate at all, due to the short growing season, poor soil, and lack of overstory shade. In Saskatchewan, when the forest is cleared, it leaves behind bizarre, barren landscapes—thousands of acres of bare rock and sand. An entire ecosystem flipped upside down, from life to death.

The timber companies come as they always do, promising gifts and jobs. But when the trees are gone, they leave; their operations are driven by shareholders, not spirit.

We are losing our places of spirit. We are losing our spirits. We are having them taken from us. We are standing by quietly as it happens, like deer pushed down by high snows to the water's edge.

Larry steers us into another harbor. The tide is out, so we anchor as close as we can and wade the rest of the way, hauling our gear. The woods swallows us, but there's one slender trail climbing from the ocean up to Ellerslie. We slip and stumble, hop across bogs of skunk cabbage and hellebore, tightrope-walk along giant fallen cedars. Ferns of all varieties lace the forest floor. From time to time we see wolf tracks.

We slog on through a kaleidoscope of green and black—electric green forest and black soil. Banana slugs glisten in the rain, gnawing away at the skunk cabbage. We spot yellow and black tiger salamanders and Pacific giant salamanders. There is an incredible smell of life amid the steady rain. It makes all manner of different sounds as it strikes the various types and levels of vegetation.

We are not prepared for the beauty of the lake, when we come upon it. The forest ends abruptly—it's startling to see sky again—and we are at the lake's edge, in a little cove.

If I cannot tell you what salmon tastes like, how can I tell you what it is like to see Ellerslie Lake for the first time? The rain has stopped, though low clouds and fog still hang above the evergreen mountains, and I can tell that any breeze will stir more water from the clouds, though there is no such stirring. I have never seen a lake as dark and still—resting—huge, untouched, and healthy.

The mountains plunge right into the lake. Islands of various sizes appear to be swimming in it, and the drift of fog tatters (there is still no surface breeze to touch the skin of the lake) gives the impression that the islands are moving. The predominant feeling you get, staring out at the lake and the mountains that surround it, is one of great peace. When you crouch to drink from the clear waters, you are drinking only two things: forest and granite.

Ten thousand years suddenly doesn't seem that long at all. The glaciers were through here just a short time longer ago than that, carving these mountains, scooping this lake out of the granite. Ellerslie Lake is perched so close above the sea—but it's one of the rare lakes the salmon could not reach, because of a waterfall, though they could pass beneath the lake at the foot of those sacred falls and taste it as they went past.

We slip our canoes into the water; we slip into the canoes and push off. The lake takes our paddles, and we glide across the surface amid silence—there is only the sound of the water trickling off the paddles. My God, it is so good to be alive.

The fourteen-mile-long lake is shaped roughly like a star with five arms, though from down on the water we cannot tell this; we can see only that it is immense. If it were not for the trickling of that water rolling off the blade of our paddles, and the soft cutting sound of the canoe's bow veering through the dark still water, we might not be convinced that we weren't imagining it all.

This is what salmon taste like, I think.

The Round River students are camped about midway down the lake, on a puny little sand beach whose whiteness, even on this overcast purple day, is made more brilliant by the dark cedars at the beach's edge. As we come closer we can see the bright primary colors of the canoes beached there, and our hearts leap, drawn as always by the opposite braid of solitude—community, and the tribe—and we paddle for a long time toward those tiny spots of color. The thin blue wisp of smoke from a campfire appears after a while. A handful of tents. The students have been here about a month, trying to quantify magic—or biodiversity, as it is commonly called—but also trying to qualify it, to *feel* it.

It's evening, and the group is cooking supper at the campfire. I recognize the field instructors from other Round River camps: Chris Filardi and Jerry Scoville. The students are excited to hear the ecology lessons and all the stories. There's no real way to prove that the students' passion for this place—their learning about it, their falling in love with it—can help save it. There's no real way to prove that an invisible thing like passion can help hold together something that is healthy—as the salmon and clean rivers once held these mountains together—or even stitch back together something that has been injured. But this is really the only card that we've got to play.

Larry tells us that tomorrow one of the Heiltsuk elders, Ed Martin, will be coming out to the lake with his grandson Benny to stay for a while; there is some healing that needs to be done. It is not my place to say what kind of healing or to enumerate the hardships and sorrows that Ed, now sixty-six, has witnessed. Let me say only that he is coming now to the lake to rest and that he has agreed to talk to us about medicinal plants and the watershed's importance as a place for healing. Dennis Sizemore's son, Paul, has come on this trip, too, and as it's his sixteenth birthday tomorrow, Ed is going to give him a blessing.

We spend the next day exploring. We strike out in canoes in different directions, determined to see and love and begin to measure what we can of this place. Some students paddle south to check on the remains of a wolf-killed deer they found—to count and sort tracks, and perhaps to glimpse the wolves. Others ride with Larry over to the west end to look at ancient ochre pictographs on cliffs that hang right over the lake, so close to the water that the artists must have had to stand up in their canoes to paint them: circles, sunsets and sunrises, thunderbirds.

Others of us head north, to the beach where a wolverine charged Jerry Scoville earlier in the summer. Jerry was paddling toward shore, still a good fifty yards away, he says, when the wolverine came running out of the bushes, snarling and hissing. It paced up and down the beach, spitting and growling, and Jerry thought it was on the verge of coming after him, not content simply to defend its beach, but desiring to swim out to his canoe and get him. Jerry turned around and paddled back to deeper water—checking over his shoulder all the way home, as if the wolverine might still be following him, like a bad dream.

We beach the canoes near an inlet at the mouth of the Polallie Valley, on the north side of Ellerslie, which, through an agreement between the provincial government and Western Forest Products, is scheduled to be clear-cut, its forest stripped from the face of the earth. We wander into the woods, following a trail worn by the feet of animals. Deer bones everywhere. We move upstream along a blood red creek, tannin tea—you can see the sand bottom of it, twelve feet down—and discover, in the root caverns of an immense spruce, an intricate series of old wolf dens: old bones, old hair, old scat. It is a lovely sight and a disorienting one, to look up at the giant spruce and then to look beneath its exposed roots and picture wolves swarming and seething there, as if they had emerged from the soil itself, simply another part of the forest.

We lie there to rest for a moment. Our faces are gold and green beneath the canopy. *Can we protect nothing? Must every place of beauty—if there are trees on it—be erased?*

Back at camp we dry our clothes as best we can by cedar smoke beneath the communal tent. The storm passes—coppery columns of light work their way down through the remaining clouds—and for the first time, the mile-high slab of sunstruck cliff is revealed.

We sit at the edge of the lake and watch the sunlight flow across the cliff, light painting itself across the naked rock. It's the largest cliff face I've ever seen. It gives shelter to the lake and its surrounding forest. Larry has been fishing and has brought back two large cutthroat trout, taken from his favorite secret spot in the lake. Some of the students have gathered tart huckleberries for a pie. Terry has spent the morning down below the falls, back out at the ocean's edge, and has netted some crabs. We sit on driftwood at the edge of the beach and eat lunch thankfully.

Later in the afternoon we see a boat approaching from far off. We watch for a long time as the boat remains tiny, the figures in it indistinguishable. Finally, closer to dusk, the boat is near enough for us to see a man standing. "Ed," Larry says, smiling, as Ed Martin and his grandson Benny, a bull of a young man, finally glide into shore, also smiling. We wade out to pull them in.

It's been a long time since he's been to the lake, Ed says, and he wants to show it to his grandson while it is still intact. We're all overjoyed when Ed and Benny come wading bare ankled through the cold water and up onto the beach, where our fire is popping. I think we feel, every last one of us, as if we have been house-sitting a beautiful home and now the owner—as much as a heart can own anything—has come home.

Around the campfire that night, the lesson for the Round River students is on biodiversity, followed by some prose and poetry reading. Ed and Benny rise and tell us goodnight, then get back in their boat and pole out toward the little forested caprock island a few hundred yards offshore, where they will spend the night. In the morning they're going to build a little camp shelter on it—a lean-to. They aim to stay here until Ed feels better.

In the morning the students are up early and soon disappear into the woods. I sit by the lake in a shaft of sun and wait for the clouds to return from their almost-hourly shuttle to the ocean and back. I nap like an octogenarian in that brief sun, beneath the wall of the giant cliff. In my half-sleep I can hear Ed and Benny sawing and hammering, building their lean-to, their recovery room. I feel the lake's huge horizontal solace lying in and over my heart, and I feel my own recovery.

A fisheries biologist had the idea of turning Ellerslie into a salmon nursery, to help beef up the declining salmon runs: to put an artificial fish ladder on the sacred falls below so the salmon could make it up to the lake and breed in great numbers. The lake's trout population would have to be killed off to allow the salmon into this place. Perhaps it could be a way to "save" the lake and the surrounding watershed: If Ellerslie were a nursery for baby salmon, then perhaps no clear-cutting would be permitted around it, because the sedimentation and runoff would destroy the fishery.

But must a thing be utilitarian—able to be measured with the span of a crescent wrench—to remain in the world, here at century's end?

The students return from the woods and don their life jackets, climb into their canoes and kayaks, and set out upon the lake. I decide to go for a hike up the creek. I want to see its headwaters, if possible. All morning I hike upstream, up a cataclysm of boulders, through cool woods. The cedar forests are the most magical. Sometimes I come to strange little clearings where columns of sunlight pour down upon rain-jeweled skunk cabbages or carpets of red huckleberry, and I realize that I'm surrounded by giant red cedars that form a perfect ring around the clearing, as if planted there to create this rare sun cathedral.

Last night Ed told us that spruce and pine wood were associated with physical things, such as strength, but that cedar was linked to the spirit. I stand in the cathedral and know that he is right. Anyone could know it, I think, if they'd just pause and listen.

As I stand there among the ferns and skunk cabbage in that bowl of old light and look up two hundred fifty feet to the top of the canopy, I think, *Please, no. Leave Ellerslie, Polallie, Ingram, Mooto alone.*

Later in the hike, higher in elevation, I come upon some small bogs and lakes. Summer-nesting ducks guard their nestlings back in the reeds. Some of the ponds are filled with lotus blossoms and lily pads. A bald eagle follows me across a meadow stippled with bear scat. The bear scats seem to be getting larger as I ascend—and fresher, too. The trees are becoming wind stunted, and after a while I crest a saddle that separates the vast uncut expanse of the Ellerslie watershed from the steep, forested elegance of the Polallie Valley.

I walk along a spiny rock crevice, the wind gusting and swirling against me, trying to see the slender ribbon of the Polallie River. Western Forest Products wants to cut that valley, primarily for its giant Sitka spruce. But the forest directly below me looks overmature, a rich and rotting mix of green cedar and dead spruce snags. It doesn't look like it would hold enough timber to be worth the price of entry. But then I remember: pulp. Those spruce snags—the eagle perches, owl cavities, wolverine burrows—can be sucked into the shredder. They can simply pulp it.

I find a tiny patch of dirt tucked into the cliffs that is laced with the white hairs of mountain goats. I sit down in the goats' bed and watch the Polallie below, connected so intimately to Ellerslie and the Mooto Valley and the ice-blue and glacier-white jagged mountains farther north.

One of the hearts of the Heiltsuk nation lies below me, and any wild or healthy thing desiring to pass north or south of here requires this anchor point, this core, to make the journey safely. There is still some uncut country to the north. There is still, barely, some uncut country to the south. I like to dream that there is even a thread of uncut wildness trailing all the way down across the border to my battered little valley in northwest Montana.

It's windy. The sun is warm on my face and arms. I close my eyes but have the troubling thought that if I blink, then the Polallie, Mooto, and Ingram will be gone.

That afternoon, back in camp, Ed performs his blessing for Dennis Sizemore's son, Paul. Ed has gone to his favorite place—past the ancient pictographs, past the good fishing spot—and dug up some hellebore plants. Now, at the ceremony for Paul's sixteenth birthday, Ed lights the green leaves of hellebore and walks in circles around Paul, chanting, bathing Paul with the blue smoke. The rest of us stand motionless, focusing our attention and respect upon Paul and upon Ed. We watch, listen to, and smell, in the scent of the burning hellebore, the care and focus being given to this young man. Dennis's eyes glisten—he stands at a distance, for this is between Ed and Paul, between the lake and Paul—and the rising waters lap at Paul's bare feet. Now some tears glisten in Dennis's beard, sunlit.

It's as real as rock, or water: You can feel the love Ed has for young people, the love Dennis has for his son, the love the lake has for life. As recently as forty-five years ago—Ed would have been about Paul's age—such ceremonies, such love, were illegal under Canada's Indian Act. But like the wisps of hellebore smoke, perhaps, ceremonies and respect may be returning.

We breathe in the hellebore smoke; we breathe in the lake scent. We have participated in Paul's ceremony—three generations of us standing right here on the beach. I think again about the elusive definitions of *diversity* and *health*.

Later that day, Ed and Benny return to their little island and resume hammering and sawing. They'll haul a wood-burning stove over there in which to burn chunks of driftwood on cold mornings. The mewing of gulls and the wailing of loons will bathe them at night, as will the brief, crackling light of falling stars.

We spend a few more days in the grace of the lake before Larry takes us back to Bella Bella. We canoe to the north end of the lake, past the impassable falls, and hike through the woods, hurrying to make it out to Spiller Inlet and our appointment with the day's high tide.

On the ride home we see animals along the shore. They stand in the rain and watch us, and we watch them: a wolf, then later an ebony black bear in brilliant green grass. A flock of murrelets, and always the bald eagles, and on the rocks, the seals.

In the year to come, Ed will fall ill and have last rites said over him twice but will recover. A bacterial blood infection will strike Larry, and last rites will be said for him—but Larry, too, will survive, and as part of his recovery, he will come out to Ed and Benny's lean-to for a while, to sleep by the lake.

We pass through slashing rain, and when we finally reach Bella Bella the sky is washed blue again, and the white frame houses clinging to the cliffs are also rain cleansed. There is a clarity to the scene that is like the clarity, the cleanliness, in our hearts. The snowy-headed eagles line the cedars at the ocean's edge and watch us with gold eyes. The water laps quietly at the dock. A lone fishing boat comes chugging in. I feel—as I have rarely felt before—that the earth has paused.

Benny has ridden in with us to take care of some business in town. He's been exceptionally quiet all week, but now he volunteers to us that this is how it always is for him whenever he comes back from the lake. I'm not just imagining it.

It's been so long since I've felt this way that at first I do not even recognize what the name of the feeling is—only the deep and surprising quality of it. And instead of trying to name it, I just stand there and try to savor it, to figure out how to hold that peace in my heart—how to take it with me, if I can.

It is not until later that I realize what the name for the feeling was. It was the feeling of having a second chance—being given a second chance.

JOSEPH BRUCHAC

Call Me Ishi

So
you say
you found me
crouching
in a corral,
cornered by dogs,
dogs no less savage
than those men
who burned the forest,
hunted my family,
killing them
like rabbits driven
out of the dry brush
into long teeth.

So
you say
I spent my last days
dismayed
in one of your museums,
making arrows,
stringing small bows,
recording for you
those few stories
and songs I would share
of my people,
my voice

the last,
the final sentence.

So
you say
in books and with
the pictures which
move light faster
and with less sense
of spirit
than my dreams.

But
I say
call me Ishi.
It means
Man, I said.
It does not
mean
you.

And then
I died.
The last one
died.
So
you say.

But
I say
this story
does not

end here.
There is another
turn in this road.
This story
walks beyond
what you thought
to be the end
was only
a bend
in the trail,
the rest of it
opens
below you
like a deep valley
cut by
a living stream.

Now,
I say,
I am walking
here among you.
My voice
is not
just in the trees,
the whisper
of grass,
the departed spirits
of old ones
watching.

I am
in your cities.

My spirit
was not caught
in any
of your boxes of light.

I am
walking
as wind
learns to walk
through canyons
of shining stone,
clear stone
like ice
between
your eyes
and mine.

I sit within
the animals
who eat fire,
whose hearts
throb with lightning
whose breath
is smoke.

Call me
Ishi.
I can speak
those words
which you
do not

understand
either.

Camera,
television,
computer,
train,
automobile,
airplane.

Placed alone
on the land
you
cannot
make
even one
of them
as I can shape
with a knife from stone
a spear
or a bow,
hunt game,
make a fire,
build a home.

You say
you see me.
Drunk
on your streets,
weaving past
a pawn shop

in Gallup,
scoring crystal meth
in Sioux Town in St. Paul,
falling through
the doors
of a Mohawk bar
in Brooklyn.

So
you say.

Say my name.
Is it
Meadow Burned,
Meadow Green Again?
Is it
Waking Up
to Dream Again?

You cannot say.

You
never learned
to say
my name.
The same
as your own.

Now
you are alone
on the land
I have sung

you there.
I say.

Ishi
Ishi
Ishi
Ishi

SCOTT CAIRNS

To Himself

from Image

When in scripture we first meet God,
apparently He is talking to Himself,
or to that portion in His midst
which He has only lately quit
to avail our occasion.

In prayer, therefore, we become
most like Him, speaking what no one
else, if not He, will attend.
A book I borrowed once taught me
how in the midst of attendant

prayer comes a pause when The Addressed
requires nothing else be said. Yes,
I witnessed once an emptying
like that; though what I saw was not
quite seen, of course. I suspected

nonetheless a silent Other
silently regarding me as if He
still might speak, but speak as to Himself.
That was yesterday, or many
years ago, and if it profit

anyone to imitate the terms
of that exchange, let the prior

gesture be extreme hollowing
of the throat, and inclination
to articulate the trouble

of a word, a world thereafter.

LÉONIE CALDECOTT

Reign of Flowers

from The Chesterton Review

As I walked down the Mall toward Buckingham Palace with my husband and children on Sunday, September 14, 1997, I couldn't help thinking of the A. A. Milne rhyme "They're changing guard at Buckingham Palace, Christopher Robin went down with Alice. . . ." A semisurreal chain of association, of the type we associate with G. K. Chesterton, began to course through my mind. The soldiers marching, the benighted royal family caught up in a tapestry of history that goes back to Henry VIII, the populace surging, equipped with the products, not of shady arms deals, but of Interflora, around the royal residences. Having observed the events of the last few weeks at a safe televisual distance, we had decided, since we had to be in London for my mother's birthday, to make our own firsthand pilgrimage to that palace, favorite haunt of children enamored of glorious pageantry, symbol of all that is secure and safe in our national ethos.

It certainly felt safe and secure. The place was crowded but extraordinarily peaceful. The dreaded automobiles were still excluded. It didn't feel like London in the 1990s. Minutes before, pigeons in Trafalgar Square had fulfilled my middle daughter's wildest dreams by flying to her hand without being coaxed and delicately picking the grain she offered them. Here at the palace, you could still smell the flowers, see the notes about Diana and "her boys." People drifted, reverentially, around the gates, talking. The extraordinary scene of English people being so unhurried, so courteous toward one another, so attentive to this privileged moment in their history, was persisting still. You could still scent grace upon the early autumn air. It was the feast of the Triumph of the Cross.

Still bemused and musing, I was struck by another oddity: Hindus in India turning Mother Teresa into a Kalilike goddess, wreathed in flowers, and the messages and posters attached to the palace railings (and, still more surreal, to the memorial of Queen Victoria) evincing the devotion of the populace to their own new-found "goddess." One large poster read simply "Diana, goddess of Peace and Love." "Is she a *goddess*, Mummy?" asked one of my daughters. Her elder sister saved me from this tricky theological conundrum. "Even Mary isn't a goddess, so it's unlikely that Diana is. But she was a lovely lady. . . ." I surveyed the mountains of flowers, such as might have adorned, in one's wildest dreams, a Corpus Christi procession. There was a picture of Christ crowned with thorns among the other cards, but it was a minority gesture at the heart of a different hermeneutic.

As I watched the flowers being slowly cleared away from the gates by a small posse of girl guides, I couldn't, however, find much sympathy for the impatient cynicism expressed by some at what they view as mass hysteria and threatened mob rule. John Henry Cardinal Newman, I reflected, would surely not have turned his nose up at the phenomenon of ordinary people expressing in their thousands their desire for something better, more loving, more beautiful than normally touches their lives in this daunting post-Christian age. After all, what does it mean when people start reinventing religion? It means that they are looking for a meaning, for something to bind the components of their lives into a purposeful whole, for something to bind their hearts to other human hearts. *Religion* means this: something that re-binds, from the Latin, *religare, religio*. Ironically, this is exactly what Diana herself was trying to do: to find a meaning, a purpose for her life. To this end the psychiatrists, the gurus, the advisers, the candles surreptitiously lit in front of—but we'll come back to that. And, yes, the love affairs with men who either betrayed her or, as it now seems, actually caused her death. Now it seems as though an entire nation is engaged in a love affair with her: the People's Princess, the Queen of Hearts. Diana has become the projection of a wounded consciousness; she has been recreated in the neopagan mind as a figure with which to assuage the scattered yearnings of a flock without a shepherd. She has been elected "Goddess of the Britons" by popular acclaim.

The Church, for her part, does not make goddesses. But she does make saints. It is worth pondering what actually makes a saint, and what function saints serve. In particular, in connection with all this, what function the actual flaws of a saint serve in making them useful to the faithful. The debate about John Henry Newman, and his agonizingly slow process toward canonization (shan't, won't, don't care, he seems to say), is one case in point. Or again, there are aspects in the character of Edith Stein, the heroic Jewish philosopher (who became a Carmelite nun and died in a Nazi camp) soon to be canonized, which do not appeal to me at all. Yet I still find myself praying to this woman, in circumstances where her qualities seem to be relevant. Then there's the case of G. K. Chesterton. Does he fit the canonizable mold? Oh yes, he'd say, if all a canon-ball need be is round. . . . But short of adopting the strategy currently in vogue and making him over as a latter-day Bacchus (any volunteers for the donkey?), we would do well to contemplate, if only for therapeutic purposes, the saintly quality of Chesterton. To my mind, this quality is displayed in his extraordinary compassion, and in his deeply courteous sense of fair play, which surfaces time and again in his writings, no matter how combative. It was this empathetic quality that engaged even the most unsympathetic interlocutor (witness the ritual jousting with figures such as Shaw). This is the quality of "radical outreach" that makes the great saints. Mother Teresa immediately springs to mind, of course. Just to show you that I am not simply paying lip service to the woman, I'll interject a swift personal anecdote.

The only time I met Mother Teresa was in my peace movement phase. The people who launched something called the Prayer for Peace had invited me to photograph Mother Teresa for them at the launch of the prayer at St. James's Picadilly, that famous haunt of liberal British religiosity. There was just one problem. They had also invited the press. I suddenly found myself, a timid portrait photographer, competing outside the church with the leather-jacketed pros from Fleet Street, replete with the latest reflex cameras and stiletto elbows. The organizers had not made special provision for me to photograph, or indeed to meet, the subject to whom they had assigned me. There was an agonizing instant on the porch of the church when they waved a hand at my direction and said airily this is so and so; she is taking photos for us (the point of this was that they shouldn't have to pay the Fleet Street photographers for their shots: I was, of course, working for free, for the "cause"). I had a straight choice: either say hello to Mother Teresa or ignore her and take a swift mug shot as the rest of the men (I was the only female photographer) jostled impatiently around me. *Carpe diem,* as they say. I chose the former option, grinning sheepishly and extending my sweaty palm. A moment later, the party had swept past me: the "photo opportunity" was lost.

As the prayer service progressed, I began to feel tortured. They were all praying for peace, but peace was not my lot. I had failed. I had failed to compete with the paparazzi, failed to deliver, failed in my duty to do my bit for the peace movement. I was too poor to afford sophisticated photographic equipment, but I had a nice Olympus OM2, with a shutter release that would waken the dead. I had also borrowed a zoom lens from a friend. So I decided to sacrifice dignity to the cause. Never say die. I crawled up to the front of the side aisle closest to the Saintly Celebrity, and I took aim. "Let us pray," said the Reverend Donald Reeves. "Clunk": my shutter reverberated around St. James's. Mother looked down at me, down there on the ground, faithfully serving the Cause at all costs. Her look was impressible. I swear she almost laughed. But her face was solemn. It was kind, too, but not given to *complaisance*. "What on earth are you doing down there?" those deep-set eyes seemed to say. Within a year or two, I had begged admittance to the Roman Catholic Church. I also swore to avoid the company of voyeurs, whether professional or amateur. Certainly, I have never forgotten that wordless encounter with Mother Teresa, and I envy Princess Diana her more elaborate conversations with her. She it was, acknowledging the dignity of those who in the eyes of the world seem to have lost it in their suffering, who inspired and validated Princess Diana's own aspiration to spiritual maternity. Thus the saints, canonized and not, have a marvelous knock-on effect in the economy of salvation. We get more camaraderie from them than we do from plaster-cast gods and goddesses.

"Lord, your child has understood your divine light: she asks pardon for her brothers; she accepts to eat the bread of suffering for as long as you wish and does not want to get up from this table so full of bitterness where poor sinners eat, before the day you shall ordain . . ." Thus wrote St. Thérèse of Lisieux, the centenary of whose death is upon us now. Some people were astonished that Princess Diana should have regularly lit candles in front of Thérèse's statue in the Carmelite church in Kensington. But it isn't surprising really. The *Sunday Times*, "breaking" the story the day after Diana's funeral, described the two as sharing a similar difficult childhood, a comment that seems a bit off the mark when we consider the loving ambiance of Thérèse's family. And yet, at a deeper level, there is an affinity between the great saint of Lisieux, who certainly had her share of emotional suffering, and the

English princess who died a hundred years later. Perhaps it was Mother Teresa, who slipped out the back door while the paparazzi-gaze of world opinion was focused obsessively on her young friend, who had told Diana to apply regularly to her Carmelite namesake. There is certainly a curiously symbiotic relationship among those who died in these early weeks of the fall of 1997. There was, for example, the great Hungarian conductor, Sir Georg Solti: perhaps he departed in order to organize a heavenly concert for the woman who didn't like only rock music. And there was yet someone else, who has received hardly a mention. That person is Dr. Viktor Frankl, author of the best-selling book *Man's Search for Meaning* and the founder of Logotherapy.

Dr. Frankl was an eminent Jewish psychiatrist who, like Freud and Adler (whose disciple he was for a brief period), practiced in Vienna in the 1930s. As the danger of Nazism grew, he refused to leave his post, and he was interned in a series of concentration camps, including Auschwitz. He lived to tell the tale: and what a tale it makes. Through his own suffering, and his observation of others struggling to remain human under the same infernal conditions, Frankl honed and refined his psychological observations. In its essence, Logotherapy is a radical departure from Freud's emphasis on the pleasure principle or Adler's on the will to power. For Frankl, the fundamental human drive is the will to *meaning:* the Logos, the Word. If men or women can hang on to the overall sense and purpose of their lives, they can suffer anything and remain sane. But once that sense of meaning, which is as unique for each person as their fingerprint, is stripped away, the human person is lost.

Some say that Diana needed religion. Some say that she needed psychotherapy. Amazing how fond people are of saying what other people need. Diana toyed with both, but they didn't quite have time to cohere. The best religious practice is the one that enters most intimately into the hearts of believers and enables them to make sense of their own particular circumstances. And the best psychotherapy enables them to analyze the mental processes that impede this—including the projections of most psychotherapists. I have the impression that Diana was not well served in this respect, and I am glad that Viktor Frankl, even if his genius was not at her service in her lifetime (who knows, perhaps she read his books, but they are not as well known in her country as they are on the other side of the Atlantic), at least departed on the same train as she did. Imagine it: the man who sat on those trains to hell now sits on a train to heaven with his ideal patient, whose life experience illustrates the universality of his theories, even for those whose holocaust was enacted in very different circumstances.

At one point in *Man's Search for Meaning,* Frankl quotes Dostoyevski: "There is only one thing that I dread: not to be worthy of my sufferings." Then he adds, on his own behalf: "These words came frequently to my mind after I became acquainted with those martyrs whose behavior in the camp, whose suffering and death, bore witness to the fact that the last inner freedom cannot be lost. It can be said that they were worthy of their sufferings; the way to which they bore their suffering was a genuine inner achievement. It is this spiritual freedom—which cannot be taken away—that makes life meaningful and purposeful." For when push comes to shove, Diana's real legacy concerns that wrestling with the angel that is interior suffering. Frankl compared suffering (with grim irony) to a gas, which, regardless of its amount, expands to fill all the available space. No one can say one person's suffering is greater or lesser than another's. This is a point that Mother Teresa made repeatedly when speaking to Westerners about their own mission field. She must have loved Diana partly because she was so representative of her generation, and of their struggles; and whatever you say about her, she did this very honestly and unashamedly. These reflections bring us back to Thérèse, who in many ways also represented her generation (a much more secure milieu, bereavements and oversensitivity notwithstanding). Except that Thérèse did something revolutionary with her own suffering: she universalized it, in order to include those whom the rest of us tend to think deserve to suffer—the murderer Pranzini, the apostate priest Hyacinthe Loison, and all the anonymous tormented souls on whom she wished to pour the balm of her own knowledge of God's passionate mercy. When her true mission began at 7:20 P.M. on September 30, 1897, she reached out also into our century: the century of atom bombs, genocide, mass abortion, the disintegration of the family, and the apostasy of millions. If she could take on these problems, she could certainly take on Diana.

So now that Diana is "on the team," so to speak, to whom does she reach out during this extraordinary period in our history? Even souls still in purgatory have their mission, as Dante made clear (funny thing, the pope was attending a reading of Dante the day Diana died, and he spoke about the Blessed Virgin reaching down to those who are struggling through their purgatories). There are, of course, all those people who lined her funeral route. There are all the victims of illness and violence to whom she reached out during her life. But I feel that she is reaching out especially to one very grief-stricken, courageous man, who like her has spent his life searching for love, for the deeper meaning of life (are not the two, after all, one and the same?). That person is her husband, Prince Charles. His role in ensuring that her funeral on September 6 was conducted with sufficient attention to her significance to the nation demonstrates the quality of the man—no matter what his mistakes and flaws. For this reason, I rather wish Earl Spencer, when he delivered his impassioned speech at Diana's funeral (which like most people I responded to—who wouldn't give their eyeteeth for such a loyal fraternal tribute?) could have tempered his indignation at the injustice done to his sister and his determination not to see her legacy rot with the flowers now composting the garden at Kensington Palace. Diana is dead. Charles is the sole surviving parent of their sons, and he is united to Diana by more than just blood. He is united to her by a crucifying, unbearable suffering. He remains here, still with us, to carry forward the lessons that her life implies, not just for the royal family, but for a giddy, gossiping, sensation-seeking nation, stopped in its track by the shock of Diana's untimely death under the flashlights of the relentlessly curious public eye. The very propaganda war waged between Charles and Diana themselves contributed horribly to the paparazzi syndrome, as Diana realized after her disastrous television interview. Now, I am certain, she wants the hurt that was done not only to herself, but to Charles, to be healed, and good to come of it all.

This is what the celestial "team" says, and this is what Diana, being irrevocably seconded onto that team, asks us to do, so that her sufferings may not be in vain. That we support, in particular, the man, the future king, with whom she was unable to make common cause in this vale of tears. That we support him with a compassion that respects the "logos" of his life, of his role, and of his unique contribution—above all, that we support him with prayer, not as the pharisees do ("God bless the adulterous so and so, may he learn from his mistakes"), but as followers of Thérèse: with a burning, unconditional love, the kind of love that exists only in the Heart of Thérèse's Master. For if Diana, in death, was worthy of Cardinal Hume's loving tribute, why can we not show the same largesse to the man, whom she was originally intended to assist, in life? Must we always wait until we are contemplating the wreckage of all earthly hopes before we behave as Jesus wants us to? What do we stand for: sacrifice, or a mercy whose quality is not strained?

STEPHEN V. DOUGHTY

A Readiness Remembered

from Weavings

Better than thirty years have passed since the summer I spent as their guest. Officially, I was their "summer student pastor," but "guest" comes much closer to the reality. They provided me with lodging, more food than I could eat, and more encouragement than I merited. Though my stated duty was to instruct and guide them, it was ultimately they, the entire congregation, who instructed and guided me. I suspect some of them knew all along that it would be this way.

Certain basics of their life stood firmly in my mind before I ever arrived in town. Their church, nestled in New England's Green Mountains, shut down in the winter. The congregation could not afford a year-round pastor. All they were able to manage was, for the summer, a seminary student with my level of experience (none) and then lay preachers into the fall. After the lay preachers came freezing weather and heating bills that even in the 1960s were too high to pay. The congregation itself, I understood, would be an unusual mix: well-off summer folk from the suburbs and cities of southern New England plus year-round residents who eked out their livelihood doing whatever they could.

"You'll find good, solid folk," I was told. The denominational official who said that spoke like he meant it. So this much I knew when I went there: good people; a somewhat unusual blend; a church open for worship part of the year; a congregation willing to take on someone, well, like myself. These things I held in mind, along with considerable excitement about the chance to be out of the classroom and on my own.

What I did not know was the rich gift that would come through this body of persons. That arose from the congregation over the next ten weeks and has continued to press itself upon me in all the years since. It came not in one way but in many. As I revisit it in my mind, I still find it too full, too ample to be defined by any single incident. And yet for all the different angles from which I have viewed the gift over the years, I am finding now it comes to sharpest focus in the gentle interplay between a stump sitter, a man who laid down his tools, and a widening circle.

The Stump Sitter

Let me start with the fellow who knew how to sit on stumps. He was only nine years old but had already become something of a prodigy at it.

My assigned dwelling for the summer was with two older women in the community. The first morning I did what I continued to do through the rest of the summer. I jogged down their driveway, along the dirt road running through the center of town, and up toward the church. And it just so happened that there he was on a stump out in front of his house, not far from the church. He was small, blond, barefoot. I waved. He sat as motionless as the stump itself, except that he turned his head slightly to watch this strange bit of business scurrying past.

The same thing happened the next morning. I jogged and waved; he watched. And so on the next morning, and the next. Unknown to me, though, something was building, and on the fifth morning it broke. As I approached his stump, the young fellow suddenly thrust an arm forward, pointed sharply at me, and called out, "You! Before this summer is over I'm going to teach you how to sit on a stump!" The slightest hint of a smile broke around the corners of his mouth. I nodded, smiled back, and kept on jogging.

When I got inside the church office certain images started to move through my mind. They were of the self-flattering type: "young minister befriends neighborhood child," and "young minister sits on stump."

The sad truth, however, is that I never took the boy up on his offer. We became friends. We laughed. We talked as much as his shyness and my awkwardness would allow. But, alas, not once did I ask, "How *do* you sit on a stump?" and then go ahead, receive of his expertise, and just sit for however long he felt a novice could take it.

The omission was my loss. I have no idea where this person is now. He must be about to charge into middle age, if that is the proper way to put it. I was middle-aged myself before I realized he was on to something I much needed to learn. Wherever he is, I am sure he is still way out in front of me.

THE MAN WHO LAID DOWN HIS TOOLS

It was midsummer now. As I recall, he not only put down the hammer he was using, he unbuckled the belt that held all manner of other tools tight about his waist. He laid the belt on his workbench and took seven or eight steps directly toward me.

Half an hour before, I had been in the office at the church. A knock came on the door. It was one of the summer residents, a jolly woman who, it had turned out, was aunt of a friend of mine in seminary. We had laughed at the discovery and at tales of seminary and at tales she told me of her nephew. Her face now was drawn.

"Steve," she said in direct and measured tones, "we just had a call from your parents. Your grandmother has had a stroke. It's not good. Your mother and father are driving on from Chicago. They said you would want to know. They thought maybe you would want to be there, too."

My grandmother lived in western Massachusetts. We had eaten dinner together every Sunday all four years I was in college. The whole family had gathered for her ninetieth birthday just six weeks before. When the cake, with ninety candles on it, caught fire she had laughed harder than any of us.

Yes. In my parent's phrase, I "wanted to be there, too."

I thanked my new friend for telling me. I went outside, got in my car, and drove off to ask the chair of the congregation if I might have some time away. He was a carpenter, year-round resident, and right now he was building an addition on the home of a summer family.

"Ed." I spoke his name through the open walls of the addition. The sun was bright and shone on his white hair. Normally he would have turned, smiled, given a few more licks with the hammer, or finished sawing a board.

"Ed." I am sure I said his name only once and not very loud. He looked directly at me. Then, without hesitation, he put down the hammer, laid aside his tool belt, and walked directly toward me.

After my explanation of why I was there, words followed from him. Kind words. I certainly could have time away, as much as I needed. Don't worry about Sunday. "Don't even think about it!" He would take care of the worship. Please, though, just let them know how matters were coming.

His words freed me to go. Some days later, when I returned from the memorial service for my grandmother, the warmth of the welcome I received lifted me. What I remember most, though, is a solitary image: on hearing the tone of my voice, and after a single look at my face, he laid down his tools so he could be completely there . . . for me.

A Widening Circle

The widening circle was at first harder for me to perceive. What I was experiencing, so up front and easy to spot, was a readiness of spirit aimed directly at me. It met me from all ages and all angles. It saw, and gently chided, my too-swift pace. It took time with my grief. It spread meals before me day after day in almost more homes than I could number. It encouraged me to take time off when I needed it. And always this readiness of spirit came through the flesh-and-blood particulars of one or another person's sensitivity, humor, gift of time.

As weeks passed, though, I realized that the availability shown to my needs was only a hint of what was going on. "Do you know what John does?" a congregation member asked me one day. I had no notion, except I knew that John, nearly seventy and a year-round resident, earned a small amount of money digging graves in the cemetery on the edge of town. The questioner explained. John, with what little he had, would periodically give to others in the community who had even less. And on those occasions when he dug a grave and a family stood about grieving, with no clergy to help and no sense themselves of what to do, John would gently come forward and offer to pray with them. He was, I gathered, never refused.

Two summer residents with a lovely lakefront cottage noted the number of young children in the area who had never received instructions in swimming, or even in basic water safety. They took safety lessons themselves, then for fifteen days opened their normally quiet residence to the dusty, then dripping bodies of children who came to learn, splash, swim along the shore.

On a ridge overlooking the town lay a summer camp for children with Down's syndrome. It had come into operation recently, and contact between the camp and town remained minimal. This particular year, congregation members determined to welcome the camp more fully into the community. Soon afterward three pews in the church filled, each Sunday now, with campers and their young adult counselors. Stating an obvious reality, but one that much needed to be named, a member of the congregation noted, "This is doing something for us." As barriers of awkwardness faded and closeness grew, the hospitality was clearly doing something for everybody.

The list of caring actions could continue here, but ultimately it was not so much the list of deeds as something else that so impressed me. I began to sense that I occupied a small point on what was a very wide circle of caring. The circle itself was formed by the members of that congregation, looking outward, sensing need, responding to a hurt, a loss, a sudden joy. Whenever one or another of the group responded, the circle grew. The love widened. And those of us touched by the love became points along the circle. Touched, and then drawn in, we ourselves became more aware of the love as it grew.

After ten weeks, I packed the car and drove off for another year at seminary. Classes were starting up. That began to excite me, as did my ever-present hopes of rekindling a rather stagnant social life. Even so, I sensed something had changed within me or, more accurately, something had been planted within me by that good and caring body of people. Though I was not able to articulate it at the time, I had come as a mendicant, a spiritual beggar to their door. They had taken me in, tended to my needs, borne witness with their way of being, and then sent me forth with lessons for a lifetime.

When now I am too much in haste, a small child still points at me from a stump. When I am in need, or when I must set aside my own preoccupations to tend to the needs of another, I still see Ed instantly lay down his hammer and belt full of tools. When, amid all the confusion besetting congregations today, I strain for a clearer vision of what our communities of faith are to be about, I see again that widening circle of responsive love.

Readiness. Responsiveness to the lives and needs before them. As a community in Christ, this was their gift. Three decades, and the memory nourishes still. . . .

ANDRE DUBUS

Love in the Morning

from DoubleTake

At the weekday mass in my parish church, I see the same people, as in a neighborhood bar. Not everyone comes every day, but I rarely see someone who is not a regular. We greet each other going in, say good-bye leaving. One morning when I parked at the church, an old woman and two old men were standing near the door I can go through in my wheelchair. I opened my car door and pressed the switch to open the box on the roof of my car and lower on two chains my folded wheelchair. The woman and men were talking about their bodies, about tests and medications. My chair descended, and the woman looked at me and smiled and said to the men: "And here comes the one with no troubles at all."

I have been at funeral masses for people I did not know. When many people are expected at a funeral, that mass is usually in mid-morning, after the daily mass. Years ago I walked one morning from my apartment to the early mass and saw a hearse outside. I went into the sacristy where the priest was putting on his vestments, and asked him if I should go home. "Oh, no," he said. "It's a very small funeral. Just sit in the back."

"Should I receive Communion?"

"Of course. It's a community. Wait till her family receives, then come."

I kneeled in the back. So did the other regulars, when they came in. That was at Sacred Hearts Church in Bradford, Massachusetts. Now I go to weekday masses at St. John the Baptist Church in Haverhill, because it is close to my house, mass is at nine rather than before eight, and it is the easiest church in town for me to push my wheelchair into. It is a brick church with steps at its front; but at both its sides, close to its rear, there are doors without steps or a curb, and the asphalted ground is level. So I roll in, between the altar and the first pew, and park in the middle aisle.

I have taken part in several funeral masses here. I push backward in a side aisle till I am at the rear of the church with the other regulars. I would feel like an intruder, if the priest at Sacred Hearts had not instructed me. Now I see a few relatives and friends in the first six or seven pews, flanking the body in the casket; then the empty pews separating them from the rest of us; the priest at the altar; the brown wooden walls and ceiling, and the stained glass windows enclosing all of us; and I think it is good for us strangers to be here as witnesses to death and life, to prayer and grief. During the mass and in the church, we are not strangers. We simply do not know one another. Entering the building has rendered us peaceable; the mass keeps us respectful; we only speak when we pray, and when the priest asks us to offer one another a sign of peace, and we take the hands of those near us and say: Peace be with you.

The mass unites us with the body in the casket, and with its soul traversing whatever it is that souls traverse, perhaps visiting now the people in the pew near the body; perhaps melding with infinity, receiving the brilliant love of God. The mass and the walls and floor and ceiling of the church unite us with the people who knew this person, with their sorrow, like the sorrow most of us have felt and all of us will feel unless we die before anyone we love dies. It unites us with the mortality of our bodies, with the immortality of our souls. The mass ends, and everyone but me stands as the family and friends follow the body in the casket out of the church. Then we leave and tell each other good-bye. We do not say good-bye. We wave, we nod: sometimes we say, "Have a good day." Earthly time is upon us again; we enter it, and go to our cars. Sometimes, in spring and fall, I do not go to my car. I push myself around the church, on the asphalt parking lot, downhill on one side of the church, then uphill on the other; I breathe deeply and look at trees and the sky and passing cars, and I sing.

The thirtieth anniversary of John F. Kennedy's murder was a Monday, a day in Massachusetts with a blue sky, and in the morning I filled a quart plastic bottle with water, put on a Boston Red Sox jacket and cap, and a pair of gloves, and went outside and down the six ramps to my car and drove to the church. On Sunday afternoon, while I was driving my young daughters to their mother's house in a nearby town, the first line of a story had come to me. I was talking with my daughters and watching cars and the road, and suddenly the sentence was inside me; it had come from whatever place they come from. It is not a place I can enter at will; I simply receive its gifts. I had been gestating this story for a very long time, not thinking about it, but allowing it to possess me, and waiting to see these characters living in me: their faces, their bodies. I do not start writing a story until I see the people and the beginning of the story. In the car with my girls I knew I must start writing the story on Monday, and before writing I wanted to receive Communion and to exercise. So Monday I drove to the church, grateful to be out of bed and on the way to mass on a lovely morning, my flesh happily anticipating exercise in the air under the sun. In that space between my heart and diaphragm was the fear I always feel before writing, when my soul is poised to leap alone.

There is only one priest at the church, and he is the pastor and lives in the small brick rectory beside the church. The rectory faces the street and is close to the sidewalk, and it is separated from the church by a driveway of the parking lot, and on some mornings in the basement of the rectory people in Alcoholics Anonymous gather to help one another. I like this priest, but liking him is not important. A priest can be shallow, boring, shy, arrogant, bigoted, or mean; during mass, it is not important. I believe most Catholics go to mass for the same reason I do: to take part in ritual, and to eat the body of Christ. If the priest is an intelligent, humorous, and impassioned speaker, then the mass includes the thrill of being entertained, even spiritually fed. I know that a homily can affect the soul. But a mute priest could perform a beautiful mass, and anyone could read aloud the prayer and the Gospel and the words of the consecration of the bread and wine. The homilies of the priest at St. John the Baptist are good; he always says something I can use that day.

I do not remember his homily on that November Monday morning. At mass my mind wanders about like a released small child. It does this wherever I am; it is not mine to hold, and I can either concentrate and so contain it, or wait for it to return. Probably at mass that morning I was concentrating on not writing the story in my mind, for doing that disturbs the gestation, and the life that may come on the page comes too soon. Once, while working on a novella, I came home from teaching and, before writing, I took my golden retriever outside to relieve himself. It was late afternoon, and we walked in a grove of trees on the campus. The dog rolled on the ground and chewed on fallen branches, and the work I meant to do at my desk began coming to me: the people and the words I would use and the rhythms of punctuation. I let it come and it filled me and I was not under a blue sky in the shade of a grove with my happy dog, I was a young woman who lived in a notebook on my desk, and the words I saw and hefted in my mind gave her a body and motion and dread and hope, and I was those, too. Then I went inside with the dog and made a cup of tea and went to my desk; but my soul, filled in the grove, was empty. I sat at my desk but did not write. I had already written, without a pen in my hand, standing under trees and gazing at my golden dog. It is part of my vocation not to worry about what I am working on, and never to think about it when I am not at my desk, and doing this demands as much discipline and focus as sitting at my desk and writing. I also keep a notebook and pen with me, everyplace where I am clothed, for those images or people or scenes that may fall on me like drops of rain.

I hope I prayed for my murdered president at mass; I do not remember. Dead for thirty years, he would not need prayers to help him on that Monday in 1993. But since reading Dorothy Day's belief that prayers for the dead can help them while they were alive on earth, I have believed it. I prayed to Kennedy later in the day, after mass and exercise and a shower and breakfast, when I wheeled to my desk. I had never prayed to him before. Moments before I wrote the sentence that had come to me in the car with my girls. I prayed: Jack, you were an active man, and probably people don't ask you to do much anymore, so will you help me with this story?

When mass ended I put on my jacket and gloves, and hung my leather bag on my right shoulder, the straps angling down my chest and back to the bag on my left thigh, which is now a stump. I left the church and put on the baseball cap and looked up at the blue sky. I went to the passenger side of the car, reached for the bottle of water on the seat, and drank. People got into their cars and drove out of the parking lot. I waited for them to leave; I do not like moving among cars in motion; my body's instincts are to step or jump out of their way, but the chair has no instincts at all. This is something I think about when I am sitting next to the stove, stirring a pot of beans.

When the people in cars were gone I pushed uphill to a tree at the edge of the lot. Behind it the hill with brown grass rose to a brick nursing home. Three young women sat in chairs outside, smoking in the sunlight. I turned right and pushed behind the church, singing "Glad to Be Unhappy." I sing while exercising so that I will breathe deeply into my stomach; I also do it because pushing a wheelchair around a parking lot is not exciting, as running and walking were; but singing, combined with the work of muscles and blood, makes it joyful. I know that, to some people, I may seem mad, wheeling up and down and around a parking lot and singing torch songs. But there were no people, and the priest was in the rectory, and I did not care if he heard me; he is a priest, and must be merciful about things more serious than someone singing off-key. It amused me to imagine watching this from the height of a hunting hawk: the nursing home, and downhill from it the church, and the singing man on wheels speeding down and turning right and passing the front of the church, then pushing uphill to the tree. Safety was not the only reason I chose the church parking lot for laps; I did not want anyone to hear me.

The people who heard me arrived in cars a quarter of an hour after I started my laps. They parked near the rectory and gathered at its rear, by the open door of the garage. In the garage are steps to the basement, and at ten o'clock these people would go down there for a meeting. But now they stood talking, men and women, most of them drinking coffee from Styrofoam cups, and smoking. I sang softly as I pushed past them, up the hill, and did not look at their faces. If I looked at their faces I would not sing. At the tree I looked up the hill at the three women sitting outside the nursing home, then turned right and sang loudly again and wheeled past the back of the church. All of us were receiving sensual and soothing pleasures: the workers at the nursing home, smoking; the alcoholics drinking coffee and smoking; me pushing and singing, after eating the body of Christ. At the end of the parking lot I turned downhill and steered as the chair rolled fast; to my left were houses, and across the street was the high school football stadium, but not the school, which is in another part of town.

When I came around the church and went up between it and
the rectory, I stopped singing and looked at the alcoholics. I felt an
affinity for them and believed that, because of their own pain and
their desire to mend, they did not see me as an aberrant singer on
wheels, but as a man also trying to mend. That was in their faces.
They all watched me going by; some of the men greeted me;
women smiled and looked. I said: "How y'all doing?" and went up
the hill, sweating. I stopped at my car and unlocked the passenger
door and drank water. A small gray bus with the engine in front,
like a school bus for only a few children, came up the driveway
between the rectory and the church. It turned left and stopped and
teenage girls and boys got out, some lit cigarettes, and they all
walked down to the gathering of alcoholics. I pushed away from
my car and went up to the tree and turned.

Going down the hill toward the street, I saw a man on the sidewalk, to my left; he was walking at a quick pace toward the church.
His overcoat was unbuttoned, and he wore a coat and white shirt
and tie; he had lost hair above his brow, and something about his
face made me feel that he did not work in an office. I turned to roll
in front of the church; he was walking parallel to me, thirty feet
away, and he looked at me. I stopped singing. He was glaring, and I
felt a soft rush of fear under my heart, and a readying of myself.
He raised his right arm and his middle finger and yelled: "Fuck
God."

He was looking at the church, walking fast, his finger up. My
fear changed; for a moment I expected a response: the sky suddenly dark gray, thunder, lightning. He yelled it again. We were
both opposite the church door, and there was no fear in me now; I
wondered if any of the alcoholics or if the priest in the rectory
were frightened or offended. He yelled again, his finger up; his
anger was pure and fascinating. By now I knew he was unsound.
We passed the church, and I turned and pushed upward, looking

at him over my left shoulder. He kept his finger up as he passed the rectory, still yelling. I moved past the alcoholics watching him; some smiled at me, and I smiled. As I pushed to the top of the parking lot, I looked up at the nursing home. The workers had gone inside. I sang, and laughed as I rolled past the rear of the church, seeing all of us: the roofs of the church and rectory, and the alcoholics talking and smoking, and me singing and sweating in the wheelchair, and the man in the suit and tie, with his finger up as far as he could reach. On that morning under a blue November sky, it was beautiful to see and hear such belief: Fuck *God.*

I wrote the story in four days; it is very short, and I knew before starting it that it was coming like grace to me, and I could receive it or bungle it, but I could not hold it at bay; and if I were not able to receive it with an open heart and, with concentration, write it on paper, it would come anyway, and pass through me and through my room to dissipate in the air, and it might not come back. That is why I prayed to Kennedy. It was strange, in those four days, to become one with the woman in the story, and the evil she chose, and the ecstasy it gave her and me. I called the story "The Last Moon," and in December I wrote it again, and in January I wrote it again. I did not look at it for days between drafts, and worked at not thinking about it, because it was hot and I was hot, and we both needed to cool, so I could see it clearly enough to take words away from it. But in January it was done, which truly means I had done all I can ever do with it, and it became something that lived apart from me. I started another story, and in a few weeks "The Last Moon" was a memory, much like meeting someone while you are traveling, and you eat and drink and talk with this person, feel even love, and then you go home with the memory and it does not matter to you whether you ever see the person again.

That winter, snow fell and fell and froze and stayed on the ground. The church parking lot was plowed often, but a coating of snow remained, and all winter I did not push my chair around the church. I live on a steep hill, and each time the snow stopped falling a friend plowed it, then I paid young men to come in a pickup truck and shovel sand onto the driveway. A friend shoveled my ramps and spread rock salt on them and chipped away the ice on top of the railings I use to pull myself upward to the house. Most days that winter I did not go to mass; I could have gone, on many days, but waking in the morning and thinking of cold air and of rolling on the packed, thin layer of snow and ice blunted the frail edge of my desire to leave my warm bed, and I lay in it.

One of the regulars at daily mass is a pretty blond woman in her thirties. On a cold and gray spring morning I drove to the church, and a seventy-eight-year-old man walked from his car to talk to me while I lowered my chair. I knew his age because once I asked him how old Jack Kennedy would be if he were still alive, and he said: Same as me: seventy-eight. On that morning in spring, after the winter of snow, I got into my chair, and the blond drove into the parking lot and stopped. We looked at her. She walked past us to the church and smiled and said good morning, and we did, and she went through the door I use. The man shook his head, grinning. He said: "If I were ten minutes younger."

Two days later he was standing outside when I drove to the church. The sky was still gray, the air cold. As I lowered my chair and got the armrest and seat cushion and leg rest from the back seat, I watched him. He was looking at the sky, at the green hill in front of the nursing home, at trees near the parking lot. I got into my chair, and he looked at me and said: "I'm looking for a robin."

I told him I had seen one this week, on my lawn.

* * *

Today is a Friday in early September, it is not autumn yet, but the air is cool and rain falls and in the rain I see winter coming, snow and ice on my ramps and driveway, on roads and parking lots and sidewalks, snowbanks pushed by plows to curbs, blocking the curb-cuts I use in my chair; and the long dark nights. While this September rain falls I want to be held, loved; but this morning I woke too late to go to mass. I have learned rarely to worry about my work, and not to write it in my mind without a pen in my hand and paper in front of me. But I have not learned to live this way, so I sit in September, listening to rain, glancing up from the page at it, feeling the cool air coming through my windows and open glass door, and I feel the sorrow of a season that has not come. This morning the sky was blue, and if I had gotten out of bed and gone to mass, I would not feel this sorrow now; it would be there, but as a shadow, among other shadows of pain; the trees that cast these shadows are mortality and failures in love, in faith, in hope; and if I had this morning received the Eucharist, all of these would be small shapes and shadows surrounded by light.

I go to mass because the Eucharist is there. Before the priest raises the disk of unleavened bread and the chalice of wine and consecrates them and they become Christ, the Eucharist is there in the tabernacle. When it is time for us to receive communion, the priest will go to the tabernacle and take from it the consecrated hosts to give to us. But the Eucharist is not only there in the tabernacle. I can feel it as I roll into the church. It fills the church. If the church had no walls, the Eucharist would fill the parking lot, the rectory, the nursing home, the football stadium. And the church has no walls, and the Eucharist fills the women smoking outside the nursing home; and the alcoholics waiting to gather, but already they are gathered, as they are gathered when they are apart; fills the man cursing God from the isolation of his mind; fills the old man watching a woman, and looking for robins. When I am enclosed by the walls and roof and floor, and the prayers and duration of mass, I see this, and feel it; and when the priest places the host in the palm of my hand, I put it in my mouth and taste and chew and swallow the intimacy of God.

Cold Comfort
from Harper's Magazine

> *Our country has wide borders; there is no man born*
>   *has traveled round it.*
> *And it bears secrets in its bosom of which no white*
>   *man dreams.*
> *Up here we live two different lives; in the Summer,*
>   *under the torch of the Warm Sun; in the Winter,*
>   *under the lash of the North Wind.*
> *But it is the dark and cold that make us think most.*
> *And when the long Darkness spreads itself over the*
>   *country, many hidden things are revealed, and*
>   *men's thoughts travel along devious paths.*
>   —Blind Ambrosius

This morning a sundog—a rainbowlike ring around the sun—looms so large it seems to encircle the visible world. As I move, it moves. I watch it slide across something stuck: a ship that has frozen into the ice of Frobisher Bay. I am taking off from Iqaluit, a town in Arctic Canada where I've been stranded for several days, and as my plane taxis out onto the runway, the sundog billows and shudders, dragging itself across black ice, too heavy to leave the ground. Then the plane does rise and so do the spectral rays of the sundog—a bright porthole into an Arctic winter's permanent twilight. I pass through its wavering hoop and it breaks.

People always ask, Why do you want to go north, especially at this time of year? There's nothing up there. But Greenlanders know the opposite is true: "Summer is lots of hard work. All we do is catch fish to feed our dogs through the winter. We don't have time to visit or see one another. In winter the fjords are paved with ice. We go out with our dogs every day. That's when we are happy." Which is why I'm on my way to Uummannaq, midway up the west coast, to travel by dogsled with ten hunters to Thule—the northernmost part of the country—or as far as we can go.

I delight in the spare landscape out the plane window—ice oceans and ice mountain and clouds full of ice. So much of what Americans live with is an economic landscape—malls, stores, and movie theaters, ski slopes and theme parks—in which one's relationship to place has to do with boredom, undisciplined need, and envy. The Arctic's natural austerity is richness enough, its physical clarity a form of voluptuousness. Who needs anything more?

The first time I visited Greenland was two summers after a near-fatal lightning strike. My heart had stopped and started several times, and the recovery from ten thousand volts of electricity surging through my brain took years. To live nose to nose with death pruned away emotional edacity and the presumption of a future, even another sunrise. Life was an alternating current of dark and light. I lost consciousness hundreds of times, and death's presence was always lurking—a black form in the corner. Life was the light hovering at the top of the sea.

Greenland's treeless, icebound landscape appealed to me so much then that now, three years later, I've come back. Its continuously shifting planes of light are like knives thrown in a drawer. They are the layered instruments that carve life out of death into art and back to life. They teach me how to see.

My plane from Iqaluit to Kangerlussuaq makes an unscheduled, early-morning departure. Every seat but two holds strapped-in cargo; the steward and I are the only passengers. It's thirty degrees below zero, made colder by a hard, northwesterly wind. In the cabin we wrap ourselves in wool blankets and sip coffee while a mechanic sweeps snow from the wings.

The blizzard that was stranding us has abated for a few hours, and by the time we get off the ground I can see a glow on the southern horizon where the sun will rise. But I am flying north, away from the sun, toward day that is like night and night that never becomes day. An old feeling of dread fills me: the claustrophobia of losing consciousness, of not being able to talk, move, or see.

We break the roof of the storm and fly east, then veer north, crossing the sixty-third and the sixty-fifth parallels. The immanent sun is marked by a neon-pink eyebrow in the southeast. "The sun is lazy in winter," an old Inuit woman at the airport told me. "It worked so hard all summer, now it doesn't want to get up. It just lies there and sleeps all day."

Days before, flying from Kuujjuaq, Quebec, I saw a ship frozen into the ice at Hudson Bay and thought of Henry Hudson's last journey in 1610–11, during which he had discovered the bay later named for him. After leaving winter quarters, some of the crew members, despairing of the continuous ice and fog and diminished food supply, refused to go farther. Moored to an ice floe somewhere in James Bay, the mutinous crew seized and bound Hudson, casting him adrift with his son and six others in the shallop. The mutineers sailed the *Discovery* home safely. Hudson and the others were never seen again.

Under us thin clouds are white rib cages threaded with pink strands of flesh. Farther east, the ice below breaks into platelets— stepping-stones on which to make one's cautious way. Out one window are the mountains of Baffin Island; a fast-moving river pours out from them, its riffles frozen in place as if to teach me lessons peculiar to the far north: that ice is time, time is light, light is speed, and speed times light equals darkness, or else more ice.

It is morning, almost nine o'clock. Between blizzards, somewhere out over Baffin Bay, a low-riding sun casts its brilliances: islands of ice shine within bodies of water that have no islands, and islands of land float within uprooted continents of ice. But out the other window, to the north, an indigo wedge has been hammered against the sea. We are flying into the earth's shadow. That is the darkness, the Arctic night for which I am bound.

"Do you see that coming?" the old woman Arnaluq asks.

"What?"

"That—out there over the sea. It is the Dark coming up, the great Dark!"

The sea is calm, and awl-like summits stand against the sky. Morning out one window, night out the other. For a moment I feel balanced between the two. Then dawn quickly dwindles to twilight. A black blank of fog lies against the horizon: the polar night advancing.

The Inuit say that only the *qallunaat*—the white people—are afraid of the dark, whereas Eskimos like nothing better than long winter days of conviviality.

"Is there a creation story, a beginning?" I once asked an Inuit archaeologist.

"That goes too far back," he said. "It was so dark then, too dark to know anything."

We land at the old air base at Kangerlussuaq, transfer to a smaller plane, and fly north to Ilulissat. There, at midday, the sun is like a fire burning on the horizon, but after a few hours it drops out of sight.

The helicopter to Uummannaq is grounded by bad weather. I stay with Elisabeth Jul, a young doctor who is chief of staff at Ilulissat's regional hospital and visits her outlying patients by dogsled. She is red faced, tomboyish, and stocky, with a physician's speedy abruptness and tenderhearted courage. Her house smells like the kitchen scraps she gets from the hotel next door and feeds to her dogs.

Three days later, the helicopter to Uummannaq lifts up through lingering snow showers that have turned Ilulissat's few hours of daylight gray. Up above, over the waters of Disko Bay, the sun burns a hole on the horizon, its long wake of light a torch striking north at the darkness into which we fly. Below, each iceberg is a miniature continent with its own turquoise inlets and long-fingered fjords, sharp peaks and sloping plains. Where an iceberg has collapsed into itself, its broken parts have curdled and are floating in black water; in other places, the ice floor has shattered into elongated rectangles like blocks of basaltic rock.

Instead of flying over the mountains, we fly way out and around the Nuussuaq Peninsula, a rough thumb of land that sticks out into Baffin Bay, separating the town of Ilulissat from Uummannaq Fjord. The idea is that it's safer to autorotate down onto ice than onto a snowy mountain. The father of my Greenlandic friend Aleqa Hammond drowned in this fjord when she was seven years old. He had been hunting when he fell through the ice with all his dogs. "I asked my grandmother why people have to die, and she told me it was something arranged by the spirits. Some people have thick candles that last a long time. His wasn't so big. And so he went down to where the goddess of the sea lives."

Once the storm overtakes us, winds buffet the helicopter, an old Sikorsky. Its one blade of hope holds us above ice, ocean, sea goddesses, and the certain death that Arctic waters bring.

Uummannaq. Latitude 70. We follow the fjord where Aleqa's father disappeared. Snow-covered cliffs rise up, wounded and scarred by glacier traffic over their rocky flanks, and the last of the twilight disappears. We pass the village of Niaqornat out on the western end of the peninsula, where the mountains turn from rock to cloud. For a moment a half-moon comes up above the storm as if greeting us. Then we auger down into a chaos of snow, falling away from the gaudy metallic glow far to the south, toward black, pitching water where a smooth floor of ice should have been.

I'm in Uummannaq again, a town of fourteen hundred people and six thousand dogs perched on a rock island, cast off from Greenland near the head of a fjord. Long ago the sun stopped rising here, and I can only wonder if it will ever come again. It's 3:00 P.M. and the lights are on all over the settlement. What is called day here is something else entirely; here the sky has not yet become a lamp for human beings. I only want to sleep.

Friends have arranged a house for me. It is reached by a long series of rickety wooden stairs over steep, snow-covered rock. At the top sits a two-room house, uninsulated and with no running water, that looks down on the town and harbor below. From my window I can see the grocery store, the post office, the warehouse, the administration building, and the bakery on one side of the harbor; on the other, the Uummannaq Hotel, the Grill-Baren—a Greenlandic-style fast-food place—and a clinic; and on the far side, the Royal Greenland fish factory. Fishing boats are frozen into the harbor, and the seal hunters' skiffs are laid helter-skelter on top of the ice.

* * *

Four P.M. looks like midnight, and the dog noise is cacophonous. Bundled up in wool pants, down parka, and sealskin mittens with dog-hair ruffs at the wrist, I trudge through a village lined with prim Danish-style houses painted yellow, blue, or green. Once, the Inuit people lived in peat, stone, and whalebone houses that in winter were lined with rime ice. When the sun returned they removed the roofs to let the rooms thaw.

Each yard has a sled, twelve or fourteen Greenlandic huskies (each chained on a long line), a drying rack hung with halibut to feed the dogs, and seal- and polar-bear skins pulled taut on stretchers and leaned against the house to dry.

Kids shoot by, four to a sled, narrowly missed by a dogsled climbing the hill the other way. Men and women push prams with babies whose tiny hands reach up to touch dangling mobiles of soft-sided whales and seals. Female dogs in heat run loose through town, as do all puppies, and as each passes through a new neighborhood of chained dogs, howls and moans erupt—the sounds of excitement and longing. I feel rather unnecessary in this world of dogs. Local taxis zoom up and down the hills, taking grocery shoppers home, and through the window of a tiny woodworking shop whose lights are on, it is impossible not to see two graphic posters—beaver shots—of naked white women on the wall.

Morning. The current crisis is that the fjords have not iced over. Without ice, there is no way to get to other villages. We are prisoners here, and my dogsled trip to the north may be doomed.

Far out near the head of the fjord there is a piece of ice shaped like a heart within a heart-shaped opening of black water. My own heart—which stopped once and started again unaided—is almost too cold to beat, and anyway, for whom? Down there in the water the sea goddess lives. Her long hair is tangled and full of lice, and no one will comb it clean. She is unhappy, the old people say, and there are no *angakkoqs*—shamans—to pacify her. That is why there is no ice.

Today I meet a man who knows all about trees but has never seen one growing. He's the local dogsled maker. Each district has a distinct sled-making style.

The shop is high-ceilinged, with handsome Danish-modern workbenches where sleds of different sizes are being constructed. As we walk between them he explains that for the runners, which must be strong but flexible for traveling over rough ice or rock, he buys whole trees from Denmark that have been split in half and air-dried. When cutting and shaping them he is careful to match the left, or outer concave, side of the log to the left side of the sled, and the right, or inner convex, side to the right side. Otherwise the runners will break, he tells me.

Sleds vary in size according to function. The long sleds used to hunt narwhal in the spring, when the sea ice is breaking up, are eighteen feet long, whereas sleds for local travel and seal hunting may be only six or eight feet long. On sleds to be used for long trips at any time of the year, he reinforces the handles and joints with sheet metal, and the crossbars that make up the floor of the sled must be fastened at alternating lengths into the runner. If not, the runner will break through the grain of the wood.

It's Friday afternoon, and already the other workers in the shop are drinking warm Tuborg beer. On the floor I lay a topographical map of the Uummannaq Fjord and the Nuussuaq Peninsula. They gather around to show me which canyon they go up to get across the top of the mountains, where they sleep at night (there are huts along the way), and where hunters the year before were rescued by helicopter after the piece of ice they were standing on broke away during a storm. They also show me where friends have disappeared through the ice—dogs, dogsleds, and all.

When I ask if the ice will come this winter, they look out the windows and shrug. Then the sled maker says, "The time between the full moon and the new moon—that is when ice always comes. When the weather grows calm and very cold. If there are no more snowstorms, there will be ice."

Qilaq taatuq. The sky is dark. *Seqineq*. The sun. *Siku*. Ice. *Tarraq*. Shadow. *Aput*. Snow. *Tartoq*. Darkness. *Kisimiippunga*. I am alone. That's my vocabulary lesson for the day from a mimeographed Greenlandic-English dictionary used by Allied troops during World War II, with words about bombs, warships, torpedoes, and German-speaking people. In reading the expedition notes of Knud Rasmussen, I learn that words used in séances are different from secular words, so that the shamanic word for sea is *aqitsoq* (the soft one), rather than the usual *imaq*.

By the time I walk home from the sled maker's shop, the skim of ice is gone and the pathway out to the annual ice used for drinking water has gone to liquid.

At my house I read about dark nebulae—immense clouds composed of the detritus of dying stars. Their function is unclear, but their effect in the universe is to "produce visual extinction." Yet the nebulae themselves are detectable because of "the obscuration they cause." I look up at the sky. The dark patches between constellations are not blanks but dense interstellar obstructions through which light from distant suns cannot pass. They are known variously as the Snake, the Horsehead, the Coalsack. Darkness is not an absence but a rich and dense presence, a kind of cosmic chocolate, a forest of stellar events whose existence is known only by its invisibility.

Polar days are almost the same as polar nights, and anyway, the streetlights in town are always on. I try to keep to a schedule—coffee in the morning, dinner at night, then sleep—but the schedule slides into the body's own understanding of constant dark. I sleep when I should eat and eat in the middle of the night. A recent study suggests that the eye may have its own biological clock, separate from the one in the brain. Now it's possible to think of eyes as circadian timepieces with resettable daily rhythms in the retina that orchestrate the ebb and flow of the hormone melatonin. In the dark and near-dark, I wonder what dances my eye rhythms are making and if, upon reentering the world of all-day sun, I will be blind.

Ann Andreasen is a Faroe Islander who followed a boyfriend to Greenland and decided to stay. Her house is next door to the Children's House she runs for children whose own homes have been marred by domestic violence or drugs. In the middle of the night a little girl is brought in. She has just witnessed the beating of her mother. The policeman who went to the scene is a friend of the family's, and, as in all Greenland towns, there is no bureaucratic tangle and no prison, just a firm suggestion that the child spend the night elsewhere.

Ann has left her own child, who is sick with the flu, to attend to the newcomer. Badly shaken, the girl is given hot chocolate and cookies, a fresh nightgown and toothbrush, then put to bed. The Children's House is modern, spotless, and cheerful with a capacious kitchen, living and arts area, computers and paints and traditional crafts for the kids. But the stories Ann can tell are a litany of tragedies—the inevitable consequences of a fiercely self-sufficient people meeting up with modern European life, despite or maybe because of Denmark's altruistic socialism.

My daily walk has been the one constant. Down the stairs from my perched green house, I stroll along the rocky edge of town, past the inlet where yesterday a wave generated by a calving glacier washed fifteen anchored boats onto the road. The Danes were so busy trying to save their pleasure boats that they forgot about the dogs tied up at the shore. The dogs drowned.

A week later. Now it's mid-January. A distant sound of thunder jolts me: a glacier calves, and waves made from the iceberg's birth undulate toward shore. Then something catches my eye: low down, from between two white cliffs, a full moon begins to rise—almost too enormous for the mountains that flank it. I stand mesmerized on the edge of the island. For some time the moon rises so slowly I'm afraid it will drop back down. But moons are not betrayed by gravity. Soon it tops the icy towers at the head of the fjord and brightens, suddenly rubescent, as if it had just been cut from ice and thrown up in the air—the absent sun's pale twin.

Morning. I'm not living on earth or ice but on rock and the sharp tooth of Uummannaq Mountain. At eleven the peak catches light like the poisoned tip of an arrow, and the cliffs that gave birth to the moon last night are pink, crimson, and gold. At noon there is a bit of light in the sky, but not enough to read by.

Later, maybe 2:00 A.M. Against the dogs' constant conversation about social hierarchy—urgent matters of food, sex, and rank, and the general angst of being chained on dirty patches of rock and snow—I lie alone in my bed. The moon is down. Unable to sleep, I drink a cheap bottle of blanc de noir—the white of the black, the foam of the night, the light hidden within dark grapes and made to sparkle. But how do they get white from black? How do they separate the two?

When all the blanc is gone there is only noir, *obscurum per obscuris,* a dark path leading through darkness. The Inuit never made much of beginnings, and now I know why. Because no matter what you do in winter, no matter how deep you dive, there is still no daylight and none of the comprehension that comes with light. Endings are everywhere, visible within the invisible, and the timeless days and nights tick by.

I am invited to dinner at a local painter's house with Ann and her husband, Ole Jorgen. Ole Jorgen arrives first to drop off a bottle of wine, and an ashtray almost hits him in the head. The artist—S.—and his wife are fighting. S. has been drunk for days. But they insist we come in. S. has recently suffered a stroke and can't walk. Holding court in his unkempt house, on a low daybed amid empty beer bottles, he looks like a doomed, deposed king, but his conversation is bright.

S.'s Greenlandic wife sets dinner down on the coffee table. It's a traditional soup made with seal meat and potatoes, accompanied by a shrimp and cabbage salad. (Lettuce doesn't survive the trip from Denmark to Greenland.) As the evening wears on, S.'s talk is reduced to expletives and non sequiturs. He adopts a British accent and says "I caun't" over and over, inserting it nonsensically between anyone's words. It's funny at first, but once I realize there will be no end to it I grow bored.

The wine has turned to vinegar; in the middle of the meal S.'s wife vomits in the kitchen sink. As we try to finish dinner fire engines roar by toward Ann's house, and we race outside after them. They pass her house and continue up the hill. My intention is to keep going, but Ole Jorgen says, "You're the guest of honor!"

I talk to S. about his paintings, and he gives me some sketches he's made of the harbor, white cliffs, and icebergs. The man can draw. When the evening finally ends, I thank him for the gifts. Alone in my green house, I bundle myself up in my made-to-order Feathered Friends sleeping bag and sit by the window. The tranquillity of perpetual night is like starch in my brain.

* * *

In winter, light sources are reversed. Snow-covered earth is a light, and the sky is a blotter that soaks up everything visible. There is no sun, but there's a moon that lives on borrowed time and borrowed light. Home late from hunting, two men pull a sledge laden with freshly killed seals up a hill, dripping a trail of blood in the snow. As I dose off, I dream that the paths are all red and the sky is ice and the water is coal. I take a handful of water and draw with it: in the frozen sky, I draw a black sun.

Later I can't sleep. The half-moon's slow rising seems like a form of exhaustion, with night trying to hold the moon's head down underwater. It bobs up anyway, and I, its captive audience, catch the illuminated glacial cliffs on the surface of my eyes. The moon's light is reflected light, but from what source? The sun is a flood that blinds us, a sun we can't see.

January 27. The glaciers are rivers, the sky is struck solid, the water is ink, the mountains are lights that go on and off. Sometimes I lie under my sleeping bag on the couch and recite a line from a Robert Lowell poem: "Any clear thing that blinds us with surprise."

I sleep by a cold window that I've opened a crack. Frigid air streams up the rock hill and smells like minerals. In sleep I hear the crackling sound that krill make underwater. Earlier in the day the chunk of glacier ice I dumped into a glass of water made the same sound.

The ice came from the top of a long tongue that spills out at the head of this fjord, as if it were the bump of a taste bud that had been sliced off, or a part of speech. Now it has melted and looks floury, like an unnecessary word that adds confusion to insight. But when I drink it down, its flavor is bright, almost peppery, bespeaking a clarity of mind I rarely taste but toward which I aspire.

When I lie back in the dark, the pupils of my eyes open.

* * *

My Uummannaq friends and I have started a countdown until the day the sun appears. After all, there's nothing else to do. Days pass. I try to distinguish the shadowed path from the shadowed world but fail. Then it's February.

The real is fragile and inconstant. The unreal is ice that won't melt in the sun. I walk partway up Uummannaq Mountain and look south. The sun's first appearance of the year will occur in three days, but for now the light is fish colored—a pale, silvery gray, like the pallor between night and day. I try to remember the feel of sun on my face, but the dark mass, the rock body of Nuussuaq Peninsula, drives the sensation away.

In the night there is none of the old terror of the sun going down and never coming up again, the terror that heart patients feel, because the sun is already gone, and I'm alive, and the darkness is a cloak that shelters me. As I walk down the mountain to the town dump, patches of frostbite, like tiny suns, glow on my cheeks. They burn like lamps, and I wonder if, later, they will cast enough light to read by, if they will help me to see.

Later I walk around the room trying to lift the dark cover of night with a flashlight in my hand, as if its fading beam were a shovel. I'm trying to understand how one proceeds from blindness to seeing, from seeing to vision.

In Greenland's early days a young shaman would come to the old *angakkoq* and say, *Takorusuppara.* "I come to you because I desire to see." After purifying himself by fasting and suffering cold and solitude, he would sit on a pair of polar-bear pants beside the old man, hidden from the villagers by a curtain of skin, and in time would receive *qaamaneq*—a light suddenly felt in his body, an inexplicable searchlight that enabled him to see in the dark.

One young shaman told Knud Rasmussen that his first experience of "enlightenment" was a feeling of rising up—literally, up into the air so that he could see through mountains, could see things far away, even blades of grass, and on that great plain he could locate all lost souls.

The next day. I don't know where I am. Wind comes through the walls. Maybe the walls have fallen away and merged with the walls of the galaxy. In this place it seems that there are only undefined distances that grow wider. I pick up a two-week-old *New York Times* science section brought from America, and it confirms this notion. "Space Telescope Reveals 40 Billion More Galaxies," the headline reads. Following the repair of the Hubble Space Telescope, which gives detailed portraits of galaxies far out in space and far back in time, astronomers learned that the universe is at least five times as vast as they had thought and is still expanding. Because of the telescope's power, many fainter galaxies are now being counted for the first time.

From the window I look into indigo space, and indigo space, like an eyeless eye, looks back at me. The thirteenth-century Zen teacher Dogen wrote, "To say that the world is resting on the wheel of space or on the wheel of wind is not the truth of the self or the truth of others. Such a statement is based on a small view. People speak this way because they think that it must be impossible to exist without having a place on which to rest."

In the harbor, we walk on crystal. Night is a transparency, and ice is the cataract over the eye that won't see. Only the finlike keels of fishing boats touch water under ice, and the fish look up through their cold lenses at our awkward boots. Beyond the harbor there is still-open water and the fjord is a wrinkled sheath of ink that has lost the word *ice*.

Later. Twilight gone to dark. I lie naked, careless, not quite destitute under a full moon on a polar night. Greenlanders thought

that the moon and sun were sister and brother who had unknow-
ingly slept together. After they discovered their incest they sailed
up to the sky holding torches, and lived in separate houses from
then on. In summer only sun, the sister, came out of her house,
and in winter only the brother moon came out. Sometimes,
though, he had to go away to get animals for the people to eat,
which is why, when the new moon came, the people were thankful
for the return of its light.

I light two candles and open a bottle of Fitou, a red table wine
from a French village I once visited. Strange that I can get it here. The
biweekly helicopter from Upernavik, a town one hundred miles to
the north, comes and goes, its pale headlights wedging a channel of
light in dark air: should I run to the heliport and escape or give up
and stay here forever? In the dark there is no middle ground.

Sitting by the window, I must look like a character from an
Edward Hopper painting—almost unmoving but not unmoved.
Stuck here on this Arctic Alcatraz, I don't know what I'm moved
to, except too much drink, and low-fever rage.

I write and drink by candlelight. No leaf, no shadow, no used-
up senses finally coming to rest, no lover's postorgasmic sleep.
Only this: a cold room where snow fallen from my boots does not
melt and the toilet in the unheated entry of the house stinks
because it has not been emptied for days. It occurs to me that the
only shadow I've noticed since last autumn is the wavering one a
candle makes, casting its uncertainty upon the wall.

Later in the evening the wind stops and a skin of ice hardens
over the water. Groups of villagers come down to the harbor to
watch and wait. An old woman standing next to me looks far out
over the ice and water and says, "If people go out, they will die.
They will fall through the ice and go down to where the sea goddess lives. No one knows about ice anymore."

*   *   *

February 3. Jorge Luis Borges reprimands us for thinking that blind people live in a dark world. Behind his blind eyes, he says, there were always colors. In *Paradise Lost*, Milton, also blind, writes of burning lakes, of inward conflagrations. I tell Ludwig, Ole Jorgen's son, the story of Ulysses and the Cyclops, how in order to escape from the Cyclops, Ulysses and his men sharpened a stick and drove it through the giant's eye, then clung to the underbellies of sheep and were carried out of the cave right past their blinded captor.

The sun is an eye. Its coming means that the boulder rolls away from in front of the cave and we are set free. Yet I'm still night-foundered, still blind so much of the time. I read John Muir's book *Travels in Alaska*. He writes of a summer day, crossing a glacier: "July 19th. Nearly blind. The light is intolerable and I fear I may be long unfitted for work. I have been lying on my back all day with a snow poultice bound over my eyes. Every object I try to look at seems double."

I'm done with daylight. It reeks of carbonous toast crumbs left behind after breakfast, of the kind of bright decor that hides a congenital blindness to what is real. Today in my house, with no lights, no water, only a view of the darkness outside from the darkness within, from the unlighted room of the mind and the unheated room of the heart, I know that what is real comes together only in darkness, under the proscenium of night's gaunt hood.

It also occurs to me that the real and the imagined have long since fused here, that it's not the content of experience that is important but the structure of our knowing.

In the next days there is more daylight, three or four hours at least, but not enough to read by—that's become my measuring stick. Tomorrow the sun will peep over the ridge, then disappear.

Now I don't want it. I've grown accustomed to the privacy and waywardness of night. In daylight all recognitions turn out to be misconceptions. During one of my many naps I dream that I can hear the sun beating behind the rocky peninsula like an expectant heart.

February 4. Sun Day, Sonntag, Sunday, Solfest. At ten in the morning light heaves up. It's seventeen below zero, and the sky over the Nuussuaq Peninsula is a pink lip trembling. The wind is sharp. Ann and Ole Jorgen spread a yellow cloth on the dining room table for our postsun feast. In northern Greenland it is still dark. Solfest will not reach Thule for another three weeks.

Here in Uummannaq it is nearly time. Panic sets in. Do the children have mittens, caps, boots on? Gitte, a neighbor, comes by in her pickup to take us all to the topmost viewpoint on the island—her house. Ole Jorgen, Ann, Pipaloq (their two-year-old daughter), Ludwig, and I jump in. At the top we run to the edge of a cliff that looks across rolling fjord waters south toward the mountains. There's a moment of utter breathlessness, then a pale light begins to move into the sky and smears itself from a sharp point of the heart-shaped mountain down into the village. Every object of Arctic clutter momentarily goes from shade to gloss—sleds, harnesses, dogs, drying racks, clotheslines, drying animal skins, cars, baby carriages, empty bottles, gravestones. House by house, the dead windows come alive. The sled dogs stand up and stretch in the sun, shaking all the secrets of winter from their coats.

Eleven forty-seven A.M. Ole Jorgen counts down: five, four, three, two . . . A spray of cloud lifts, lit from below and fired to the color of salmon. From behind the upside-down arch of rock, incandescent daggers spike the sky. In the square notch between two peaks, a tiny crack crescent of sun appears, throwing flames onto the forehead of morning.

"Look, I can see my shadow!" Ole Jorgen says. His son runs to the wall of the house, affectionately touching the elongated body of his father. "That's you, papa!" he says.

Do shadows prove existence? "*Sono io,*" Gitte yells out across the valley as if yodeling. "I am."

For six minutes the sun burns inside the notch like a flame. When it scuttles behind the ridge again, our shadows dwindle to nothingness. I am not I.

Everyone goes inside to eat and drink: *kaffe,* tea, *mitaq* (whale skin with a quarter inch of fat), rye bread, cheese, smoked salmon, and a dark Dansk liqueur that tastes like night. Outside, the sky is still bright and the sun pushes west behind the mountain as if behind the back of a giant, almost appearing again in a crack, then going blank again.

We toast Knud Rasmussen, polar explorer and ethnographer extraordinaire: we toast the return of the sun. After all, we're still alive despite our various bouts of cancer, tooth loss, divorce, marriage, childbearing, barrenness, and, in my case, lightning. As I drink down my liqueur, it occurs to me that there are all kinds of blindness and all kinds of seeing, that a dark world is not emblematic of death but of a feral clarity. And so I must wonder: in this sudden flood of sun, have I seen anything?

Afternoon. The pink light is going, not down but up, a rising curtain lifting light across the face of the village, up the long tooth of Uummannaq Mountain, leaving in its wake the old darkness. The diesel-powered lights of town come on as we stumble home. Dogs are fed. An old man chips away at an iceberg, carrying a chunk in his pail to melt for drinking water. The world has returned to its dark normalcy.

Walking back to my perched house, I see that out in the bay a collapsed iceberg holds a tiny lake in its center, a turquoise eye glancing upward. The moon comes up in the east as if it were a sun, and for the second time in one day, the mountains go bright.

Today winter was a burning lake and I watched it catch fire.

Ilulissat. Mid-February. The dogsled trip to Thule has been canceled until next year. Again I land on Elisabeth Jul's doorstep.

"You must go dogsledding at least once while you are here," she says on the phone from the hospital. It's noon and she's already performed surgery, delivered a baby, dispensed condoms. By evening she will have performed an autopsy on a policeman from Sisimuit who committed suicide. "After all," she says, "that's what you came for."

I sleep much of the day. Elisabeth is late coming home from the hospital, and I ask if it isn't too late to harness the dogs. "Why not?" she asks. "If it's dark, it's dark. Who cares what time it is?"

We put on layers and layers of Arctic clothes—fur over Polartec over down over Polartec—and start catching and harnessing the dogs. They are frantic with delight at the thought of being freed from their chains. One by one, Elisabeth leads them up the hill to the sled, where I am tying a frozen reindeer hide to the frame for us to sit on. She pushes the dogs' heads and legs through nylon harnesses, then ties their long blue lines to the central knot near the front of the sled.

My job is to keep the dogs from running off. "*Nik. Nik. Vinta,*" Elisabeth says. I repeat the commands to stay and sit. She hands me the long reindeer-hide whip, which I shake at the dogs that move. They cower in mock displays of fear. As soon as Elisabeth ties the last dog in, they quiver with expectation. "Better sit on the sled and hang on," I am warned, though I'm not exactly sure what I should hang on to and Elisabeth doesn't say. When her hands touch the sled handles the dogs erupt in a snarling fight, then jerk forward and take off feverishly. She jumps on the back of the sled and we are flying.

Cars come toward us and veer off quickly. The dogs, which are hooked up in the traditional fanlike array, don't step aside for anyone or anything. If pedestrians don't get out of the way, the dogs will go right over them. We turn left at Knud Rasmussen's little red house (now a museum), follow the path to the center of town, fly past the bank, the brottlet (an open-air market), the tourist shop, then leave the harbor behind on the road that goes out to the airport.

"This is called the 'Round the World Loop,'" Elisabeth yells. When she commands the dogs to stop, they stop. There are no reins. Nothing to hang on to. If you fall off the sled and the dogs run off, you walk home. We bump up and over a lip of plowed snow and follow a trail into the mountains.

In Rasmussen's day, sled runners were made of walrus bone covered with reindeer hides. Now they are metal and emit sparks as we scrape over rock. The sky clears. I think of Milton's line from *Paradise Lost:* "No light, but rather darkness visible." Away from the all-night lights of Ilulissat, we can see the stars and guide ourselves by them. "I wish you had a cabin out here and we never had to go back," I tell Elisabeth.

The ground is uneven—rock and snow and ice and more rock. When the dogs come to the top of a ridge they know to stop so that Elisabeth can get off the sled and look over to find a safe route down. As they tire, their speed is more negotiable—they settle into a steady trot. I try to jump off the moving sled and stand, all in one movement, but fail and roll in a ball through the snow, laughing. I run to catch up with the sled, grabbing the handle to pull myself closer, then Elisabeth jumps on and rests while I "drive," though the truth is the sled is dragging me as I pump my legs on uneven ground in heavy oversize Arctic boots.

Finally we stop to let the dogs rest. Elisabeth's face and hair are frosted white and her round cheeks are bright red. It's twenty degrees below zero but we're almost hot—Elisabeth wears neither gloves nor hat. "I only do that when it's really cold," she says. The dogs sleep curled in little knots—white and pale yellow on snow. The Big Dipper is laying its ladle down on our heads, and we know we're headed north.

When we start off again, Elisabeth jumps on the sled and crouches behind me, her arm around my shoulder to keep from falling off. In that moment I experience an extraordinary sense of well-being. Bundled into polar rotundity, linked and crouching, we fly from abyss to abyss. We look up: the northern lights flare, hard spotlights focused on dark nebulae and nothingness. They expand and contract like white laces being pulled tight and extending so far up into the sky that they appear to be holding the universe together.

Darkness reconciles all time and disparity. It is a kind of rapture in which life is no longer lived brokenly. In it we are seers with no eyes. The polar night is one-flavored, equanimous, without past or future. It is the smooth medium of present-time, of time beyond time, a river that flows between dreaming and waking. Behind the dogs, in the streaming wake of their flatulence, we move over white ground fast. The ground is alive like a torrent, a wild cataract. Which one is moving?

"I'm still not sure where we are," Elisabeth says, "but we're not lost. It's impossible to be lost. That would mean we were nowhere." We cross ridges, slide down icy slopes, zing over snow-less patches, striking rock into sparks as if our sled runners were trying to light our way. But the moon does that, and anyway, seeing in the dark is no longer a difficulty.

To our disappointment, the lights of Ilulissat flare up ahead of the team. "Let's not go home," I plead. But we have to. We bump over a plowed cornice of snow and hit the road near the airport that leads back into town. On ice the sled fishtails, wagging with a kind of unspoken happiness, and as the dogs go faster and faster, I am swept forward over the glass eye of the earth into the full sun of darkness.

The Good Life
from Notre Dame Magazine

I first heard the phrase "the good life" at the University of Chicago, where I was an undergraduate in the middle 1950s and where it was Topic Number One. I don't know how it is today, but during those days at the University of Chicago only two philosophers truly mattered, Plato and Aristotle, and they represented what Francis Bacon called "First Philosophy" and also "the springhead" of all important thought. Other philosophers—Aquinas, Augustine, Kant—while taken seriously enough, were also understood to be so much commentary on Plato and Aristotle. And Plato and Aristotle, no matter where one encountered them—in the *Dialogues*, in *The Republic*, in *The Ethics*, in *The Politics*—were really talking, ultimately, about how a human being ought to live. Which is to say that they were talking about the good life. What is the proper relation between man and state? What is happiness? When is the soul in healthy balance? All these are really questions about the good—I am tempted to add here the "freakin'" good—life.

Mind sharpening and immensely elevating though all this talk was, both in and out of the classroom, there was more than a slight air of unreality about it. The city of Chicago was not exactly a Greek polis, and the concept of the good life seemed to grow more than a little hazy when set in the complex context of the twentieth century. What I chiefly knew as the good life was that, while a student at the University of Chicago, with its grim winters and gray Gothic buildings, I almost certainly wasn't living it.

Yet the University of Chicago, even though no one quite spelled it out, did make plain what qualified, by its lights, as the good life.

Any attentive student could not miss that four things—and four things only—qualified: being an artist, being a scientist (which did not include anything so grubby as being a physician in private practice), being a statesman (of which, of course, then as now, there were none extant), or (most likely choice) being a teacher of potential artists, scientists, or statesmen. If you were none of these things, if you were merely, say, a clever lawyer or an immensely successful businessman or a courageous Navy test pilot, you were, in the University of Chicago analysis, rabble, just another clown sweeping up outside Plato's cave.

Of course this was greatly unrealistic, impractical, ridiculous really. Yet lots of people believed it. As it happens, I was one of the people who did. Besides, after the University of Chicago, after all that Plato and Aristotle, I was rendered perfectly unfit for a career as a CPA, mortgage banker, or jockey. Since I had no skill at science, no illusions about my capacity for governing, and no appetite for putting myself through the torture of acquiring a Ph.D., all that was left for me in the way of a good-life choice was artist—more specifically, literary artist—and that, over the past nearly forty years, I have attempted to become.

I haven't many regrets about this. I have had the exceptionally good luck to have people pay me to do what I want to do anyway. I have got my share of attention. I hope I have got something close to the most out of my slender talent. And yet, and yet, and yet. Being a writer seems a funny kind of life—living for making sentences, for telling stories, for recording experiences, wringing what is known as copy out of life. Can this be the good life?

Flaubert, himself engaged lifelong in the wrestle with language, is supposed to have said, when one day coming upon a happy peasant family, that they were living *dans le vrai,* or "in the true." One can sense the envy in Flaubert's phrase; it is the envy for those who live a natural life, among children and spouses and in nature, as opposed to those who worry endlessly about such trivial matters as the formation of style and the formulation of ideas. Who was living the good life, Flaubert or those peasants? If pressed, Flaubert, I suspect, would have said that those peasants were. Tolstoy is likely to have concurred. Neither man, of course, would have traded places with them, *dans le vrai* or no. Nor, let me add, would I. And yet, and yet, and yet—one longs for what one thinks of as life lived more directly than through the mind, and one is a bit dubious that such a life quite qualifies as the good life.

As a sometime university teacher, I frequently talk with students who come to me to discuss their futures—or what I call, to myself, their brilliant careers. Those among my students who worry me most are the putative idealists, who wish to do something, as they are only mildly embarrassed at putting it, for the good of society. There was a time when such kids, after an eighty-thousand-dollar education, wished to become forest rangers. Today some still speak of doing one or another sort of environmentalism. Others talk about a career in law with an eye to social justice, taking on class-action suits, defending the poor, and so on. Wicked man that I am, I gently try to persuade them not to worry overmuch about society. "I may be wrong about this," I say, "but it seems to me that any work you do well—provided it does not entail regularly stepping on the next fellow's neck—is giving society all the help it needs."

Sometimes, to italicize my views, I tell them a joke I once told, over the telephone, to Thomas Sowell, the conservative economist. It's the joke about the airplane in difficulty whose pilot announces that the plane is carrying too much weight and he will have to ask one person to jump out. He and the crew have talked this over and have decided to ask that person to jump who is of the least use to society. At which point—so the punch line goes—a disc jockey and a used-car salesman get out into the aisle and begin fighting.

At the end of my telling of the joke, utter silence at the other end of the phone.

"You didn't care for that joke, I take it," I said.

"No," said Sowell, "I didn't. I would have liked it much better if the punch line went, 'At which point, a curator of contemporary art and a psychotherapist get out into the aisle and begin fighting.'"

I had to allow that Thomas Sowell had a point. His point is not so different than the one Wittgenstein makes in *Culture and Value:* "I look at the photograph of Corsican brigands and reflect: these faces are too hard and mine too soft for Christianity to be able to make a mark on them. The brigands' faces are terrible to look at and yet they are certainly no farther than I am from a good life: it is just that they and I find our salvation on different sides of such a life." The good life, I take Wittgenstein to be saying here, is not everywhere, or for everyone, the same.

I have lately been reading the novels and stories of Willa Cather, and in *The Professor's House,* one of her darker books, she has her protagonist, Godfrey St. Peter, remark to a classroom of students, "Art and religion (they are the same thing in the end, of course) have given man the only happiness he has ever had." St. Peter would seem to be speaking for Cather here. And yet not really, for in other of Cather's fiction the good life, or something very close to it, is lived by immigrant girls working at domestic jobs, grandmothers who have given themselves over to the happiness of their families, missionary priests, young men and women who are able to live outside themselves—or, more precisely, for something larger than themselves. The good life, Cather makes plain, can never be the selfish life. The first step to achieving the good life seems to be to forget about one's own good life. I myself fear it may even preclude thinking too much about what constitutes the good life.

The second step seems to involve understanding that it is the journey not the destination that matters: the way not the end that counts. "The greatest good luck in life, for *anybody*," the sculptor Henry Moore has said, "is to have something that means everything to you . . . to do what you want to do, and to find that people will pay you for doing it . . . if it's *unattainable*. It's no good having an objective that's attainable! That's the big thing: you have an ideal, an objective, and that objective is unreachable."

My own view of the good life is that one can only judge—and then but obliquely—if other people are living or have lived it. One is probably not in any position to judge if one is oneself living it. One knows well enough when one is living a bad life, but as soon as one thinks one is living the good life, it is almost certain that one isn't, else one wouldn't be so damn smug as to think one is. Maybe on one's deathbed, if one can say, without too great self-deceit, there are not too many things I would have done differently, then, maybe, just maybe, one has lived a decent, possibly even a successful, life. As for having lived the good life, that alas remains, as Auden had it, "the heavy-lidded riddle."

The Very Short Sutra on the Meeting of the Buddha and the Goddess

from Yoga Journal

Thus I have made up:

Once the Buddha was walking along along the
forest path in the Oak Grove at Ojai, walking
without arriving anywhere or having any thought
of arriving or not arriving

and lotuses shining with the morning dew
miraculously appeared under every step
soft as silk beneath the toes of the Buddha

When suddenly, out of the turquoise sky,
dancing in front of his half-shut inward-looking
eyes, shimmering like a rainbow
or a spider's web
transparent as the dew on a lotus flower,

—the Goddess appeared quivering like a
hummingbird in the air before him

She, for she was surely a she
as the Buddha could clearly see
with his eye of discriminating awareness wisdom,

was mostly red in color though when the light
shifted she flashed like a rainbow.

She was naked except for the usual flower
ornaments Goddesses wear

Her long hair was deep blue, her two eyes
fathomless pits of space and her third eye a
bloodshot ring of fire.

The Buddha folded his hands together
and greeted the Goddess thus.

"O Goddess, why are you blocking my path.
Before I saw you I was happily going nowhere.
Now I'm not sure where to go."

"You can go around me," said the Goddess,
twirling on her heels like a bird darting away, but
just a little way away, "or you can come after me.
This is my forest too, you can't pretend I'm not
here."

With that the Buddha sat supple as a snake solid
as a rock beneath a Bo tree that sprang full-leaved
to shade him.

"Perhaps we should have a chat," he said.

"After years of arduous practice at the time of the
morning star I penetrated reality, and now . . ."

"Not so fast. Buddha.
I *am* reality."

The Earth stood still, the oceans paused,

the wind itself listened—a thousand arhats,
bodhisattvas, and dakinis magically appeared to
hear what would happen in the conversation.

"I know I take my life in my hands," said the
Buddha. "But I am known as the Fearless One
—so here goes."

And he and the Goddess without further words
exchanged glances.

Light rays like sunbeams shot forth so bright that
even Sariputra, the All-Seeing One, had to turn
away.

And then they exchanged thoughts and the
illumination was as bright as a diamond candle.

And then they exchanged mind

And there was a great silence as vast as the universe
that contains everything

And then they exchanged bodies

And clothes

And the Buddha arose as the Goddess
and the Goddess arose as the Buddha

and so on back and forth for a hundred thousand
hundred thousand kalpas.

If you meet the Buddha you meet the Goddess. If
you meet the Goddess you meet the Buddha

Not only that. This: The Buddha is the Goddess,
the Goddess is the Buddha.

And not only that. This: The Buddha is emptiness
the Goddess is bliss, the Goddess is emptiness the
Buddha is bliss.

And that is what and what-not you are. It's true.

So here comes the mantra of the Goddess and the
Buddha, the unsurpassed non-dual mantra. Just to
say this mantra, just to hear this mantra once, just
to hear one word of this mantra once makes
everything the way it truly is: OK.

So here it is:
Earth-walker/sky-walker
   Hey, silent one, Hey, great talker
Not two/Not one
   Not separate/Not apart
This is the heart
   Bliss is emptiness
   Emptiness is bliss
Be your breath, Ah
Smile, Hey
And relax, Ho
And remember this: You can't miss.

FREDERICK FRANCK

The Stereopticon
from Parabola

The meaning of life is to see.
—Hui Neng (seventh century)

Grandfather's house was full of treasures: the enormous rolltop desk of shiny mahogany matched the bookcases with their beveled glass doors, which contained all the classics in gold-embossed bindings. The greatest treasure by far, however, was what Grandfather referred to as his "stereopticon." To this contraption, more properly known as a "stereoscope," I probably owe my Weltanschauung, my way of perceiving the world. The antique contrivance consisted of twin lenses set in a leather-covered housing lined with red velvet. From this housing a kind of wooden slide rule jutted forward, with a device at its end in which you placed twin photographs. Then, pressing the velvet edge to your face, you saw through the lenses an oak tree, not flat, as in a picture, but all in the round: a living presence. For hours I could sit and watch the miraculous three-dimensionality of cows in a meadow, of lovers dallying under lilac bushes full of white doves, of Princess Juliana of the Netherlands riding her piebald pony, and even a few of languid, well-fed ladies in provocative old-fashioned garb.

And so it came about that sometimes, when on the long solo hikes I loved I got tired, and fields and hedges began to look listlessly flat, two-dimensional, I found I could command my eyes: "Now, look as if through the stereopticon!" And suddenly every blade of grass sprang to life again and stood there in a space all its own; clumps of trees broke up into individual living beings, each one rising from its own roots deep in the earth. People, when observed through my virtual stereopticon, underwent an extraordinary metamorphosis: they too became impressively unique, mysterious beings. What looked at was just a waiter, a sumac, or a cow became a poignant living presence when seen stereoscopically.

I found this discovery of seeing stereoscopically such a precious secret that I never mentioned it to anyone, but practice it I did, as often as I could, and so I learned that seeing things and beings in this way is an excellent substitute—to say the least—for lots of thinking and reading about them. Grandfather's gadget, I now realize, was the mute master who initiated me into seeing, who gave me the first hints that one's everyday eye can become an awakened eye, an eye that can do infinitely more than merely look at things, recognize, classify, label them. This awakened eye could see the Ten Thousand Things as they are, in themselves, each in its own truth. When all appears as déjà vu and dull, one has only to command one's eye to see stereoscopically, to awaken it from its habitual slumber to fully conscious perception.

There are drawbacks to this eye awakened: you can't cut down that sumac that is in the way and that is "only a sumac" . . . the waiter is waiter no longer once you see the tremor in that hand . . . the cow is no more "cattle" when you have drawn those eyes. . . . Stereoscopic seeing may make you relatively harmless; it also makes you vulnerable.

St. Bonaventure distinguishes "the eye of the flesh, the eye of reason, and the eye of contemplation which sees unto liberation. . . ."

There is for me no legitimate reason for drawing, painting, sculpting, other than in this intensified awareness of the eye awakened from its half-sleep, no more valid criterion of what is really authentic in the visual arts, regardless of the dictates of fashion. *I see therefore I am!*

* * *

The stereopticon's revelation was to make me into the incurably compulsive image maker I am to this day. It must have started when I was five or perhaps six years old. My mother and her friend—I had to address her as Aunt—had taken us children to the little tea garden with swings and seesaws on the edge of our town on the Dutch Belgian border. It sported the elegant French name Les Champs Elysées, "the Elysian Fields," the fields of celestial bliss. I can still see, yes, even hear, the trio that was playing sentimental "salon music" on the rickety bandstand: the elegiac violinist in his patent leather shoes, the balding pianist with his pince-nez, the blond lady in white tulle with the cello clamped between her thighs.

The other children were still swinging and seesawing when I got bored, and as Mother and the pseudoaunt with her Pinocchio nose were absorbed in the music—which did not prevent them from chattering rapturously in loud whispers—I saw my chance to escape across a narrow stream, and found myself in a sun-drenched meadow. I lay down in fragrant, swaying grasses, tall enough to make me invisible, listening to the piano's arpeggios, the cello's moaning in the distance.

Then, suddenly, there was a loud zooming close to my ear. I was terrified. A big velvety bee circled around my head, almost touched it. But then it ignored me to land on the purple flower that was so close by that it looked huge and vague, and started to suck.

At that precise instant it happened: suddenly all my fright evaporated, but with it the bee, the sun, the grass, and I disappeared. Sunlight, sky, grasses, bee, and I merged, fused, yet somehow remaining sun, sky, grass, bee, and I. It may have lasted for a heartbeat, an hour, or a year; it was timeless. Then, just as abruptly, the grass was grass again and I was I again, but filled with indescribable bliss.

The trio was still playing the tune I remember to this day. I could whistle it for you. . . .

I had probably come as close to Reality as ever I would in the eight decades that followed. But the older I get, the more faithful I seem to become to the child I was then. It is the child who draws and who even dares write this down, trusting that the child in the one who reads it will find it true. In every life, I believe, there must be such a moment of consciousness awakened, however forgotten, however blotted out it seems to be by the buffetings of life.

In what occurred in the meadow, I find in retrospect a first glimpse of Zen experience, of that seeing into nature that includes one's own nature. Once having experienced it, some of us apparently are driven to recapture this timeless moment of bliss, against all odds, by any means at hand.

And so it could happen that just a week ago, I felt for a second as if on the point of recapturing it when I stopped my old vw—illegally—at the curb on the corner of 36th Street and Seventh Avenue and started to draw the riddlesome processions of people crossing the street in both directions, interrupted only by changes from green to red. The procession coming from nowhere disappeared forever behind the corner where I sat drawing. I was aware that as I was drawing, these men, these women appeared on my paper, the pen was touching each one for those few seconds on their trip from birth to death. I was drawing mortality, that of the sprightly young ones, the old tired ones, the self-assured ones in minks and trench coats, the ones in shabby sweaters and dirty baseball caps. It was, so to speak, as if I were bestowing blessings in some quiet trance, perhaps something close to Blake's "catching a joy as it flies," a joy perhaps frayed by pain, by pity. But I was catching it on Seventh Avenue. Apparently the demarcation line between real estate and the Fields of Bliss has never been clearly established. . . .

A few months ago in Europe I went looking for the little tea garden without much hope of finding it again after two world wars. All I found was a street sign that read "Champs Elysées Straat" on the corner of a neat street between white villas that had been built on my meadow. It had all disappeared without leaving a trace, as had my mother and the aunt. Only the tune was still ringing in my inner ear.

Wittgenstein says, "If we take eternity to mean not infinite temporal duration, but timelessness, eternal life is theirs who live in the present."

What Are You Looking For?

from First Things

In Genesis 37:15 we read the story of how Joseph arrived in the town of Shechem in search of his brothers and his father's flocks that they were pasturing. Joseph had been sent by his father, Jacob, to Shechem, not just to bring back word about his sheep and goats, but, primarily, to give Joseph a chance, away from his father's presence, to reconcile with his brothers and to mend a relationship that had been sundered after Joseph's arrogant dreams and Jacob's lavish gifts to Joseph.

Joseph's brothers were not in Shechem when he arrived there, and just before turning back, his mission unfulfilled, we read in the Torah, "a certain man found him and behold he was wandering in the field." That man (or was he a man?) asked Joseph a two-word question, *ma t'vakesh*, "What are you seeking?" Joseph answered the man, "I seek my brothers. Tell me, I pray thee, where they are feeding the flock." The stranger (or was he a stranger?) said to Joseph, "They are departed hence; for I heard them say, 'Let us go to Dothan.'"

And we must ask, "Why is this incident in the Torah at all?" Who cares if Joseph found his brothers in Shechem or Dothan or Brooklyn? Why would a narrative as concise and spare as the Hebrew Bible, the Tanakh, take time to recount Joseph's false start in finding his brothers? The answer, of course, is to be found in Lewis Carroll's *Alice in Wonderland*. At the beginning of *her* journey Alice asks the Cheshire cat, "Would you tell me, please, which way I ought to go from here?" The cat answers her, "That depends a good deal on where you want to get to." It's too bad Joseph did not meet the cat. He might have realized that this great short question, *ma t'vakesh,* was not a question about the location of his brothers, but a question about the location of his life. And the stranger who met Joseph in the fields of Shechem may also have been deceived about the real purpose of their meeting. He may have thought that he was just helping a stranger find his flocks, but what he was really doing was helping the Jewish people find a future.

For consider this: If Joseph does not meet the stranger he returns home and is not sold into slavery in Egypt, *which means* that he would not have become a big shot in Egypt, *which means* that he would never have been able to provide a safe haven in Egypt for his family during the famine in Israel, *which means* that his family would not have become the Jewish people over four hundred years of slavery, *which means* that the Pharaoh would not have tried to oppress us, *which means* God would not have sent Moses to take us out of the house of bondage with a strong hand and with an outstretched arm and with many signs and wonders and through forty years of desert wanderings to the land flowing with milk and honey, *which means* that we would not have been able to establish a Jewish kingdom under Saul, David, and Solomon, who would build the Temple in Jerusalem, *which means* it could not have been destroyed by the Babylonians who would exile us to Babylonian cities like Sura and Pumbadita where Jewish life could begin to create tools like the siddur and the Talmud to adapt Jewish life to the realities of diaspora existence, which really began in earnest after the Romans destroyed the Second Temple, *which means* that there never would have been the impetus for the rise of Christianity, which saw the destruction of the Temple as a sign that it was now the new Israel, *which means* that Helena, the mother of the emperor Constantine, could never have made

Christianity the religion of the Byzantine Empire in 325, *which means* that Muhammad would never have organized the Arabs under the new religion of Islam to reclaim the holy sites, which led to the Islamic empire of the eighth century, which saved all the texts of the Greek philosophers because Greece and Rome were covered by drooling vandals and which gave us relative freedom, *which means* that the Christian leaders of Europe would not have turned against us as infidels, like Pope Urban II, who ordered the first crusade in 1095 where Crusaders massacred Jews in Worms and Speyer and Cologne and Mainz, and like King Ferdinand and Queen Isabella of Spain, who expelled us in 1492, *which means* that we would never have gotten to the Ottoman Empire just in time to open trading routes for the sultan in Poland and begin the building of the vast and thriving Jewish life in Russia, Poland, and Lithuania, *which means* that the Jews who fled Spain to the north would not have gotten to Amsterdam just in time to share the fruits of the Dutch East India Company's voyages to the new world, finding places like Curaçao, Martinique, Tobago, Barbados, and Jamaica, which gave us a head start on getting all the good hotel rooms for the winter season, *which means* that when twenty-three Jews fleeing the Inquisition in Recife, Brazil, landed in a Dutch colony at the mouth of the Hudson River called New Amsterdam in 1624 they would not have been let in because the governor of New Amsterdam was a raving anti-Semite named Peter Stuyvesant, however he received a fax from the Dutch East India Company saying, in effect, "25 percent of the stock of this company is owned by Jews, are you nuts! Let the Jews in and treat them well, or you will be swabbing the deck on a pepper ship to Bombay," to which Peter Stuyvesant responded, "What would New York be without Jews, welcome to America, please name a high school after me!" *which means* that when Eastern Europe got really dangerous because the industrial revolution never got there and the economies of Russia and Poland were collapsing and pogroms like Kishinev swept the area in 1904 we would not have been able to move to America, *which means* that we would not have been able to start the garment industry, and eventually Ratner's, *which means* that we would not have been able to save a few bucks to find a nice apartment in Queens and move out of the tenements, *which means* that we would not have eventually decided that our kids need a yard and good schools, *which means* that we would not have been able to buy in the new Levitt development out at exit fifty of the Long Island Expressway in a place called Dix Hills which was really Melville but we called it Dix Hills because we thought it sounded tonier, and where Levitt sold some Jews a plot of land cheap to build a shul because he couldn't get zoning to build a strip mall, and where the shul fifteen years ago said, "I think this guy Gellman will be good for us," and where I said, "I think we will both be good for God," and where we were both right and where I have finally had a chance to explain to you that none of this would have happened if that stranger didn't meet Joseph in the fields and didn't ask him, *ma t'vakesh.* "What are you seeking?"

And what happened to Joseph in the fields happens to us in our lives. We meet angels and they change everything. The man who met Joseph in the fields of Shechem was of course not a man, he was an angel, or to say it more precisely, he was not only a man, he was also an angel. Judaism has always taught that it is quite possible to be both at the same time.

The Bible is constantly confusing people with angels. Abraham receives three men into his house who suddenly deliver messages from God. Indeed, the midrash recounts that the three men were three angels, each with one errand (one to announce the birth of Isaac, one to destroy Sodom and Gomorrah, and one to save Lot), and the reason for this according to the midrash is that "An angel is never sent on more than one errand at a time." Jacob at the Jabbok River wrestled with a man who suddenly turns out to be an angel, and this man/angel changed Jacob's name to Israel, which means "one who wrestles with people and angels and who survives."

The reason for this confusion is simple. In Hebrew, the word for angel is *malach,* which means "messenger," and so for Judaism any person with a message from God is a *malach,* an angel. Now you must understand that there are two kinds of angels: the *malachim,* the angels who are human beings recruited into God's messenger service, and then there are the angels who inhabit the *olam habah,* heaven, and who are not and who never were human beings. These heavenly angels also communicate with us, but their main role is to be minions of the Holy One Blessed Be He who inhabit the world to come always hovering close to the divine presence. Angels like Gabriel or Uriel or Uziel or Michael have specific names and functions and personalities. The Bible describes two angels with fiery swords standing guard at the entrance to the Garden of Eden, and other angels overpowered the prophet Ezekiel with powerful visions of a heavenly chariot, but they are all part of the *malachai hasharet,* the angels who serve God. These angels come equipped with wings and music and white robes and halos and with signs and fearful portents. They are very easy to spot in a crowd. They also tend to be terrifying. The poet Rilke wrote, "If the archangel now, perilous, from behind the stars took even one step down toward us, our own heart, beating higher and higher, would beat us to death." So all in all it is a good thing that there is a division of labor amongst the angels.

The angel who met Joseph in the field was not winged or terrifying, he was just a messenger angel—a man who was also an angel from God. Joseph surely did not know that this man was an angel, and the man himself may not even have known, yet he was a *malach,* a messenger bearing a message from God that was both important and fragile. Important because it was a message from God and hearing it changed Joseph's life, but fragile because Joseph might not have heard it. He could easily have dismissed the stranger's directions to Dothan, figuring that he might have confused his brothers with some other shepherds heading that way. Angels present us with a message but also a choice—the choice of whether or not we can hear the message.

I know that you risk appearing like some kind of new age goofball if you say you believe in angels, but I do believe in angels, along with all of Judaism up to those German rationalist Reform Jews who, starting in Frankfurt in 1823, introduced a lot of good things into Judaism and also killed a lot of good things that were already in Judaism. What they killed was everything that did not fit with the historicist and rationalist and idealist philosophies of nineteenth-century Germany. The idea that God revealed the Torah was rejected, Jewish mysticism was rejected, the world to come was rejected, angels were rejected, indeed for a while having a Torah scroll in a Reform Temple was also rejected. Unless you think Hegel, Fichte, Schelling, and Kant are the last word of human wisdom and that the Prussian state was the epitome of human culture, you are going to have to move on, as our movement itself has done, and reclaim the authentic Jewish beliefs our movement ignorantly rejected and in doing so left us naked to the worst predations of secular humanism, positivism, and the spiritually desiccating equation of Judaism with political activism.

I want you now to reconsider your naive and erroneous belief that angels do not exist. If God's care and love for us are so strong that even the death of our bodies will not end that love, then the *olam habah* is real, and similarly if God did speak to us somehow someway through the Torah it is just not reasonable that the Torah is God's last word to us. God needs a way to speak to us, to chastise us, to direct us, to encourage us, and to nudge us. God has given each of us unique gifts, and God needs, from time to time, to show us how to use those gifts to help the world. One of the ways God does this is by sending angels into our lives to ask us the great short questions. Lincoln referred to "the better angels of our nature," and he was just right.

Look around you. Even in this secular culture we are in the middle of a literary and cultural angel explosion. Surveys indicate that almost 70 percent of Americans believe in angels. Five of the ten best-selling paperback books are about angels. Tony Kushner won a Pulitzer Prize for his play *Angels in America,* in which an angel visits a man with AIDS. Harvard Divinity School even has a course on angels (which I will admit is one powerful argument *against* their existence).

But I do not believe in angels because the survey data support belief in them. I believe in angels because the Torah and our sages teach us that angels are real, and I believe in angels because I have met them just like Joseph met one in the fields of Shechem, and so has each and every one of you.

I want you to think about the angels who have come into your life. I want you to call to mind right now, among all the thousands of people you have met, those handful of people who clearly and absolutely changed your life for the better—not just parents and family, but often total strangers whose simple advice or gift or suggestion or admonition or question changed you forever. Perhaps it was the person who first gave you a book about science and sent you off on the road to become a scientist. Perhaps the person who told you that you would make a good lawyer or teacher or mother or friend or confidant at just the time when you had no intention of becoming anything like that. Perhaps it was the person who told you to watch out at just the time you needed to watch out. Perhaps it was the prayer in a hospital of a stranger whom nobody saw on the floor but who came to your bedside and said everything is going to be all right and then it was all right even if the doctors did not understand why or how.

When we are about to lose our way it seems to me absolutely obvious and unarguably true that God will send someone into the fields of our lives to ask us, *ma t'vakesh,* "What are you looking for?" If there is such a God, and there is, then there are angels and there is a life after death where we will meet all of them and then you can slap your spiritual foreheads in wonder and say, "It was all true. Everything that Rabbi Gellman ever taught us was true." That is when you will know for sure what you may have some doubts about now, that there are angels sent to us by God along our way in this life, so that we will get the message that God would not give each of us special and unique blessings unless God wanted those blessings to be used.

Another purpose for angels is that God always needs to teach us how to listen better. Angels teach us how to listen because if you know that every person you meet might be an angel, you are going to listen to that person not just with the ears in your head but with ears in your soul. This is the reason I give to beggars. I know that my coins and dollars have probably bought crack and booze, but I still give because my money might, just might, have bought some baby food or diapers or soup, and I can't take the chance that I have stiffed an angel. Indeed, rabbinic legends teach us that the Messiah will appear on earth as a beggar waiting for some act of kindness by a stranger before announcing himself. If you can learn to see street bums as potential messiahs, you can learn to see angels when they meet you in the fields of your life.

* * *

I want you to leave here and do something. I want you to write a letter to your angels. I want you to try to find a person/angel who came into your life at just the right time, and I want you to write that person a letter and say, in your own words, thank you for appearing in my life and for changing everything for the good, for helping me to find what I did not even know I was looking for.

And then some day when I pray you are 120 and God takes your breath away, and your soul begins its glorious eternal life in the world to come, when the two angels with the fiery swords guarding the entrance to the Garden of Eden, the portal through which all souls must pass, say to your soul, "You can go right in," and when you arrive safely in the place where there are no questions only answers, no pain only love, no death only life, then this is what will happen, I believe. All the angels who have appeared in your life will appear before you then, and some of them will be holding the letter you wrote to them after this *yontif,* and they will embrace you, and you will know why, and they will say, and you will hear, "I didn't need the letter, but thank you anyway. Now let me tell you everything."

And they will tell you everything as they lead you into the green pastures beside the still waters where all the flocks have come home to rest and where all brothers and sisters and parents and children have found each other at last. They will explain that this is the place you have been looking for ever since the day you realized that the world is full of angels.

Ma t'vakesh. "What are you looking for?"

Dog Bite Enlightenment

from Yoga Journal

There is a Zen story about an old monk who practiced for over forty years in a monastery and then became disgusted—I'm getting nowhere, he thought—and decided to leave. As he walked down the path to the gate, with his few belongings on his back, he noticed that the walkway looked a bit messy. He went to get a rake to smooth it out. As he raked the dirt, one pebble flew out, hit some standing bamboo nearby, and made a sharp sound. The instant the monk heard that sound, he became fully and completely enlightened.

I have been having terrible trouble this summer with my house out on the mesa. First, it was the mice. Every day, I caught three in my Have-A-Heart mousetrap. This went on for a month. At the end of August, teaching a two-week writing workshop at the Mabel Dodge Lujan house in Taos, I came in to class and explained why I was late:

"As I was leaving the house, I heard the trap snap close again. I thought, that poor mouse will have to be in it all day. I better take her out now. So I put down my car keys and my books, walked her down the long drive, crossed the road, aimed her at Michael's house, and let her out."

Each morning the class wanted to know how many were caught. I told them I was getting the funny feeling I was catching the same ones over and over. Kate Green, who was teaching with me, said, "Well, you set out a meal for them each night. Why wouldn't they come back? And then in the morning, you give them a little ride to the end of your driveway, and they get to jog back and have a little exercise." It was true—the night before I couldn't find anything else in my refrigerator, so I set out gourmet almond butter for them.

One morning before I left to teach, the phone rang. "Eddie, I could swear the same mice are in the traps every morning."

"Nat, didn't you ever hear Mary's story? She was married to a man who had a cabin on an island in Rainey Lake, in northern Minnesota. He'd catch mice and take them in his canoe and let them off on another island. He'd say to Mary, 'I could swear they're coming back.' So he started to paint their toes with different colors of nail polish. Sure enough, when he started catching them, they had polish on them."

I shrieked. "You're kidding!"

I drove across the mesa to class that morning, thinking D-Con, the poison that mice munch and then run from the house in search of water. Last night, I saw four mice whiz across my living room as I read a book. It seemed to me they were almost frolicking, content from being well fed. I grew increasingly paranoid—I thought every shadow was another one. I read little that night. D-Con, I thought, and cackled as I turned my car toward Taos at the blinking light. I was tired of being the Bodhisattva of mice.

When I got to class, I told them Eddie's story. Very straight-faced, Jane raised her hand. "Are the islands inhabited that he was rowing them to?"

"I don't know. Why does that matter?"

"Well, if there was a house there, too, maybe that owner was catching them and bringing them back over to the other island."

On the way home from class that night, I stopped at Smith's and bought new and improved D-Con—two packages. I placed a box under the kitchen sink and another in the bathroom where the mice had been feasting. I lay awake, imagining I heard them crunching on the poison, imagining I saw their small white ghosts arising right outside my bedroom window. I felt terrible and guilty. I finally dozed off at three A.M. I woke up at four to a long, terrible animal cry. I was certain it was the mice dying. Then I was sure it was a cat who caught a poisoned mouse and he, too, was dying. I'd moved up the animal chain. I was ruining the entire neighborhood.

The next morning when I woke up, there were no mouse turds. I looked gingerly around the house. No mice had dived into the toilet bowl, desperate for water. Okay, I had one sleepless night, I thought. I'd be okay.

Two days later, I took a bath—finally, my new well was working, though the water was still a bit muddy. I thought I smelled something burning. Kate was over; she was reading me some of her new poems as I lounged in the brown water.

"Go check the barbecue. Maybe it's something out there."

She came back. "Nope, everything's fine."

"I still smell it. Check the kitchen."

"Oh, my god," she shrieked. "Nat, the house is on fire. The water heater—it's in flames."

By the time I slid wet across the tiles Kate had thrown water and put out the fire.

I stood there in a towel, looking at the smoldering remains of my Aquavac On-Demand Water Heater.

I became very calm. I wonder if there were mice in there, I thought.

On Tuesday, the plumber came to replace it. I went over everything with him. When he left, I sighed. "Now I have everything. The heater's replaced. My well runs, and the mice are gone." Twenty minutes later, as I spoke on the phone to my friend Cynthia in Santa Fe, all my telephone lines went dead.

I knew I was going crazy as I drove across the mesa to teach my afternoon class. I passed my plumber, who had gotten a tire blowout after he left my house. I waved, asked him if there was anything I could do, and then kept going. I parked at the post office. I thought I'd walk slowly across Kit Carson Park to the class. I needed to gather my wits. Nat, I kept saying to myself, breathe. These things happen.

I walked into the classroom. I told them about the phone going dead. Then I told them about the old monk who became fully enlightened when a stone hit some bamboo.

Then I paused for a brief moment. I held up my hands. "What a fool I've been. That phone going dead! There was my chance! I could have turned everything around! That was it—in the face of distress, I could have become totally enlightened. Oh, my god, what a jerk I am!"

Jane raised her hand. "Why don't you become enlightened now?"

"No, that was my moment! You can't do it later. I missed my moment."

Late one night in Amsterdam, a friend told me, leaning over the table, "You know, Natalie, I began studying with Katagiri Roshi when I was twelve years old. During one *sesshin,* I became enlightened, but I didn't know it. When I was seventeen, I told a friend about it, and I realized it had happened, so I went to Roshi and described the experience."

"What did he say?" I asked.

"He nodded, yes, sounds like it."

"So?"

"But I didn't know it then, so it didn't count." He laughed.

But I think I did become enlightened for a while, once. I was quick enough, alert—no, that wasn't it. I was big; I wasn't myself. My cells had been tossed up in my skull and fell down in another pattern. I saw things from a different angle, outside myself, my needs, my desires.

I was in southern France with Thich Nhat Hanh, in June two years after my first retreat with him. I was now forty-four years old. Each morning, Thay (Vietnamese for teacher) lectured for three hours. I came early to the zendo and sat right in front of him. I was ready to have the teachings poured into me. He talked about the Diamond, Lotus, and Avatamsaka Sutras. Halfway into each morning, he switched the subject and told us another episode of when he fell in love as a young twenty-four-year-old monk with a twenty-year-old nun. He said it was an accident—he was a monk; she was a nun. It was not supposed to happen. "Falling in love is an accident," he said. "Think about it: the expression *falling;* you trip into it." Because he did not act upon it in a romantic way, as we normally do, he examined these strong feelings with mindfulness, and forty years later he shared the benefit of that with us. I realized he was teaching the nature of love, of how to love well.

I flip through my notebook now and see the notes I took then. They seem to glimmer off the page: "Your first love has no beginning or end. Your first love is not your first love, and it is not your last. It is just love. It is one with everything.

"The present moment is the only moment available to us, and it is the door to all moments.

"When we practice mindfulness, we emit light. We create more time and space.

"The miracle is to walk on the earth.

"No coming. No going. Everything is pretending to be born and to die. That is a lie.

"This self has no self.

"A king once asked, 'Is there anything, any attachment, that will not cause suffering, anxiety, grief?'

"'No, Lord,' said the Buddha.

"It is okay to suffer in the process of love."

I heard these things during those three weeks, and they poured into me. I received them. I knew them to be true. I didn't try to understand them, figure them out with my logical mind. I walked differently on the earth because of them, and it continued after I left the retreat. But out in ordinary life, it felt as though I was tripping on LSD—I wasn't, though I did have my share of European chocolate. I felt a tenderness toward sidewalks, loved the tall sycamores lining Cour Mirabeau in Aix-en-Provence, where I went after the retreat, ate slices of pizza I bought in the streets like they were part of the Last Supper.

Then, on July 8, two weeks out of Plum Village, I was bitten in the back of my right leg, above the ankle, by a trained guard dog who had been hiding when I walked up to a private house, thinking it was a café. My friends and I had wandered off from one another—we were in St. Remy, near the monastery where Van Gogh committed himself for a year. I was bitten badly. No little teeth indenting my skin—this was a chunk, a big one, hanging out of my leg. I didn't know this until I was halfway over the hill, moving fast through the woods, toward the monastery. I stopped, turned my head, lifted the pale green cotton pant leg. Oh, my god! I must be hallucinating. It can't be as awful as that or I couldn't be walking. I dropped my pant leg and got to the monastery office, banged on the door, yelling. There was a rush of women inside; the door opened.

"Un chien!" I yelled, in my impeccable French, and made the motion with my hands together opening and closing, like a crocodile's jaw (I didn't know the French word for *bite*) "mon jamb!" I pointed to my pant leg. I did not lift it, though. I did not want these nurses and nuns to collapse in a dead faint.

"Un grand chien?" they asked.

"No, un grand bouche." I was in a panic. "Aidez-moi!"

They called an ambulance.

Now the remarkable thing: Not for a moment did I feel hatred for the dog. At the moment of our confrontation, I felt compassion for him. Thay had lectured us about "looking deeply." Looking deeply was instantaneous for me. The dog had been trained to do what he was doing. This was no act of personal violence. This was the result of the lineage of private property, of ownership, of fear of loss of possession—I do not mean to sound high-handed here or even political—I just saw into the depth of the act, where and how it came about. The dog bit once—deftly, swiftly—and retreated. I fell on my left knee. He growled fiercely, as though to warn me, "Get out of my space." I crawled out of the range of his chain.

In the ambulance—it was an old car carrying me to the hospital in Avignon—I sat in the back, my leg up along the length of the seat. "Dépêchez-vous," I called to the driver. She lit a cigarette. We passed groves of bamboo and fruit trees. I had left a note at the monastery for my friends: "Meet me at the hospital."

In the back of the car, I thought, if Buddhism's gonna work, it's gonna work now. "Breathing in"—I inhaled—"I know I am breathing in." "Breathing out"—I exhaled—"I know I am breathing out." I am always breathing in and out, but it is rare that I am aware of it. "Breathing in, I *know* I am breathing in." Actually, I was delighted to be aware of my breath. It gave me something to do besides freak out about the possibilities of what had just happened to my leg.

I remembered my friend Teijo—that was her Zen monk's name—I knew her originally as Roberta Munnich. She was in a monastery in Japan for several years and wrote a letter back to the States. "People ask me what I learn. I don't know. Not much, maybe. But yesterday, as I walked into the town from the monastery, carrying my begging bowl, I noticed I was facing in the direction I was going." I never forgot that. To slow down that much, to notice something that simple, that real and ordinary, something so elemental that we usually neglect to see it. "I noticed I was facing in the direction I was going."

I noticed I was breathing in. I noted I was breathing out. We turned the corner into the hospital parking lot. I was put on a gurney and wheeled into a small room.

Two nurses came in, lifted up my pant leg. "Oh, mon dieu!" they yelled, their eyes wide, their hands thrown across their open mouths.

They ran and got other nurses, orderlies. Everyone was emotional. Obviously, professional distance and cool were not practiced here in this French hospital.

"Un grand chien?" was the only medical question that was asked.

Breathing in—I was scared. Breathing out—I was afraid. High school French failed me. "Un docteur?" I moaned.

A man came in, wearing a white T-shirt. He looked; he said, "It all right." It was the most perfect English I had ever heard. "It okay." He put his hand on my leg.

"Oui?" I pleaded.

"It okay." It was the only English anyone spoke in the whole hospital. He made the motion with his hand that he was going to have to sew.

I nodded, yes, I understood.

He left.

I lay there, waiting. What does "okay," my leg okay mean?

I looked away as the doctor worked. A second felt like a year. He hummed a little. We were alone in the room. Okay, Nat, what are you going to do now? Breathing in and knowing it wasn't quite enough. I was facing the wall. I began to sing a song I'd learned at the retreat. I sang it loud. The lines, "I'm as solid as a mountain, as firm as the earth," comforted me the most. I repeated them over and over and skipped the rest of the song. Here I was, lying out on the table in a French hospital, my leg torn, my pants bloody, the only English I'd heard was "okay," I was alone, and at the other end of my leg, a doctor was performing unspeakable acts while I looked at the wall—and I was singing. Was this possible? I was filled with joy. I felt such gratitude to be alive. The air shimmered. I wanted to turn to the doctor and touch him, thank him.

This all happened in the moment, instantaneously. There was no lag time. I didn't realize a week later that I was okay or that everything was all right. The moment was all right when it was the moment, not later.

He was done. I turned. "Combien?" I asked. "How many?"

He made a face. "Beaucoup."

I held up ten fingers. "No." He shook his head. He flashed twenty fingers. "Vingt soutures."

I nodded.

The nurse came in who earlier had given me a tetanus shot. She showed me a card. I had to get another shot in a month. Another in a year.

My friends Rita and Phyllis came to the door. "I can leave," I said. We were so happy to see one another.

I sat in the back seat of our rented car.

"Let's sing," I said. All three of us had been to Plum Village.

We drove through the countryside. ". . . And I know there is space deep inside of me . . . I am free, I am free."

"We should go back to the hotel. You're in shock." Rita was driving.

"No, I want to go to these medieval towns I've been reading about," I insisted. I looked at the map. I wanted to live every moment now.

We drove down winding, thin, country dirt roads. "Pull over," I said.

We got out of the car and looked around. There were fruit trees—three of them—in tall grass near vineyards. I walked over to them and looked up. Cherries. This was a cherry tree; all ripe, many having fallen to the ground. No farmer was going to gather this crop. I grabbed fistfuls, hobbled with my bandaged leg from clump to clump, my hands dripping red.

"Aren't you afraid a guard dog is going to come?" Rita called, standing by the car, snapping a picture of me.

"Naa, no dog wants to harm me. That was a Mu dog, a Zen dog, that bit me. He said, 'Wake up!'" I laughed. "Rita, these are *Bing* cherries. Bing. Do you understand? They are my father's favorites. I always imagined they grew on vines, not trees." Phyllis stood under the tree, too, grazing alongside me.

I filled a big bag full of them. We drove in the dusk past a faded *chocolat* sign overlooking a beautiful valley and were stopped in Cavaillon by truckers, drinking wine out of bottles, their massive semis parked in the road—a blockade. They were demanding more lenient license laws. They let us pass. We drove on and on, the car carrying us back to Aix. We stopped at the all-night bakery next to our hotel and ate éclairs.

"The best I ever had," said Rita. She smiled. She had light brown freckles across her white skin, and black eyelashes.

I told her she looked familiar.

"How come?" she asked.

"You're Irish-Catholic. My father served them at the bar he owned during my childhood," I said.

She choked on her éclair, laughing. "Yeah, I bet he did."

I climbed the long flights up to room number twelve. Phyllis held my arm.

I loved the Hotel Splendide. I loved my room, with the window opening on the orange tile roofs of the city. Just that morning I had lain there looking out, carefree, the swallows scissoring the morning sky. Both legs intact. Now the Novocain was wearing off. A dog had bitten my leg.

The next day I stayed in bed. Rita brought me quiche and purple flowers. Phyllis drew my portrait. I read *The Great Gatsby* in its entirety. I'd bought it two days before at an English bookstore. The cover photo was black-and-white, a sleek boulevard with a man and woman leaning against a thirties sedan. In a foreign country, I discover the American classics again. I look over at that continent where I was born and wonder, Who am I anyway? And what is the American dream?

I finished the book, and I looked down at my leg, then at the water-lily wall painting the owner of the hotel had done, and I knew I was in my own dream.

The next day, Rita and I went to the emergency room of the Aix Hospital. I needed to get my wound dressed, and no one at the other hospital spoke enough English to tell me what to do. We found a doctor there who spoke some English.

"It maybe come infected. Maybe okay. Maybe you need operation. They take skin from your hip"—he pointed to my hip—"and put on leg." He pointed to the dog bite.

Rita and I looked at each other. It wasn't going to heal in ten days, in time for me to fly to London? I was going to have to leave and return to the States. A reality map spread out in front of me. Suddenly Rita and I were bewildered young girls together in a foreign country. She told me about her father's funeral in New York. "You know it's going to happen someday, but there you are picking out a coffin. 'Whose life is this?' you think."

We turned into a travel agent's. I made reservations to get a flight the next day from Nice to Minneapolis—my close friend there is a doctor—and change planes in New York. I packed.

I had an idea about the way my life should go. My plan to fly to London to meet my friend Henry and travel around Scotland was just an idea—even though I had made travel arrangements—it was a concept, a future moment. It did not exist, except in my head. In a moment, your whole life can change. "It is not because of impermanence that we suffer, but because of our ideas about permanence." (Thich Nhat Hanh)

Event followed event. I called Henry and told him I couldn't come, but I was not suffering. I miraculously was not holding onto any plans, and I did not know it was miraculous. I was living my life. I was in it in a way I'd never been in it before. It was burning pure white.

The plane had engine trouble near London, and we had to come down. I was taken in a wheelchair—my leg had become swollen— to a bus that drove us from Heathrow to Gatwick. I looked out at the green grass of England, at the sturdy homes. I had to board another plane, and we landed in New York too late to catch a plane to Minneapolis. There were long lines as Delta figured out hotel and plane reservations for all of us at Kennedy. I sat in a wheelchair. The porter went ahead of the line and got me new reservations. Then he told me I had to wait with the rest of the group for a bus to go to the Holiday Inn.

"Will the bus be outside?" I asked.

"I suppose so," he answered.

"Well, could you wheel this outside? I'll wait there. I need real air. I've been in planes and airports for nineteen hours." He brought me to the front door and left me outside. The air was humid, the sky hazy; it was a New York summer evening. And past the hustle of taxis and sweaty people of every color and language, wearing shorts and thongs and baseball hats, greeting one another, grabbing arms and hands, was the full moon, like an ancient call, big and fat, out there in the dark. I looked up, and my heart flew to it.

The porter came back ten minutes later. "Wanna come back in? It's hot out here." He put his hand to his neck. "Air cool in there." He nodded toward the door.

"No, thanks," I said. "I'd like to sit here with the moon." He laughed, looked up at it, wiped his brow, and left. I remained in my wheelchair, my right leg stretched out, my blue nylon suitcase hanging from one arm of the chair, and my red nylon purse hanging from the other, until the bus came twenty minutes later.

In Minneapolis, my leg was a waiting game. Would the flap that they sewed back in France survive? I could walk or lie down, be straight, vertical, or horizontal; sitting cut off vital blood flow. I lay on my side in Carol's living room and colored in the chair I had drawn while waiting for Phyllis at Deux Garçons, the café where I wrote in Aix. I wanted it to be a predominantly gray painting. It ended up being a bright yellow and red one.

I read a memoir by David Muir, *Becoming Japanese*. I had known David when I lived in Minneapolis eight years earlier. It was a good book. I thought of Japan, the land I hadn't yet been to, and of Roshi, my Zen teacher, who had died in Minnesota two years earlier. I loved all of Japan, because that country had produced that man. I sat in the suburbs of Minneapolis all day, alone, while Carol went to work. Sometimes I lay on her front lawn and looked up at the trees, elms and maples. Big ones. They had to be the most beautiful things. I was in the Midwest again. I walked to the mailbox, down those asphalt streets, the early afternoon so still and empty. A man looked out his window, his lawn perfectly trimmed, his shutters white, his sprinkler poised for action. The sunlight waved the tree leaves in shadows across me. The mail was picked up at two-fifteen every day but Sundays, and on Saturdays pickup was at twelve. They wrote *noon* on the inside lid of the blue metal mailbox.

I hobbled to the Lincoln Deli each day—five blocks away—for matzo ball soup. On Wednesday they had a special: a bowl of soup and half a sandwich for $4.95. As I leaned my head over the steaming bowl, I noticed that the same old people were there every day. There was a retirement community four blocks away. A few days earlier, I had been in France, land of Manet, Monet, Matisse, Picasso, van Gogh, Cezanne. Now I was in the suburbs of the Midwest with old people, an ulcer on my leg, glad for my chicken soup. I remembered an old Jewish joke whose punch line was: I know where I *want* to go, but I don't know where I'm going.

I walked back to Carol's, ate some cappuccino yogurt, looked for the mailman, did a few paintings the size of postcards. One was of a small dog with a large mouth. I wrote on it, "Un chien n'est pas grand, mais la bouche est grand." Another was of a traffic intersection with the signs saying SLOW and YIELD, ending at Heaven Café. In the foreground were three ducks and a green lawn, and it was raining on them. "Il pleut tres bien," I wrote below them.

Carol, who was a dermatologist, came home each day and told me about the patients she saw: a Russian immigrant with a boil on her neck, an old man who was an activist and had just come home from a march in Washington. "'Clarence,' I told him, 'that march enlarged the ulcer on your foot.'

"'I couldn't not go. People's rights were at stake.'"

Carol and I went for long slow walks along the abandoned railroad tracks. I told her about Jack Kerouac working for the railroad and how writing happens, how it's over at your side, not directly in front of you—gnawing at your insides, calling you out of yourself, wanting something of you that is not right in your face, but coming up from the whole underworld.

I'd met Carol ten years earlier in a Hebrew class when I lived in the Twin Cities. After I left, we had become traveling partners. Every two years or so, we would meet for a month in Czechoslovakia, Amsterdam, Portugal, Israel. Now I was back in

Minneapolis with her. I asked her, "This is your life? Every day you go to work? Regular and real?" She laughed and nodded. Each night she patiently helped me with my dressing. After she went to sleep, I'd open the shade of my bedroom window and smell summer through the screen and see the moon reflected on the thin square of wires that kept out the flies. "The Midwest," I'd whisper, "the Midwest," and I'd feel the corn in distant fields turn out of its seeds.

Carol had a day off in the middle of the week. "Let's go to Lake Rebecca," I proposed.

"Nat, where's that?" she asked, interested. The old adventurer, she loved anything new, even in a fifty-mile radius of her home.

I told her it was nearby. I would direct. She should just drive and not remember the directions. It was a secret place, I told her. We put down the back of the passenger seat so I could remain horizontal and my foot wouldn't swell. As we rode through the green countryside, past fruit stands and gas stations, I told her, "You'll see, no one will be there. Minnesotans are chauvinistic about their state. Yes, there are good things here, but they miss what the *real* good things are. For twenty years, Katagiri Roshi lived here in a little zendo on Lake Calhoun. No one ever came! What they missed! Then everyone whips up to northern Minnesota to get nearer to mosquitoes. They don't know the true beauty is in the southern part of the state. Rolling hills, big red barns."

I was on a harangue. I loved to carry on about the Minnesotans. The people I loved and hated, how could they be so good and so dumb. It drove me crazy when I lived here for six years. I'd always had the strange urge to take off my clothes and run down their Main Streets, screaming. But go away from them, move to another state, where every car driving its roads carries licenses that herald the Land of Enchantment, and even though it's true, with New Mexico's pink cliffs, red earth, sky as big as the world, and light falling on cottonwood leaves like the last remains of God visiting Moses on Mount Sinai, I missed the Minnesotans—their rootedness, their sincerity, their gentle, easy openness, their tendency toward the spiritual embodied in good old American virtues of truth, honesty, and justice that the rest of us have all about forgotten.

I went on to tell Carol about the bank in Owatonna, two hours south, that I always visited. "Everyone thought I was nuts. 'A bank?' they'd ask. It was designed by Louis Sullivan. He called it a color form poem, and it was one of the most magnificent buildings I've ever seen. It had a beautiful mural of cows inside."

"Cows?" she laughed. Carol was brought up on a farm in North Dakota.

"Precisely," I said, "cows. You Midwesterners don't know what you've got."

We drove through the town of Maple Grove. I lifted my head from my horizontal position to look over the bottom edge of the window. This was the town Neil and I drove out to in order to get a special chocolate wedding cake for our marriage a zillion years ago. A woman baked them out here in her home. I was quiet after that. I thought of doing a painting of that wedding cake: six tiers, a plastic man and woman on top, yellow fringe hanging from each layer, the chocolate icing dark and laid on thick, packed with sugar to keep it stiff. Then my mind skipped over to a painting of a softball diamond, girls and boys playing together, green trees, the team would be called "The Tygers," spelled like William Blake's poem. It would be a Midwestern painting, the world Neil brought me to.

Carol parked the car. I was right. The park was empty. I slung her old blue bed sheet she had in the car trunk over my shoulder, and we walked down the path I knew that brought us to swans in a far-off pond, to an old white barn with a black roof, through prairie grass, past beehives standing in fields. My pace slowed down more and more. Neil and I used to come here all the time and lie naked in the open fields, the only place in Minnesota we felt safe to take off our clothes outside. I remembered walking hand in hand, slightly bored, relaxed, no beginning or end to the afternoon. He would hum a tune, his thin red freckled hand in mine. Sometimes he would tell me a story about his grandmother, Chloe, in Kankakee. I loved that man, I thought to myself. I loved him deep and long, and it would be forever, though we had divorced twelve years earlier. I felt sad and happy that we had known the kind of love we had together: simple, real, something pure in its innocence—the kind of innocence that eventually destroys itself.

Carol and I walked on and on in silence. The sky was a big gray, and a slow wind moved the tall grasses. I spread her bedsheet on the ground, and we lay down. We sipped at the bottle of water. I mentioned Neil. She told me about traveling to Europe for the first time after college and hitting every capital she could in a month. Then she told me how her mother worked on the farm, stronger and longer than any hired hand. Then she imitated for me again how her Rumanian boyfriend pronounced her name, how the *r* rolled out for a long time, and he said, "I want a bad mood," and she corrected him: "I'm in a bad mood," and he said, "Yes, I want a bad mood," and we lay on our backs, giggling.

Two days later—suddenly I wanted to revisit old places—I went to the Croissant Express. It wasn't the Croissant Express anymore. It was some other name, equally as corny, and they'd rearranged the counter so it blocked some of the great windows, and they now had a nonfat yogurt machine, and the chocolate chip cookies weren't half as good, but I sat down there in one of their seats for a moment anyway, there on the corner of Hennepin and Lagoon.

And sure enough! I'd been right about this place ten years ago when I wrote here every day. It was a power spot in the Midwest. There was an energy field here in this little dessert place. Here was another example of a place the Minnesotans missed when they were touting their state. When Carol came home from work that night, I told her, "I want to buy a bra. I haven't worn a bra since I found feminism and I was twenty. I'm forty-four. I want a bra." A bra and the Croissant Express had nothing to do with each other, but it happened on the same day.

"Okay, Nat, let's go to Dayton's." Dayton's was the department store in downtown Minneapolis that my mother had loved when she came to visit twelve years earlier. "Now this is a good store," my mother had said, her eyes bright, as she turned to look up at me. I was one stair higher up on the escalator that was moving down.

Carol parked in the underground lot. She insisted on getting in some compact space that was at an odd angle. Then we went up in the elevator to the third floor. The whole back of the floor opened out into lingerie and undergarments. Section after section of bras. Athletic ones, evening ones, seamless, nylon, lace, day, morning— any kind you wanted, for any occasion. No wonder my mother loved Dayton's. Every desire could be appeased.

The place was empty. Carol veered off. She saw something on sale. "Natty, just go on. I'll meet you."

I was left alone under the fluorescent lights with aisles of undergarments. I called out. "Is there a salesgirl here? Help."

A young woman popped her shiny face out from behind a rack of slips. "Yes?"

"I'm looking for a comfortable bra. I haven't worn one in twenty years."

She stayed professional. She didn't wince.

"Okay, we'll try several different kinds and see what feels good." She buzzed all over the department and grabbed bras with her right hand and handed them to me, trying to follow behind her. I was growing paler, thinner. I was regressing to that adolescent back in childhood, when I began at twelve to feel myself bound in.

Carol met me in the dressing room. I had regressed by now to a gorilla. Nothing female fit. I "wanted a bad mood."

"Let's see," Carol said.

I turned around like an ape.

"No, Natty, not those. Let me find you one. Just wait here a minute."

I waited.

She came in with three. I chose one easily.

"I'll buy four of these, so they'll last the rest of my life." We stood at the cash register. It was the same redheaded salesgirl, the only one on the floor.

"I've been working here ever since I graduated from school. You come to love all these garments," she told us.

"How old are you?" I asked.

"Twenty-eight." She saw my shocked expression. "Yes, it's been ten years. My friends call me June Cleaver, and I know they're right."

"Back where I live, in Santa Fe, if anyone did something consistently for ten years they could become governor," I told her.

As we left the department store, my bras in hand in a bag, I turned my head, looking back at the salesgirl. "Carol, I'm telling you, it's a foreign country here. A women of twenty-eight says proudly she's like June Cleaver! She's from another world!"

At the end of two weeks, I went to my third visit with the plastic surgeon. I felt so confident that the flap had gotten enough blood and was healing that I told Carol I'd go to the doctor by myself. I'd see her after work.

I took a taxi to the medical building. I went into the office with great confidence. Two weeks earlier, I'd known nothing about dog bites. Now I thought I was an authority. The nurse took off the bandage. I looked at it all the time now; when I first arrived in Minneapolis, I'd been afraid to look. The stitches were in the shape of a tongue but larger—the size of a coffee mug. And just like Frankenstein, with his stitches accentuated across his face, those stitches that the French doctor gave me were visible. You could count each one and even see the knot where he ended. The thread was black. He'd had a regular sewing bee in the operating room.

I said to the doctor when he walked in, "It's my professional opinion that it's doing really well. Carol and I conferred. Her only concern is that the flap skin is a little yellow."

"Let's have a look." He bent over it. "Hmmmm." He tapped and poked. "It's not making it. We'll have to cut it out."

Everything went blurred at that moment. A nurse assisted him. It happened fast. The whole flap was cut out, everything the French doctor had sewn back in. It didn't survive.

"You'd better look," the doctor said. "You are going to have to dress it every day."

"No, I can't." I had my head turned to the wall. "I just can't. I'll do it some other time. Carol will look at it."

"It would be better to look at it now, while I'm here."

I heaved my head around. "Oh, my god!"

When I was in fourth grade, and we went to visit my Uncle Manny in Brooklyn, who was a doctor, I snuck into his office after dinner, before dessert was served, and looked through his medical journals. The pictures were so horrifying they burned holes in my brain. They were so fascinating that I couldn't stop looking. This is what the hole in my leg looked like when I glanced at it—like the pictures in Uncle Manny's magazines.

The plastic surgeon actually held me. I felt his comfort flow into me. He understood my fear. He had a tenderness that amazed me. Carol had told me that he had fought cancer and survived.

I went back to Carol's in a cab. All I said to her was, "Please take me for a malt."

We sat outside on the patio of an ice cream parlor near Lake Harriet. I spooned chocolate shake into my mouth. I began to sob. I fell over the table and cried and cried. Now this was another miracle. I'd been living right there with everything in front of my face, moment by moment, since I had been bitten by the dog in France, but now who was I crying for over my malt? Not for me, though I was scared. I felt inside me, like a column of white light, overwhelming gratitude for my life and for the tenderness of that doctor. I would live. That was certain. I could walk out of his office with a bad leg. There wasn't a question of life and death. I was lucky, but I felt the life of my teacher, Katagiri Roshi. Roshi went in and out of the hospital right across from the medical building I had just been in. Chemotherapy treatments, radiation, infection. Life and death. Life and death. I felt him in his car after a treatment, exhausted, dauntless, a Zen student driving him back through the winter streets of Minneapolis to his apartment above the zendo, his wife of thirty years in the back seat next to him. She told me once that for that whole year, they were never outside. In hospitals, in cars, in beds, in bedrooms, away from harsh weather, drafts, breezes.

When I quieted down, Carol asked quietly, "How are you doing?" She was good about crying. She just let it happen.

"You know, Carol." I felt shy. After I cry, I feel as though my face is ripped off. "Roshi didn't make it. I just now felt physically what he must have gone through, moment by moment." I sighed, pushed the malt away from me. I didn't want any more. "I am so lucky to be alive."

My friend Carol nodded.

I was leaving Minnesota to return to New Mexico. The Saturday before I left, Carol and I drove down to the Zen land on the bluffs of the Mississippi near New Albin, Iowa. Katagiri Roshi's ashes were there. We arrived at midday, the sun hot, the air thick and humid—it had rained earlier that day. I told Carol I needed to go up there alone, and I climbed the high hill where his monument was. I went slow, my right leg bandaged, the grass tall, thigh high. There is a ceremony you're supposed to do when you visit the memorial—with water and thick scrub brushes, incense and offerings. You are supposed to carry all this up. I carried it all maybe a quarter of the way; then it became too hard; I dropped the buckets of water, let go of everything, and hobbled up the rest of the way empty-handed. I collapsed on the smooth granite that his name was carved in. I looked out over the valley. The spruce trees we'd planted for future generations ten years ago, as soon as we bought the land, were now way above my head. I could see the brown tar-paper roof of the zendo and the porch around it, the bell, the kitchen beyond it, the slow Winnebago Creek, the supply room, Roshi's cabin.

"Pretty nice, pretty nice," I said. It was an expression I'd picked up years ago from a newspaper article when I lived here. I read that an old woman's house, in Blue Earth, Minnesota, was destroyed by a tornado, and the townspeople got together, surprised her, and built her a brand-new house. When they brought her to see it, her only comment with a smile was, "Pretty nice, pretty nice." I took that as my comment about everything in the Midwest. "Pretty nice, pretty nice," I'd say, so as not to get too excited, too enthusiastic.

I sat on the memorial of my great dead teacher, looked out on the great world, and commented, "Pretty nice, pretty nice."

Then I turned to him. "Roshi, you know I'm a fuckup." Then I began to laugh. What a terrible and devoted Zen student I had been. He knew all about me. I'd been his student for twelve years. "Sorry, I don't have the incense and the scrub brushes." I laughed some more and felt a bitterness, too. He wasn't in the flesh to laugh with me.

Then I sighed and just sat there for a while. It was hot, probably the worst part of the day to be sitting up there. I began to get up, and then I sat down again. "Roshi, what do you think about love?" I asked.

A slow joy, a trickle of heat was in my chest. "To love is a good thing," I heard him say.

I threw him a kiss. "I love you forever," I said and began my slow walk down the hill.

A moment later, I heard a terrible snorting. I flung my head around. Oh, no, animals were going to attack my leg—a deer! a beautiful, chestnut-colored deer leaped out from Roshi's hill. I never would have seen her except she snorted. She ran like a dancer, all four hooves were in the air, and then she disappeared in the forest.

Deer were my favorite animals. But I thought they came out only at dusk and stood at the edge of daylight. She was in full sun, in full view. Pure energy broke from my heart.

I whistled the rest of the way down the hill and picked up the buckets and brushes near the bottom.

EDWARD HIRSCH

Simone Weil: Lecture on Love
from Image

I would speak to you about supernatural love,
which touches creatures and comes only from God,
though I am unworthy to speak of divine love.
God's pity for us is not a reason to adore God
but to know ourselves, for how else *could* we love
ourselves without the motive—the reason—of God?
I am a stranger to myself, whom I cannot love,
when I have fallen away from knowledge of God.
Is my wretchedness a sign of His eternal love?
I believe not, though I am understood by God
who recognizes the porousness of human love:
the divine Word descends and returns to God.

I speak to you from a chastening solitude.
You must never allow yourself to be soiled
by human affection. Preserve your solitude,
though everything vile, everything soiled
and second-rate, revolts against this solitude:
the naked fantasy of those who are soiled
wishes to dirty the abundance of solitude.
To touch is to be sullied, revulsed, soiled,
to relinquish power over your own solitude.
Possessing another—to be possessed—is soiled,
since only purity can restore our solitude.
Sentiment offers fertile ground to be soiled.

Not by accident you have never been loved,
for love no longer knows how to contemplate,
only to possess (disappointment of Platonic love).
Carnal love, which Plato would not contemplate,
is a degraded image—a parody—of divine love:
to love gloriously, to adore and contemplate
the distance between ourselves and what we love,
the void between what we love and contemplate,
the Lord Himself. But how can we possibly love
ourselves with the Word of God to contemplate?
Agape: to be delivered into a divine love—
what He divines in us is strange to contemplate.

I will know that my adoration of God is truth
when joy and suffering inspire equal gratitude;
affliction is our warrant, the deepest truth
of human existence, which fills me with gratitude.
Belief in the existence of others is a truth
to be acknowledged—like faith, like gratitude—
and may even demonstrate a desire for truth
beyond the confines of self. We show gratitude
when we acknowledge our vulnerability as truth,
the mark of existence that marks our gratitude.
We have touched the flames of supernatural truth,
and now can burn with the fires of gratitude.

It is always a fault to wish to be understood
before we have made ourselves clear to God
or to ourselves, who can never be understood
unless we offer our contradictions to God.
We must relinquish the desire to be understood,

annihilating our need to want anything from God.
Our affliction can be realized and understood
as a form of opportunity proffered us by God
who knows us as creatures He has understood;
we must sacrifice ourselves to this inhuman God.
George Herbert called prayer "something understood":
I would have us shattered by understanding God.

RODGER KAMENETZ

Silence at the Heart: The New Landscape of Jewish Meditative Practice

from The New York Times Magazine

For the past seven years, I've been searching for a Jewish practice that works for me. I've studied kabbalah and Jewish meditation with mystical Jews and joyous feminists, prayed in every flavor of synagogue, and met with thousands of my fellow Jews. One thing I've learned: in my very individual search for a new serious way to be a Jew, I'm not on my own.

My search began, oddly enough, in Dharamsala, a remote hill station in northern India in 1990, following an encounter with the Dalai Lama. The Buddhist leader asked a group of Jewish leaders: What is your inner life? How do your practices benefit people in their everyday lives? In particular, and this was the deepest question: How does practicing Judaism help you deal with affliction, pain, sorrow, trouble? The questions the Dalai Lama asked Jews, then, are precisely those American Jews are asking themselves today. My account of this dialogue, *The Jew in the Lotus,* which seemed far-out even to my publisher when it first appeared in 1994, surprised all of us by becoming a Jewish best-seller of the decade. The margins have moved to the center, and with them have come questions of the Jewish inner life.

There are many names for this shift in Jewish focus, but the meaning is simple enough; Jews very much want their Judaism to work, even if for many, especially among the more secularized, the actual mechanics are rusty and the synagogue itself far from inviting. In fact, for a growing number of American Jews today, the private search for religious meaning—what is loosely called "spirituality"—is taking place outside the synagogue. This search is often individual rather than communal or is happening at the margins of the Jewish community, beyond the reach of and, until fairly recently, outside the notice of traditional Jewish institutions. In some ways this is very good news: American Jews whose accomplishments have largely been in the secular arena, are looking in Judaism for answers to their deepest inner questions. But the grassroots and individualistic qualities of this search are catching many traditional community-based Jewish institutions off guard, and they are now scrambling to respond.

I knew something was up when I was asked last January to speak at the United Jewish Appeal–Jewish Federations of Manhattan about the Jewish-Buddhist dialogue. The UJA is the bulwark secular institution of American Judaism and the largest philanthropic organization in the world. Yet there at Judaism central, for an hour and a half I fielded questions about Jewish meditation, the Jewish renewal movement of Rabbi Zalman Schachter, about kabbalah, and about comparative mysticism. Finally, one older gentleman who seemed a bit bewildered by the discussion raised his hand and asked, "What does this have to do with supporting the state of Israel?" I smiled and said, "Absolutely nothing."

The old exoteric—outward-looking—agenda of institutional Judaism was heavily focused on supporting Israel, along with such enduring issues as anti-Semitism, the Holocaust, the rescue of Soviet and Ethiopian Jewry. And while these issues remain vital to many, especially older Jews, for a new generation, for whom the immigrant generation is a fading memory, the outward struggles have turned inward.

This shift has implications for how and where Jews worship. At Ansche Chesed, an innovative influential upper west side Conservative synagogue, Rabbi Michael Strassfeld has been experimenting for the past year with meditation and *niggunim* (wordless melodies) for a weekday service. This fall he introduced an hour-long meditative service in prime time just before the Sabbath morning prayer service. He was influenced in part by a meditation workshop for rabbis sponsored by the Nathan Cummings Foundation. But the demand for such practices is not coming from rabbis. According to Rabbi Strassfeld, "There's a growing interest within the Jewish community in meditation and Judaism as a spiritual practice."

It sounds odd to speak of Judaism as a spiritual practice, as if this were a new emphasis, but for many mainstream Jews, it is. During my visit to UJA I also met with a group of rabbis just returned from a conference sponsored by a major Jewish foundation. What was the subject? I asked. One rabbi answered, with no apparent irony, "Making the synagogue a spiritual place."

The fact is, the synagogue isn't perceived as a spiritual place by many Jews. There's currently a gap between the yearnings of individuals and the institutions that are supposed to be serving them. You can feel the disconnection at both ends. When I spoke to Professor Gary Tobin, who directs the Brandeis Institute for Communal and Religious Life in San Francisco and who consults often with Jewish communal organizations, he told me flatly that "spirituality is a buzz word," "a Christian concept," and "faddish." The evidence for it, he said, is "strictly anecdotal."

I was taken aback. In speaking around the country, I'd been inundated with questions about Jewish spirituality. The Jewish renewal movement of Rabbi Zalman Schachter, a network of small prayer groups whose national headquarters, Aleph, is based in Philadelphia, is growing in popularity on its own and is gaining influence far beyond its numbers among more mainstream denominations. Two new organizations dedicated to Jewish meditation have sprung up on the West Coast. In the spring of 1996, San Francisco's Chochmat Halev held a major conference on meditation attended by over 550 Jews. Metivta, based in Los Angeles, held a similar conference in December 1997. Books on kabbalah, hasidism, Jewish meditation, and Jewish-Buddhist dialogue are enjoying unprecedented sales, according to a November 10 article in *Publisher's Weekly.* Says Rabbi Lawrence Kushner, a Reform rabbi and author known nationally for his mystical writings, "I don't have data on the number of congregations that do meditative things: chanting *niggunim,* sharing personal stories, sitting in silence or formal silent meditation for long periods. But there's been a change. Twenty years ago if someone did that, people would think they were nuts. Now they would say, that's interesting, we do that, too."

The sound of this silence has penetrated even the hallways of the UJA, that most secular of Jewish organizations, precisely why I was asked to speak there. If you visit the busy offices in Manhattan you still can feel the tremendous commitment and willpower and sheer muscle of a philanthropic organization that raises over two hundred million dollars a year. Yet top fund-raisers have detected a shift in attitude, at least among the younger generation of donors. Alan Bayer, a fifteen-year veteran of Jewish communal organizations and a senior staff member, told me of a recent conversation with a donor in his forties. "He said, 'I have a dozen different ways to be philanthropic. What I need from UJA is to make my philanthropy connect me to my religion.'

"That is not what his father would have said or his grandfather," Bayer told me. "UJA for them was the insurance policy: to insure Jewish safety and survival here and around the world. But the notion that giving to UJA would have a religious component is emerging as a major theme for the new generation of Jews." This is surprising for an institution never previously regarded as providing religious services. Likewise, the UJA Western Region sponsored in the fall a two-day conference on prayer and spirituality in Santa

Monica, attended by over five hundred Jews age forty-five and under with more than one hundred applicants turned away. Similar conferences have been sponsored by the Wexner Foundation for young Jewish leaders. The young donors and *machers* of the Jewish community are suddenly interested in studying, of all things, God and prayer.

Yet if committed young Jewish leaders are turning inward, the vast majority of Jews aren't doing so in synagogues, which may account for Professor Tobin's skepticism. According to statistics gathered by him and other demographers, only 15 to 24 percent of the Jewish population are synagogue members at any given time. Moreover, it's acknowledged that only a small core of that already-small group attends services on a regular basis. While Tobin points out there's a parallel decline in affiliation among Protestants and Catholics as well, the Jewish figures are the lowest of any American religious group. The fastest-growing denomination of American Jews is unaffiliated.

It seems contradictory, then, to say that Jews are turning inward, and yet these same Jews stay home from the synagogue. I found one explanation when I asked Tobin, who is himself quite active in the Jewish community, about his own religious life. "I try to go to synagogue. And I have a great rabbi, as charismatic and inspirational a rabbinic leader as you can want, and the services are deadly and take three and a half hours. As my Uncle Marvin says, 'Why would any God want people to noodge him that much?'"

Professor Shaul Magid of the Jewish Theological Seminary describes this as a widely shared feeling. "People are realizing Jewish prayer is not happening. It's not working, the liturgy is not inspiring, the prayer communities are not inspiring." Rabbi Simon Jacobson, a best-selling author who calls himself a "yarmulke-wearing, beard-wielding traditional Jew," told me the same holds in Orthodox circles. "We live in a highly materialistic society. We have so many distractions. We are not naturally going to gravitate to that quiet moment of serene communion with God. This has seeped into all communities, even those that traditionally pray three times a day. I would say assimilation has affected all of us; none of us is immunized from it. Personal intimacy with God is what Judaism is about. When that's not experienced, everything begins to ring hollow, it becomes technical. Prayer without *kavannah* [inner intention] is like a body without a soul." Many who are searching for *kavannah* are turning to the study of long-dormant meditative practices of kabbalah, or Jewish mysticism.

Jewish meditation has a very long history, yet many quite knowledgeable Jews in the mainstream will state with great conviction that it does not exist. This paradox is perhaps best explained by Rabbi Zalman Schachter, the acknowledged leader of the Jewish renewal movement, who has inspired and taught many of the current crop of Jewish meditation teachers and who has written an introduction to the subject of meditation and Jewish prayer, *Gate to the Heart*. For most of Jewish history, Rabbi Schachter says, the number of Jews involved in meditation was small, perhaps in each generation "less than a minyan." That is because meditation was elaborated in medieval times primarily by kabbalists, who tended to be secretive or whose texts were obscure to the uninitiated.

Indeed, much of the mystical tradition has been oral and underground. However, Talmudic texts show that early practitioners of meditation include the Talmudic sages, such as the first-century Rabbi Akiba, and his contemporaries, known as "chariot riders" or *merkabah* mystics. Their meditations focused on the visionary book of Ezekiel. In succeeding centuries, such techniques were often taught orally, but in thirteenth-century Spain, kabbalah, and with it meditation, came more into the open when the Zohar, a mystical Torah commentary and narrative, first appeared. After the 1492 expulsion of Jews from Spain, kabbalah flourished in the small community of Safed in northern Israel. There the kabbalah of Rabbi Isaac Luria developed into a highly elaborate system of meditations. However, it was only with the popularizing movement of hasidism in the eighteenth-century Ukraine that both kabbalah and meditative techniques became accessible to the average Jew. And while these teachings and practices continued to be preserved within hasidic groups that survived the Holocaust, only in very recent years have they been brought out more widely in a very different context, a largely secular and assimilated American landscape. This process began in the late sixties among countercultural Jews who prayed together in small groups, known as *havurot.* Later, through the offshoot of the *havurah* movement known as Jewish renewal, kabbalah and hasidism have been smuggled into unorthodox circles and have begun to take root.

Much of the smuggling was done by Rabbi Schachter himself, over the past thirty years, as a leader of Jewish renewal. Born in pre-war Poland and coming out of the mystical and ultra-Orthodox world of Chabad Hasidism, he fully embraced the culture of a new age starting in the sixties. Rabbi Schachter insists on both tradition and innovation: what is old will be new, but what is new will be sacred. Thus in Jewish renewal circles one finds an emphasis on both meditation and feminism, both contemporary ecology and kabbalah. For instance, Rabbi Schachter speaks of kashrut in terms of "eco-kosher"—asking whether meat produced under conditions that destroy the rain forest or produced under inhumane conditions can really be considered kosher.

When I asked Rabbi Schachter once why so many Jews these days are interested in meditation, he described the change in terms of a grammar of Jewish participation. "In synagogue I'm there because it's genitive; my poppa belong to the shul, I'm of it. I'm an accusative Jew because a Gentile calls me that. . . . But unless it gets into the nominative, I'm not a Jew. From that first-person place, people who want experience become meditators."

A first-person place. I did not come to these questions in any official capacity. Perhaps, indeed, there is only anecdotal evidence that I or others like me exist. I only know that after encountering the Dalai Lama, I returned home most impressed by a quality the Tibetans call the "quiet mind." I knew I didn't have one. My mind was more Philip Roth novel than meditation manual. There were competing voices inside that argued and joked, imprints of old family arguments, and the Jewish culture style of humor, aggression, insult, and irony summed up in the word *chutzpah.*

Yet I was convinced that it was really impossible to develop a spiritual life while dominated by the demons of aggression and anger. After the massacre in the mosque at Hebron and the assassination of Yitzhak Rabin, murders committed and in some cases applauded by traditionally observant Jews, this point became quite obvious.

I started searching for a Judaism that spoke to my heart. That search brought me in spring 1995 to Rabbi Jonathan Omer-Man. Ordained by Rabbi Schachter, Omer-Man is a sixty-seven-year old founder of Metivta, a school of Jewish wisdom in Los Angeles that in the past seven years has taught over three thousand Jews the rudiments of Jewish meditation.

An English Jew who made aliyah to Israel in the fifties, Rabbi Omer-Man was a secular Zionist living on a kibbutz when polio paralyzed his body. In the early sixties in Jerusalem he began to study kabbalah with the great Hebrew University scholar,

Gershom Scholem. But he soon moved from academia to practice, with Rabbi Adin Steinsaltz and with teachers from Jerusalem's *haredi* neighborhood of Meah Shearim.

In 1977 Rabbi Omer-Man began teaching in Los Angeles at the request of the Los Angeles Hillel council as part of an outreach program. These days Metivta has grown into an organization sponsoring three meditative retreats a year, a daily morning meditation group, and a healing center. Plans are afoot to create an urban retreat center. Central to Metivta are classes in beginning Jewish meditation. There's been such a growth in interest nationwide that Rabbi Omer-Man is currently conducting a year-long school to train twenty teachers of Jewish meditation.

"There's a demand out there not being answered," he told me in a recent phone interview. "For a long time the Jewish establishment denied there was spirituality. But I hear it everywhere: Demands. Requests. Sometimes inarticulate. Someone will come to the rabbi and say, Teach me Jewish meditation. Ten years ago they said there was no such thing. Now they've heard about it. It's coming more and more from communities as well. Last week I got calls from Kansas City, Phoenix, and New York. I don't know who to refer them to.

"Of course you can be a good Jew without meditation," he adds. "But in the ecology of the Jewish people this is an essential niche. One of the tragedies of our time is that people don't deepen the inner life except through therapy. Judaism has an incredibly rich, a profound, language of the inner life."

That language, as taught by Rabbi Omer-Man, stresses silence. Many Jews associate silence with Eastern practice. Yet there is also a profound Jewish silence at the heart of Jewish prayer. "The awareness of the profound knowledge of the divine in the world is acquired in a place of stillness," Rabbi Omer-Man taught me, "not in a place of activity. It complements, it does not replace, it isn't instead of prayer, it isn't instead of mitzvot [the Jewish commandments]."

At times our interactions were both frustrating and amusing. Silence did not come easy for me. In fact, I was pushy for equanimity, stalking Elijah with a kind of chutzpah that just doesn't befit a student of meditation. I remember in an early lesson, Omer-Man was teaching a meditation on the Shema, and I began peppering him with questions. I asked him how long one would do it.

"I don't answer that question," he said.

"Are you supposed to watch the distraction from the performance or the performance itself?"

"Yes."

"You're not going to answer my question?"

"That's always my answer to that question."

Undaunted, I tried one more question. "Is there a meditation before davening [Jewish prayer]?"

"Watching your breath," he said, finally, "watching your breath. Just emptying."

I came to understand that here was one area in Jewish life where chutzpah was not the answer. A busy, anxious mind would never be prepared for prayer. Indeed, the Talmud describes a group of hasidim, in this context pious ones who emptied out an hour before and after each hour of prayer. "The pious ones of old would be still one hour prior to each of the [three] prayer services then pray for one hour and afterward be still again for one hour." What were they doing in those hours of silence? No one knows for certain, but it seems clear from the commentary of Maimonides they were practicing a form of meditation. I found my own answer in the Jewish prayer service, a prayer that reads, "purify our hearts that we may serve You in truth." If these ancient sages needed an hour to purify their hearts so as to focus properly on prayer, I knew I needed many more than that to get rid of the distractions, the lusts and angers, of my noisy American Jewish mind.

Clearly, as meditation practices move from the margins to the center, there will be difficulty inserting an essentially inward and introspective practice into American Jewish secular style, which is full of humor and, frankly, words. This came home to me a few years ago, when lecturing to a very knowledgeable Jewish audience in Miami about *The Jew in the Lotus.* I asked the group of five hundred if anyone knew the Hebrew word for equanimity. There was a very long silence.

Finally someone called out from the back, "What's equanimity?"

We all laughed out loud, but the question of equanimity, for many Jews, is serious and real. That is certainly what I found among Rabbi Omer-Man's students in Los Angeles. His meditation classes included therapists and teachers, Hollywood scriptwriters and social workers. Some came from Orthodox and ultra-Orthodox backgrounds; others were veterans of years of training in Buddhism or Hinduism.

I was struck, though, that many came out of very personal motivations, often through a door of pain. One student was an ex-felon; another lost his daughter to leukemia and needed to learn "how to pray Jewish." Another, a successful Jewish academic administrator, simply felt an absence of meaning at the core of his life. "Most people past the age of twenty have broken hearts," Omer-Man told me. "There's no way you can't—if you are a whole person in the world. Whether of people very important to us dying, going mad, abandoning us, or just—I don't like the life I'm living, I'm disappointed, my life seems meaningless. Nobody denies having a broken heart."

The broken heart is exactly, I believe, what the Dalai Lama was referring to when he spoke to Jews about our practices for transforming "afflictive states of mind." It's a search compelling to many Americans these days. But for Jews it must also be a search for Jewish practices, a search not only for the Hebrew word for equanimity (which, by the way, is *hishtavut*), but, even more, for a Jewish language of the soul.

ANNE LAMOTT

Why I Don't Meditate

from Yoga Journal

I have been reading books on meditation with great enthusiasm since 1975, but have not quite gotten around to becoming a person who meditates. The only times I remember practicing with any regularity were during my drug days when I'd find myself awake at 4 or 5 A.M., which are the hours of the black dogs even under the best of circumstances. I remember lying in bed many nights after all the cocaine was gone, feeling and maybe looking like Bobcat Goldthwaithe, grinding away at my teeth like a horse, lockjawed, weepy, considering the wooden bedpost as a possible teething device, idly wondering what it would feel like to close my hands, slowly, around the sleeping boyfriend's throat. But all of a sudden I would start saying Hail Marys or a mantra, thousands of times in a row, to quiet my feral mind. It always worked, maybe not as effectively as a little something from the Schedule III column, but usually, at some point, I would be able to sleep.

Perhaps a purist would not consider this true meditation. At any rate, right around the time I got sober, I discovered the books of Jack Kornfield, who writes about meditation and compassion. And they were so wonderfully written and wise that I became utterly committed to meditating. To the idea of meditating. Now, while my commitment remains firm, I cannot actually report any real—what is the word?—progress. I still don't meditate. I still just pray like a mother, in the mo-fo sense of the word. My mind remains a bad neighborhood that I try not to go into alone.

But the last few times I've gone out on a book tour, Jack Kornfield has been waiting for me in various cities when I arrived.

Maybe not exactly in the flesh, maybe a little bit more like the face of Jesus in a tortilla, but any port in a storm, right? And he's been a reliable birth coach who keeps showing up even when I am at my most narcissistic and mentally ill.

In a month or so, Sam and I will travel around from city to city by plane, and I will try to get people to like me and buy my books. I'll do readings and Sam will lie on his stomach in bookstores and draw. I'll talk about writing and Jesus and the new book, and discuss my personal problems at length, secretly trying to con my audience into having some sort of awakening—spiritual, creative—so that we can all save the world together, and Sam can grow up and have children and provide me with grandchildren. (Or Sam can grow and be as gay as a box of birds and provide me with someone who laughs at all my jokes and makes me nice snacks.) Sounds like fun, right?

But the problem, the reason I rely so on Jack, is that I do not travel well. Sam does; he thrives. He loves bookstores and hotels, which all have nice floors for drawing, and he loves Spectra-vision, and snacks from the mini-bar. He even likes flying. I, on the other hand, do not believe in flying, or at any rate, am deeply unclear on the concept. I believe that every plane I get on is doomed, and this is why I like to travel with Sam—so that if and when the plane goes down, we will at least be together, and almost certainly get adjoining seats in heaven—ideally, near the desserts.

Then when we do arrive safely at a bookstore, there are either hardly any people in the audience, at which point my thoughts naturally turn to suicide, or there are so many people, so expectant and so full of love, that it fills me with self-loathing, makes me just anxious as a cat. I start to see myself as a performer or a product, or a performer pitching a product, as if I'm up there at the podium trying to get people to buy a Veg-O-Matic. It's like the Martin Buber line from *I and Thou:* "This is the exalted melancholy of our age, that every Thou in our world must become an it." I become an it, with really, really bad nerves. I seek refuge in shutting down, in trying to hide behind my false self like it's some psychic Guard-All shield.

So this is where Jack has helped me more times than he can possibly be aware. When I first show up at each bookstore, I've usually either stopped breathing or am wheezing away like a dying asthmatic pug. But a number of times, something has nudged me over toward a copy or stash of Jack's books, and they whisper this subversive message to me: Breathe. Pay attention. Be kind. Stop grabbing. And I always end up feeling like I've somehow gotten a grip, or a little grippage, as the French say.

I was in St. Louis once in a bookstore where only ten people had shown up, and of course I was just a little bit disappointed. I peeked around a stack of books at those ten people and imagined mowing them down with an AK–47. I know that makes me sound a little angry, but I had jet lag, the self-esteem of a prawn, and to top it off, I had stopped breathing. I sounded just like the English Patient. But it turned out I was standing in front of a shelf full of Jack's books. I opened one and read one sentence, words to the effect that life is so hard, how can we be anything but kind. It was as if God had reached down with God's magic wand, because I looked out at the crowd, which by then had swelled to twelve people—a third of them guilty, beaming employees of the bookstore—and I gave one of the most joyful talks of my life.

I have walked into tables while trying to hide from crowds and rows of empty seats, and knocked over stacks of his books. I was once handed one of his books to use as a tiny desk while autographing something for someone in Seattle. He keeps showing up when I need the message most, when I feel most like Mr. Magoo at the top of an unfinished high-rise, about to step into empty space but finding instead a girder rising up beneath my feet. I show up in crowded bookstores so stoned on myself and adrenaline that I could chase down an airplane, and I read about quietness, peace. I show up to a sea of empty metal chairs, and I read about the fullness of an open heart, and I'm suddenly a sea anemone unfurling her tendrils again, after the danger has passed.

Maybe what I like best about Jack's message is that it's so subversive. The usual message is that there are all kinds of ways for you to fill up, so you'll be strong and nourished and no one can get you; but when you're fortified, fortification by its very nature is braced, and can break. So you're still vulnerable, but now you're anxious and shamed too. You're going to be vulnerable anyway, because you're a small soft little human animal—so the only choice is whether you are most going to resemble Richard Nixon, with his neck jammed down into his shoulders, trying to figure out who to blame, or the sea anemone, tentative and brave, trying to connect, the formless fleshy blob out of which grows the frills, the petals.

It's pretty obvious stuff. And it's wonderful chutzpah not to be afraid of the obvious, to know it instead as a great teacher, to know that right behind the cliché is the original message. So many other people trick it out with draperies and garments and piercing glances; while Jack, in his simplicity and kindness, returns you to yourself; and maybe that's all we have. To know that the simple truth, of love, and the moment, is here to be passed around and around, like a polished stone from the sea, only because it is of itself, and for no other reason. You don't hang words onto it, and you don't need to, because it's got the great beauty and smoothness of having been whacked around for eons. It's beautiful in a muted way, beautiful through feeling, the way it's been smoothed and roughed up and relaxed on the shore, and you pick it up and feel the stasis, the beauty of something lifted out of its ordinary flow, that's gotten its beauty by being tossed about.

I got to meet him finally, just last month, introduced him at one of his readings. He had actually asked the bookstore if it could get me to introduce him, because he cares for me. I couldn't believe it. My heart soared like an eagle. But I showed up feeling self-conscious and anxious anyway. There was a huge crowd. Sam immediately lay on the floor in the back of the bookstore and began to draw. He's simple people. But I went up to the front of the bookstore and in this sort of gritchy, obsequious mood, introduced myself to Jack. You'd have to use the word luminous to describe him. One has the impression also of sandalwood, so smooth and brown, giving off a light, delicious spicy ancient smell. He looked at me with such affection that I might have been a child of his, one he hadn't seen in a while. I thought about all those times in other bookstores, when I was out there trying to get people to buy my book, and out of all that tension and lumpiness something graceful and baroque appeared. And this amazing thing happened: I felt lovely all of a sudden, in a goofy sort of way, exuberant and shy. Clingy scared old me made beautiful, made much more elegant than what's going on—all that self-consciousness and grasping—and I moved from Richard Nixon to a sea anemone, which is something I love. They're so funny and clownish, absurd and lovely, like a roomful of very young girls learning to ballet dance, all those long legs in white tights, or a boy lying on his stomach, drawing on the floor.

Into Your Hands, O Lord, I Commend My Spirit

Into your hands, O Lord, I commend my spirit. Utter, absolute faith. Utter, absolute letting go. No holding on to personal rectitude, moral virtue, or any kind of superiority. No more do-it-yourself-ism. And no more holding on to old sins, tired guilts. Offering it all, every bit of it, to the Creator, to the one who made all. Into your hands.

The prophet Isaiah says, "See, I have not forgotten you! I hold you in the palm of my hand."

One late spring weekend I was conducting a retreat. Spring is always a hefty time, when meeting after meeting is scheduled, when there is a rush to get everything done before the summer slump. I was very tired, and in the afternoon I lay down to rest for a few minutes and drifted into sleep. And into dream, or vision. I saw the entire universe, multicolored galaxies, bright as jewels, radiantly beautiful, and all held in a single hand. The hand of God.

Into your hand, O Lord. EVERYTHING HAS TO GO: worn-out beliefs, smug ideas, even our deepest hopes and fears. Complete surrender to the One in whom we trust, the only One in whom we have absolute trust.

I speak fairly frequently in evangelical colleges, where I have learned much about spontaneity in prayer, openness before God and each other. I have become comfortable and at home in this atmosphere. But my evangelical friends have one grave worry about me. They are deeply concerned that I may be a universalist. Now, I used to think that a universalist is someone who thinks that Jesus is good, and Buddha is good, and Muhammad is good, and so forth. But no, that's not it at all. It took me several years to figure out what their version of universalism is about, and once I had figured it out I could say, No, I am not a universalist. What the evangelicals mean by universalism is that all of a sudden, and for no particular reason, God is going to wave a magic wand and say, "Okay, everybody, out of hell, home free." So, no, I say, I am not a universalist; that plays trivially with free will.

A while ago I was at Evangel College, in Springfield, Missouri, run by the Assembly of God, and during a question-and-answer period I was asked the question "Are you a universalist?" and I replied that I am not. But the student was not satisfied. He said, "But your books do seem to indicate that you believe that God is forgiving."

"What an extraordinary statement!"

Quickly he qualified, "No, no, what I mean is that your books do seem to imply that ultimately God is going to forgive everybody."

I give my best answers when I don't have time to think and get in the way. I heard myself saying, "I don't think God is going to fail with Creation. I don't worship a failing God. Do you want God to fail?"

Well—no. But, he said, There has to be absolute justice.

"Absolute justice?" I asked. "Is that what you want? If you die tonight do you want absolute justice? Don't you want the weensiest teensiest bit of mercy? Me, I want lots and lots of mercy. Don't you want any mercy at all?"

That had never occurred to him. He had been saved, and the idea of mercy hadn't occurred to him. And maybe it is a frightening idea. It means admitting we have made mistakes, that we are faulted and flawed, that we don't always love as we should. It means saying, "I'm sorry. I'm truly sorry." It means accepting forgiveness. From ourselves, from God. It means letting go all our ideas about God and how the kingdom is to come. It means accepting that we may be completely wrong about everything we believe and everything we hope, and knowing that all that matters is God's love, God's total, unqualified love. It means putting ourselves entirely into God's hands. The ultimate surrender. The ultimate giving up, letting go, falling into God's love. Jesus showed us how.

Into your hands, O Lord, I commend my spirit.

Indeed, Jesus' birth, life, death, resurrection, is "ex-quisite," is beyond any answer, is even beyond all questions.

Tonight, if it is clear, I will go out with the dogs after dinner when dark has fallen, and I will look up into the night sky. It is tinged a little on the horizon with lights from Hartford, Torrington, even New York, but the stars on a clear night are still magnificent, and the Milky Way streams like a river of light across the dark. When I look up at the glory of the night sky, I am looking not only across vast reaches of space, but vast reaches of time. I am excited by that supernova discovered a month or so ago, a star exploding all those thousands of years in the past—and we are seeing the violence of that explosion just now. I won't be able to see that exploding star from the Litchfield Hills, but I will see stars that are seven light-years away, and seventy light-years away, and seven thousand light-years away. The glory of Creation never fails to excite me.

One of my earliest memories is from when I was visiting my grandmother at her beach cottage in north Florida. It must have been an unusually glorious night for someone to have said, "Let's wake up the baby and show her the stars." Someone came to my room, perhaps my father, and untucked the mosquito netting, picked me up, and carried me out onto the beach, into the night. And that was my first vision of night, of the glory of the stars, my first totally intuitive understanding that there is more to this world than the ordinary dailiness that makes up the small child's world, and in which, as grown-ups, we are often stuck.

An old Southern woman said to me, "I don't mind cooking, 'cept hits jest so damn daily."

Dailiness is wiped out when I look at the stars in all their glory. When my faith falters, when I feel God's absence, when I am moving through the night of the soul, if I can see a sky full of stars my heart always lifts. When I was living in New York after I got out of college, working on my first novel, I was so hungry for stars that I would take the subway uptown to the planetarium.

According to the British astrophysicist, Stephen Hawking, the beginning of all things, the moment of Creation, came from a sub-sub-sub-atomic particle, so tiny as to be nothing. And this infinite smallness opened up to become all of the stars in all of their courses. How marvelous!

Just about a year ago I was at Berea College in Kentucky, and one of the students asked me, "What do you think of creationism versus evolution?" And I just laughed and said, "I can't get very excited about it. There is only one question worth asking, and that is, 'Did God make it all?' If the answer is yes, then why get so excited about how?" And I continued that as far as we can tell, in our present state of knowledge, some form of evolution seems by far the most likely explanation of development on our planet. But if I should find out tomorrow that it all came about in a completely different way, that would have no effect on my faith, because my faith is not based on anything so peripheral. Thank God. If it were, I'd never have made it through the past year.

My faith is based on the trust that God did, indeed, make it all, make it and call it good, and love it so much that the incredible Power that began everything came to live with us, as one of us.

Anyhow, what about those biblical seven days? In whose time are we counting? Earth time? Solar time? Galactic time? God's time? What matter if the first day took a few billennia, and the second day a few billennia more? What is amazing is how the scriptural account follows so closely the process of evolution as we understand it today.

Einstein wrote that anyone who is not lost in rapturous awe and amazement at the power and glory of the mind behind the universe is as good as a burned-out candle.

Think of the incredible power in that newly discovered supernova. Think of the power in our own sun, which is constantly bursting with hydrogen explosions. The very violence of our sun is what makes our green and pleasant earth. But how could all this power, power beyond our puny comprehension, willingly limit itself to the form of a tiny baby, growing up like any child, walking the dusty roads, being bitten by flies, feeling the heat of the sun, simply being one of us? That is awesome beyond explanation. That bursts the bounds of any kind of reasonableness. What a totally unreasonable thing for God to do! What a totally loving thing for God to do! Would'st thou witten thy Lord's meaning in these things? Wit it well. Love was his meaning.

Love that was willing to come, to share, to eat and drink and laugh and talk. To walk away from his friends and those who had come to be healed, and to go into the hills to be alone with God, to be refilled with the power of Love. To be recognized as who he was by the demons, but not by the scribes and pharisees. To be betrayed, abandoned by his friends. To weep, as we all at times must weep. To cry out in anguish, My God, my God, why have you forsaken me?

And then, knowing that despite the seeming failure of his mission, he had finished the work he came to do, Jesus gave it all up, all of it.

Into your hands, O God, I commend my spirit.

Into your hands. Into total love.

Amen.

PHILIP LEVINE

When the Shift Was Over

from Image

When the shift was over he went out
and stood under the night sky a mile
from the darkened baseball stadium
and waited for the bus. He could taste
nickel under his tongue, and when he swiped
the back of his hand across his nose
he caught the smell of hydrochloric acid.
There were clouds between him and the stars,
not ordinary ones but dark and looming,
and if rain had begun to fall, he thought,
could it be black? Could a halo form
on those fine curls his Polish grandma
loved to brush when he was a boy, cupping
a hand under his chin? How silent
and still the world was after so much
slamming of metal on metal and the groans
of the earth giving way to the wakened fury
of the earth and the separate cries of people
together for these nights. How odd that he,
born of convicts and soldiers, of men
and women who crossed and recrossed the earth
carrying only the flag of their hopes,
should stand numbed by the weight
of a Thursday shift and raise his head
to a heaven he had never seen and sing
in a hoarse voice older than his years,

"Oh, Lordy Lord, I am, I'm coming home!"
He, who had no home and no hope, alone
on a certain night in a year of disbelief,
could sing to the ranks of closed houses
and cars, could sing as clear rain fell.

BARRY LOPEZ

God's Love on a Darkling Plain

from Portland Magazine

Many years ago, camped on open tundra in northern Alaska with a friend and waiting for a bush plane to pick us up, I hiked away across land that stretched on for miles. The rolling and tree-less vista that I scanned as I ambled is what biologists call mesic tundra, an ecosystem of cold-adapted sedges, forbs, and other plants living in damp soil during a brief summer, vegetation that rises no more than a few inches from the ground. That same few inches below the surface, the ground is permanently frozen.

Under a solid deck of low gray cloud (a cover that made locat-ing us too dangerous and haphazard a task for the pilot meant to fetch us), the tundra palette was a hundred shades of brown and tan. Tiny pindots of red within it, and of yellow, white, and purple, were too minuscule to register on the retina unless close at hand. The long, simple sketchline of this landscape, the flat light and lack of color, and the absence of any animals in that particular hour—no snow geese skying over my head, no pair of ducks alighting on a melt pond of matte-black water, no distant drift of browsing caribou, no wolf or fox loping through—gave the plain a melancholy look. The dreariness and chill air might have inspired Sibelius's *Swan of Tuonela*.

I've attended to enough landscapes the world over to know the sadness I perceived here was culturally induced, that it was a pro-jection. The land has an intrinsic nature, and in that moment I was aware of only a sliver of the reality spread out before me. The gloomy prospect, nevertheless, urged the feeling that grows from the contemplation of human messes, the sentimental pessimism about human failure the Germans call Weltschmerz. As I pursued a looping hike that day across the shallow ridge-and-swale of damp tundra, a phrase hung before me: *peccata mundi,* the sins of the world.

I don't know what called the words up. The melancholy aspect I'd fixed on in the landscape, of course, triggered the thought. But the phrase gathered strength because it was reinforced by the memory of terrible cruelty I'd witnessed in public streets everywhere: drunken belligerence, abandoned children, mutilated animals, starvation, goon violence, the commonplace evidence of a destructive and apparently ineradicable waywardness in us.

Confronting the viciousness of human life in places like Nairobi or Manaus or Karachi or Sarajevo or the Bronx, one quickly condemns the perpetration; but that day, brooding over it on the tundra, I felt compassion for humanity more deeply. We're as noble as we are base, as intent on serenity as revenge. We injure when we mean no harm, we destroy the things we love, we succumb to prejudice even as we strive for justice.

It's a Church phrase, *peccata mundi,* and strictly speaking a concept of sin is not universal. Wanting to forgive humanity its transgressions, however, I can imagine is a universal impulse. To look deeply into one's self is to discover the capacity to produce horror; it may be our belief that it is morally wrong completely to condemn our own nature that makes us feel compassion and forgiveness toward others, even strangers.

I don't remember what specifically I was reflecting on that day on the tundra, but it could have easily been Buchenwald, or the Turkish slaughter of Armenians three decades earlier, or something as prosaic as the destruction of indigenous culture in the Mato Grosso today, the quotidian work of mining, logging, and construction enterprises and well-intentioned missionaries. But I remember the impasse of this conundrum: I don't know how to forgive the Gestapo and the Schutzstaffel for what they did at Buchenwald. I don't know how one forgives the capitalists who have wreaked cultural and environmental havoc on the Parana River in the country of the Guarani. But I know you must.

To condemn what individual human beings perpetrate but to forgive humanity, to manage this paradox, is to take on adult life. Staring down *peccata mundi* that day on the tundra, my image of God was this effort to love in spite of everything that contradicts that impulse. When I think of the phrase "the love of God," I think of this great and beautiful complexity we hold within us, the pattern of light and emotion we call God, and that the rare, pure ferocity of our love sent anywhere in that direction is worth all the mistakes we endure to practice it.

To walk away from the shelter of the tent that afternoon, to see what lay before me on the seemingly dismal and monotonous tundra, was to seek after God. It may be a conceit to maintain that the landscape speaks to us, that it might sense our plight, but I believe it does. And to express love toward a landscape that influences us, to seek intimacy with it and to become vulnerable to the world in its presence, is but the impulse to love God. It is to hope, once more, for redemption.

An Offering

from The Christian Century

Mother is furious. An aunt and uncle have asked my sister and her husband to drive them the twenty-five miles to our Christmas gathering, a service my parents have grown accustomed to receiving themselves. "They have absolutely no consideration for other people," Mother sputters, and I murmur sympathetically. Always in charge ("an iron fist in a velvet glove," she used to call my father's mother, but her own glove has sometimes been forged of chain mail), she seems increasingly to respond to the complexities that escape her grasp—her beloved brother has just died of prostate cancer, her husband has developed a second skin cancer, a daughter and a granddaughter have incurable degenerative diseases—with anger, often deflected onto tangential issues.

Even a few years ago, Mother would have made sarcastic remarks about Their Royal Highnesses, no doubt, but without openly acknowledging her irritation. I can speak with some assurance here because this was also my emotional style until my daughter told me one day that my greatest flaw was my indirectness: a family trait, perhaps even a cultural one, since we descended directly from the Puritans who settled the communities in which we continued to live. In our household, any outpouring of sentiment, even delight, was dismissed as "dramatics," and overt hostility, even the sort that bursts out between siblings no matter how close they are, was quickly quashed. Other people might crow or wail or shout, but We Knew Better.

Although Mother can now admit to anger, it still constitutes an unruliness to be mastered, as her next comment makes plain: "I've got to get hold of myself, or nobody will like me very much." Socially, anger is viewed as a menace. Just look at the verbs we use with it: erupt, explode, blow up, boil over. Keep a lid on it, we caution, even though, as anyone who's overheated a pressure cooker can attest, the tight lid is exactly what causes the device to spew bits of potato from floor to ceiling.

"Don't worry about that," I reply. "We all know what it's like to be angry. Just open up to it, really feel it, and then let it flow on out and away." The process, a sort of spiritual exercise that has grown out of what my husband and I humorously call our Zen Catholicism, sounds so simple put into words. But how hard it is to part with righteous indignation. It feels so, well, right!

I tend to learn life's lessons only through tedious drill, but the one about anger came to me all at once. During mass one Saturday evening several years ago, when George neglected to hand me a hymnal, I was suffused by irritation, which masked, I suppose now, the dread that choked me throughout his treatment for metastatic melanoma. From long experience, I knew that an evening of sullen silence stretched before us. Although I didn't want to pollute whatever time might be left us, I felt mired in a pattern thirty years in the making. Having heard traditional Catholics refer to offering some distress up to God, I decided to give this puzzling practice a go. "Well, God, I'm certainly stuck," I said. "Can you help me get over this anger?" Nothing much seemed to happen, but when it was time to depart in peace, I said to George, "Grocery shopping seems like a bleak activity for a Saturday night," the only time during the week he could squeeze it in. "Why don't we catch a bite and then do it together?" He shops more efficiently and economically, no doubt, when I'm not spinning up and down the aisles in a whirlwind of impulses, but we spent a pleasant evening anyway.

Although in my clumsy prayer I had asked only for a tranquil evening, not a lifelong transformation, perhaps that's what I got:

not immunity from anger (and complaint and jealousy and all the other mean-spirited responses to life's events that sicken the soul) but the belief that whereas the great Working Out I know as God is utterly beyond my comprehension and control, my attitude is not. Acceptance feels more soothing than anger; rejoicing delights me as moaning never can.

"Oh, well, I don't suppose it really matters." Mother sounds less than persuaded.

"No, it doesn't," I agree. "What matters is being together for Christmas." What more can I tell her? I certainly can't advise her to offer her anger up to God. She gave up on God long ago, beginning perhaps with my father's sudden death, at Christmastime, when they were both younger than my children are today. With Mother I can speak out of but not about my faith.

Like children everywhere, especially those who have lost one parent, fear the loss of the other and with her all hope of survival, I feel anxious when my mother seems out of sorts. I can still recall my awkward attempts, as a child, to comfort her when she was ill or seemed downhearted, and I have borne vestiges of that child into adulthood. I want to please Mother. I want to make her happy. But maturity teaches that another's happiness lies beyond control. I guess I'll just have to offer Mother up to God.

FREDERICA MATHEWES-GREEN

Embarrassment's Perpetual Blush

from Christianity Today

As I saw my children swept up into the night sky I knew I had made a terrible mistake. I held the baby in my arms, but the two older ones—Megan, seven, and David, four—were locked behind the bar of a Ferris wheel in a shopping-center carnival. They had begged and clamored until I agreed to let them board the contraption, but now, as they rose into the night, they panicked and began to scream. David's little legs were kicking as he skidded sideways on the slick metal seat. I saw how easily he could slip beneath the narrow bar and fall to the asphalt below.

That was more than a dozen years ago. One revolution of the Ferris wheel was more than enough for my kids, thank you, and within thirty seconds they were safely on the ground beside me again, breathing hard and shaking. I think this was the most terrifying moment in my life as a parent. Nothing else even comes close. Yet looking back now, I can remember it without feeling frightened at all.

It's a funny thing about past emotions. I can remember a time in my life when I was burdened by depression, but I can view it now without feeling sad. I can remember being furious with someone, yet without once again growing angry. I can even remember having a crush on Ringo, and I have *no* idea what that was about. But when it comes to embarrassment, I can't remember the incident without wanting to crawl under my desk. Embarrassment bursts forth anew at the moment the memory appears, bursts like lemon meringue pie in the face. It's a nearly intolerable feeling, a cousin to outright pain.

* * *

I think the reason embarrassment is ever fresh is that it jars our self-image in a way other flaws do not. Embarrassment is the flag flown from the ramparts of pride. For quite a while I didn't get this. I thought embarrassment was the opposite, an emblem of humility, perhaps even evidence of repentance. The sequence seemed to be I remember doing something stupid, and I'm agonizingly sorry I did it. But the sorrow is not actually that of remorse. It is rather the phenomenon we spot so easily in others: sorry about being caught, sorry about being revealed as thoughtless, lazy, greedy, or rude.

Yes, above all, sorry about having flaws *revealed*. "Oh, no," Embarrassment whispers. "People will think . . ." People are going to think I'm such a fool. Well, the truth is I *am* a fool. I just did the stupid thing in question, didn't I? What do I need, a certificate? And the fact that I'm a fool is not exactly classified information. God certainly knows it, and the Devil does too (and relies on it). It's a pretty good bet that everyone who knows me knows it as well. Apparently the only person left out of this information loop is me.

I don't find the word *embarrassment* in my Bible concordance. (*Shame* is there, but shame has a slightly different meaning, associated with dishonor and military loss.) There are certainly biblical instances of it, though, one of the most familiar being the fear of embarrassment that caused Herod to execute John the Baptist. He had made a heedless, drunken promise to his stepdaughter, but "because of oaths and his guests" he followed through.

One of my favorite stories from the early church describes a positive use of embarrassment. When the father of Origen, a third-century theologian, was arrested for being a Christian, the son—then only seventeen—was aflame with the desire to follow him and share in glorious martyrdom. His mother pleaded with him not to go, but the headstrong boy did not want to listen to reason. His quick-thinking mother did what she could. She hid his clothes. Though Origen stormed and protested, she wouldn't reveal where they were hidden. He couldn't leave the house, and so he was unable to volunteer for martyrdom.

What strikes me about this story is that Origen was brave enough to be martyred, but not brave enough to go outside naked. Stepping outside sans clothing would have sped up his arrest and imprisonment, but it was a step he was unwilling to take.

The embarrassing moments in our lives, and the still-painful memories of those moments, give us a bracing opportunity to "see ourselves as others see us." They knock down walls of pride like a bulldozer. I wonder if in heaven there will be a *Funniest Home Videos* night, where we get to see ourselves at our most absurd. Then, with all the books opened and every secret known, there will be no more reason to cling to scraps of false dignity. The truth is out: we're fallen like clowns in the mud, and we're beloved and saved by Christ's glory. Watching those moments again in the company of all who love us, we will hear a rising chuckle of mirth. We won't want to cringe under a twist of pain anymore; instead, we'll lead them all in a big belly laugh.

WILLIAM MEREDITH

A Vision of Good Secrets

from DoubleTake

If the kept secrets of our finished lives
Some day rise up, what a doomsday they will have:
From the numberless houses, deserts, caves
Of its human stay, each whole anatomy
Of the man's affection, and the woman's, each family
Of true deceptions, will be reunited, abler than old bones
To sing, and with more to sing about—a valley
Of buried secrets, rising to claim their own.

"Why were we secret?" one of the true may ask
Among the yawning bodies of affection
That wake on the valley floor. "Why did I risk
My blood and hair and bones in that deception?"
Or another, more thoughtful secret ask, "Hence-
Forth how will a person relish hate or shame,
Or manage love without its reticence,
And everybody calling things by name?"

But then a voice will silence all who had slept
And the host of the false secrets will tremble
As the names are read of those that were well kept,
Of all with honest reason to dissemble.
All generous and well-intentioned lies,
All expensive silences, will earn eternal silence then,
But all vain secrets will that voice expose
Like the flaming souls of wicked medieval men.

Therefore, my secrets, shades of hate and fear
And love (who outnumbers all the tribes
As, when the names are published, will appear)
Prepare yourselves, so live that when that blast
Of bright exposure rends your flimsy robes
And you stand named and naked at the last,
One judging will say, after your long sleep,
This is my faithful secret, him I will keep.

Why I Pray

from Esquire

I was an inpatient at a psychiatric hospital in Queens in July of 1987, being treated for depression and related complaints. This was where I first heard a sensible word on the subject of prayer. I was on the adult ward—a catchall locale for those who didn't entirely qualify for the drug-treatment ward one floor up or the adolescent unit down the hall or the chronic-care ward above the teens. Among my ward mates was Donny, an Irish doorman whose drinking was so bad that he had, for example, waked from a blackout on a plane to the Caribbean without having, until that time, ever set foot out of the tristate area. Donny had also done a little time in the county lockup, for brawling and public drunkenness. One night, in the dining room, over a game of checkers, we got on the subject of prayer, on whether prayer would do any of us any good. Donny loudly expressed (loud was his only setting) some pragmatic reservations about prayer as we commonly experience it here in Western culture, and these reservations stuck with me long after. He said, "After I was in jail, I never felt like that *posture* you're supposed to pray in was gonna work for me."

This had been one of my problems, too. In order to pray, you had to be on your knees.

My early religious training was conventional. I grew up mostly in the Connecticut suburbs. These towns, and others like them, were the bedrock on which the Protestant branches of the Christian church founded their ministries. Episcopalians, Presbyterians, Lutherans—each sect had there its vibrant and social congregations. I was probably five by the time I got my first taste of my family's Episcopalianism. St. Luke's, the parish, was near my elementary school. The interior of the church was cool and dim, with the requisite stained-glass panels and altar flowers. The rows swelled with the faithful.

I was shocked by the first prayer I observed at St. Luke's. I noticed adults lowering themselves in the pews and clasping their hands—some palm to palm (as in Albrecht Dürer's famous drawing), some with fingers laced. There was a solemnity to the moment—it was during the Lord's Prayer, as I reconstruct it, though there ought to have been prayers earlier in the service—but this solemnity didn't seem to include me. Though I was capable of aping the posture of these Sunday-best-dressed families of Darien (there were the Sutherlands two rows up!), though I was able to keep my eyes downcast, to maintain a pious mien, I learned right away that the dialogue implicit in prayer would be, in my case, one-sided. To whom was I mumbling these words? (I hadn't yet memorized the Lord's Prayer, so my version was full of stray syllables and patches of humming.) And why was there silence when I was done? The whole notion of prayer seemed founded on falsehoods and prevarications.

In my parish, there were unclothed emperors wherever I looked. Adults prayed to a God (whoever or whatever that was) who never answered, and they prayed for the kinds of virtues that they rarely manifested in their own lives, or they prayed (I believed) for stuff, for rain or good health, with results that were inconclusive. My grandmother, who was always after us to pray before bedtime, had never gone to church as far as I knew, and her husband never went, and my father disliked going. So what were the theories behind all this talk of prayer and church? A pattern emerged on Sunday mornings around the Moody household. My brother and I would get up at the crack of dawn and sneak into my parents' bedroom in order to turn off their alarm clock. It often worked. Sunday school and prayer and church would then be set aside in favor of *Wonderama* and *Davey and Goliath.*

This squares with the experience of a lot of people I know who came of age in the sixties and seventies. We grew up watching television on Sunday mornings. We never said grace. We crowded into the back of a church, if at all, on Christmas Eve. And we weren't aware in ourselves of any manifestation of spiritual need. Physical hunger you can satisfy with meals. The drives for food, shelter, and clothing all have a pragmatic basis, as does the sexual drive, by which a society reproduces itself. But what exactly is a spiritual need, and how does prayer gratify or articulate it?

It took me a long time to formulate compelling answers to these questions. It wasn't until I went away to school, at thirteen, that it even occurred to me to try to do so. My boarding school was intent on a core curriculum that was in disrepute at that time, the midseventies. It featured a yearlong study of the philosophical underpinnings of European culture entitled "Origins of the West." As part of Origins, we had to design a civilization, and as part of this civilization, we were told by our instructor, we had to have an *ideology*, a system of beliefs. What, Mr. Kellogg asked us, did we believe? What would the people in our civilization believe, and how would they express that belief? (Benjamin Cheever, the son of the novelist John Cheever, told me a similar story. As a young man in the Episcopal congregations of Ossining, New York, he was occasionally disinclined to say the Nicene Creed, that antiheretical portion of the Protestant ceremony. His father suggested that if he didn't approve of the creed, he make up his own, since he would "have to believe in something.")

Belief wasn't something I, or my peers, believed in. At best, we felt strongly about experimentation with drugs and about certain bombastic kinds of rock 'n' roll, and we believed that other people should leave us alone to pursue these interests without interference. Any belief in romance and its transports was, at the time, out of the question—by reason of teenage awkwardness, at least in my case. Thus, I started seriously getting high when I was fifteen, and I did it with a zeal that I hadn't applied to anything else. Within a couple of months of first smoking marijuana, I'd already experimented with Seconal, PCP, hash, Thai stick, all manner of booze, and LSD.

It was the last of these that enabled me, all at once, to find myself in a situation in which prayer seemed logical. I'd had maybe a dozen trips before my first "bad trip," a six- or seven-hour bonanza of anxieties and melancholies and punitive nightmare images in which I was tortured by *deranged clowns,* in which I was adrift in a sea of eyeballs, et cetera. With LSD, this kind of experience, though terrifying, is often routine. The amazing part of the afternoon, though, after I submitted myself to the care of a minister on campus, came when I actually had a conversation with God.

Mysteriously, the silence I had known hitherto in my infrequent dialogues with the Divine was temporarily suspended. I was able to talk freely with him. (I'm using the masculine gender for lack of a better option: I'm pretty sure he doesn't have a Y chromosome.) I prayed to him to bring a halt to my terrifying hallucinations. I prayed to him to help me. To make me a better, less awkward, less panicky human being. He responded in that deep voice you associate with Charlton Heston's biblical movies. (And he happened to live, in my hallucinations, in a church remarkably like the chapel right on campus at St. Paul's School.) But here was the thing. When I asked God directly for help, because my simple, LSD-inflected prayer had no purpose other than as a request for aid, God's response was similarly direct: *You cannot be helped.* That's what he said. While I was underneath the kitchen table belonging to the Reverend Alden Flanders of Concord, New Hampshire, God told me that I was a lost cause.

* * *

No surprise, then, since I'd had no success with God on *my* terms, that I applied myself to oblivion for a good ten years. I managed to get into an Ivy League school and to take a lot of courses pass/fail and even to do a short stint in graduate school, but my more thorough and systematic investigation was into mixology. I was frequently drunk, I had binges on speed and cocaine, I slept with anybody with a pulse, and I was a militant atheist. *God is the transcendental signified,* they used to say in the semiotics program at Brown University, where I studied, meaning that God is a theoretical repository for the idea of meaning, nothing more, a repository who reflects meaning back onto a scarily empty system of signs. You can't pray to that.

At the end of this ten years, this spree of primitive liberty, I was in the psychiatric hospital in Queens with Donny the doorman; Al, a heroin addict who had once been limo driver for Michael Jackson; Brian, an A&R guy for one of the major record labels who was a cocaine addict and who had been sexually abused by his brother; Margie, a secretary at NBC who was manic-depressive and believed that Mickey Mouse himself had led a parade through her house in Astoria, Queens.* And others.

The prayer that comes first to all who learn to pray in earnest is *the prayer of desperation.* On the Fourth of July, 1987, I was allowed out of the adult ward at my hospital for a couple of hours. It was the kind of summer day in New York City when the pavement buckles and the traffic to Jones Beach grinds to a halt. I was out in back with one of the nurses and two other recent admissions to our ward. We were all sitting in the shade, drinking sodas that we'd been permitted to purchase. One of our number was a young woman from Long Island. She was bulimic and had wrists

These names have been changed.

that were crosshatched with self-inflicted wounds. Inside of a week, her insurance would run out and she would be shipped to the state hospital, where, she told me, you might be left for days in a holding cell with vagrants and schizophrenics.

The nurse who was watching us had a transistor radio, which, as I recall, was playing Elton John's "Candle in the Wind." The live version. It was a song from my childhood, and I was struck, in the sway of Elton's saccharine melancholy, by how far I had fallen since I was a kid. I had a family who loved me, I had the best education you could get in America. I was full of promise. But I was in a psychiatric hospital in Queens where a nurse was trying to teach me how to make eye contact in conversation.

I wept. In front of the others. I wept.

And then I prayed. I prayed solitarily there outdoors, and later in the room I shared with a cocaine dealer for the Colombian mob. I prayed over meals, whenever there was a spare second, after group therapy, before cognitive therapy, whenever. I prayed the prayer of desperation. *God,* I prayed, *whoever you are, get me out of this. If you're there, work a miracle. For a change.*

There are no atheists in foxholes, the celebrated formulation goes. It's an observation that even the least spiritually inclined of my acquaintances occasionally makes. And, indeed, when I ask friends if they ever pray, their experience is mostly in the category of these *foxhole prayers.* Lily, a producer from northern California, once spoke to me of praying during the Oakland fires, when her parents' house was in danger. "I prayed to God all night and the next day. I prayed that the house wouldn't burn, that everyone would be okay, that the fire would stop." Lily wasn't and isn't a regular churchgoer, doesn't take her children to church, doesn't *believe,* and yet she found solace in that moment. Another friend, a novelist, spoke of praying in the middle of the night during dark times: "I wake and simply murmur, 'Help me.' Who else could I be speaking to?" Cynthia, a prominent magazine columnist, told me of praying during her father's struggle with cancer. She adapted a line from Saint Augustine: "Whisper in my heart, tell me you are there."

These days, on this side of the Atlantic, our military foxholes are few. Yet aren't there still the metaphorical foxholes, the inevitable pointless deaths or business reversals or romantic failures? And if foxholes, whether metaphorical or actual, continue to exist, then won't prayers continue to be mumbled in the dark bedrooms of America or in the first light of small-town mornings? When I got out of the hospital, when I was living alone in a converted filling station in Hoboken, New Jersey, when I was showing up for work and little else, when I was still suffering, in spite of medication, with a number of vexing complaints—then, though I had never gotten down on my knees (as Donny the doorman was unhappy about doing) for anyone or anything, though I had never admitted the possibility that I couldn't solve my problems myself, though I had never submitted that merely human agencies were not entirely effective, then I began to pray. Regularly. My prayers were unadorned, without *thees* and *thous*. They were simple prayers: *Give me a chance, please.*

The epiphany in this story, therefore, is backward. I never believed in God and, as a result, never prayed to glorify his or her or its name. Instead, I prayed because I was desperate, and thereafter I believed in whoever it was I prayed to—mainly because *prayer did me some good.* Life improved—as life has also improved for my acquaintances who pray, whether or not they go to church or believe in a Christian God or anything else. My friend David, an expert on new technology, put it this way: "It's been common for me, at the moment I start freaking out, that the recognition that there's a power greater than myself and that I can address that power has caused the moment to shift."

Thus prayer, as William James put it in *The Varieties of Religious Experience,* "is a process wherein work is really done, and spiritual energy flows in and produces effects, either psychological or material, within the phenomenal world." Though I had no comprehensive idea of the recipient of my prayer (in fact, I would often mumble this while praying—"I have no idea who you are"), I prayed nonetheless, on my knees, and in praying found that I felt better, that I passed some days without hopelessness, that I was calmer. This process I'm describing doesn't necessarily lay to rest all questions about the existence or lack of existence of God (and you will answer that question better if you answer it for yourself), but what I'm saying should make clear a couple of very fundamental American attitudes about the Divine: You'll know It when you see It. And: If It ain't broke, don't fix It.

I pray, therefore, because prayer works.

Early in my spiritual investigations, I learned that to speak of these things, of prayer and of a belief in prayer, was to risk ridicule and even contempt. *Prayer* implies *church* to most people, and *church* implies an inherited or unenlightened notion of God, and thus, in liberal circles, *prayer* all but implies *fundamentalism.* Prayer, in this formulation, has become a language for bigots who pray that gay people might convert to heterosexuality or that Jews will accept the message of Jesus; prayer is for lost causes, for the comatose to rise or for the dead to live. And yet that's not how it was always practiced. It was once a language that was available to everyone (as it is, say, in the book of Psalms)—available not only to the elect but also to the damned; not only to the Pharisees but also to the heathens.

I consider myself a good example of this democratic aspect of prayer. I use the more-than-occasional four-letter oath. I am not opposed to sexually explicit renderings in film or literature. I have a tattoo. I favor same-sex marriage. I have made a lot of mistakes, and I expect to continue doing so. Yet, most mornings, and sometimes on the subway or in cars or on airplanes or in the silence before a movie starts, I engage in this dialogue in which I ask to stay alive and not to do anything dramatically stupid in the next twenty-four hours. (And I emphasize this aspect of *dialogue* in prayer, because prayer, unlike meditation, is best understood as a two-way transmission. In prayer, you speak; in meditation, you listen.)

I have read widely in the literature of prayer and even attempted to crash a prayer meeting at the parish in Brooklyn where I sometimes go to church. In the books on the subject, there is often really insipid language ("Dear Lord Jesus, in my better moments I want nothing more than to be like you"), and often there are over-simplifications of some of the powerful themes of prayer (praise, remorse, celebration, desperation). But at the same time, there are all around us supple ideas about how prayer might look to intelligent, informed, contemporary persons. In Thomas Merton, for example: "Learn how to meditate on paper. Drawing and writing are forms of meditation. Learn how to contemplate works of art. Learn how to pray in the streets or in the country."

Among prayer-group types, meanwhile, you expect mainly older or more troubled people. When I went recently to the prayer meeting in my neighborhood, I arrived at the darkened, double-bolted entrance to the church at the appointed hour to find that there were no petitioners but me. Just as I was leaving, a pair of older women ambled up the walkway, similarly stranded. We chatted for a few minutes—no one had a key—and then went on our ways without having convened our prayer group at all, without exchanging much more than pleasantries. Is this the face of prayer now?

At the same time, though, in a group of Somewhat Younger Adults (their term) at the same parish, a recent Sunday-morning trip to the summit of Bear Mountain, New York, to celebrate the

Eucharist was booked to capacity, with young media workers and stockbrokers, with childless couples, with Ivy League grads decked out in Timberland shoes and khaki shorts and ready to hike and to pray.

All the things I thought about prayer as a child are still true: It takes place in silence, and silence is the response you get, and mostly while you are doing it, you feel like doing something else. Merton has an insight here as well: "The most usual entrance to contemplation is through a desert of aridity in which, although you see nothing and feel nothing and apprehend nothing and are conscious only of a certain interior suffering and anxiety, yet you are drawn and held in this darkness and dryness because it is the only place in which you can find any kind of stability and peace." You are thinking of the calls you have to return or the bills you have to pay or something you said erroneously last night or someone you hurt. But in silence and motionlessness can come perspective and calm and resolution and manifestations of a better, more reliable self than the one who first hit his or her knees this morning, who first closed his or her eyes in meditation. Silence, it turns out, is redemptive, is generous. Silence is perhaps what a relationship with the Divine *is* these days. You could do a lot worse.

For brief moments in American cultural history, it has been *cool* to pray. The late sixties, for example. At Woodstock, they prayed for rain to end, all five hundred thousand of them. Later, Allen Ginsberg prayed (with reporters covering the story) for the Pentagon to levitate, in the hope that this would end the war in Vietnam. Though these prayers were superficially facetious, they indicated a value for prayer, an esteem for endeavor, that the nineties, this era of bargain-basement pragmatism and low-level depression, may never endorse. Nonetheless, as the fifties gave way to the sixties, perhaps the nineties will give way to a more adventurous and experimental fin de siècle, in which the expressions of humility and joy and acceptance that are at the heart of the language of prayer will again be valuable on a larger scale. Gandhi prayed. Tolstoy prayed. Martin Luther King, Jr., wrote some of the finest prayers of this century. I see signs of activity among any number of people my own age, signs that spirituality is not simply Harmonic Convergences or Pyramid Power or the vegan lifestyle, signs that there's more to the Western spirit than a limitless arcade—a place fashioned of opportunities to purchase stupefaction.

Often, these days, I pray for particular results (because I'm not smart enough to do much better), and therefore I pray sometimes for a renaissance in this ancient discourse, because the mysteries engendered by prayer are inspiring to behold. Inspiration is good. It's all around us. *Lux in tenebris lucet et tenebrae eam non comprehenderunt.* "The light shines in darkness and the darkness has not understood it."

Mystic Clouds and Natural Spirituality

from Orion

I live on top of a hill. When I awoke this morning, I looked out over many miles of rolling valleys and ridges, a thick mist settling among them like the waves of a vast ocean. The low-lying fog touched and mirrored the red-edged clouds of the sky. Mesmerized for a time by the beauty of that morning sky, I then recalled Botticelli's famous painting of spring, *La Primavera*, where the god Mercury points with his magic wand to overhanging clouds, an image of his own shifting nature. Clouds also evoke the realm of spirit that in Botticelli's painting is intimately engaged with the lush gracefulness of the green and floral garden-world of Venus.

The clouds in Botticelli's painting have long charmed me because they represent a certain sublimation of the rich life of nature into a higher level of experience, yet one that is not stratospheric in its loftiness. Clouds hover. Where I live in New England, the mountains are small in comparison to those in the west, yet with my family I can make a modest climb and still be higher than the clouds. Clouds dwell in a midrealm between the infinite sky and the familiar earth, and in that midrange they give image to a kind of spirituality that I aspire to—one that never completely abandons the lower levels of ordinary life and yet at the same time offers a degree of contemplative loft, a perspective and a vision that is not swamped by things earthly and quotidian.

One significant implication in *La Primavera* is the idea of spirituality as an emanation of earthly life, or a sublimation, not in the Freudian sense of a defensive transformation of raw emotion, but in the Jungian and alchemical sense of a rising of plain experience into subtle forms of thought, image, fantasy, reflection, and memory. In this sense, the spiritualization of nature does not escape earth's full physical presence and wild concreteness, but rather is a subtle refinement of nature as it meets the human imagination. Contemplating nature, we find lessons about life in general that give a foundation for a spiritual perspective, qualities such as its overwhelming beauty, immense powers of destruction, unimaginable reaches of time, the extraordinarily small and the unfathomably great, the unpredictable and the complex. Like Mercury standing firm on the earth and raising his wand into the sky, nature shifts our gaze from the literal world at our feet to the higher, spiritual implications of that world.

This nature-rooted brand of spirituality has the advantage of not creating a dualistic way of life where body is opposed to mind and matter separated from spirit. Classically, the midrealm of Mercury was known as the domain of the soul, which has both material and spiritual elements. In the world of Marsilio Ficino, the Renaissance priest-philosopher I take as my guide in these matters, and who historians say may actually have had some influence on the themes of *La Primavera*, the soul lives both in time and in eternity.

UNNATURAL SPIRITUALITY

In recent decades we have come to think of the spiritual life in such abstract terms that it seems almost by definition to be opposed to the mundane world. Generally we emphasize belief, not faith—an intellectual attachment to certain ideas, values, and opinions rather than an open-ended, deep trust in life.

This highly mental approach to the religious and spiritual life tends to be anxious and defensive; for as much as we study nature and human life, we simply can't answer the ultimate questions. Death remains a profound and confronting mystery. In spite of our advances in technological medicine, illness still arrives as a shock and a mystery. Even in our daily emotional lives, we are confronted by inexplicable depressions, loss of meaning, and the sense of failure. In the face of these mysteries, we tend to latch onto a comforting explanation, theory, or spiritual program and give it our loyalty.

Often, it seems, the provisional answers given by science or religion serve simply as palliatives to the fundamental anxiety of human life. We hold them tightly because they are all we have in the face of threats to our safety, health, happiness, and indeed our very existence. We defend our spiritual positions, feel wary about anyone who takes a different stance, perhaps try to convert everyone to our point of view, or at least champion our particular spiritual organization or leaders. These days, in many places, including the United States, many people go so far as to hope for a hagiocracy, a government that imposes the values of a certain belief system, blind apparently to the fact that spiritual fervor can easily turn into intolerance, violent action, and suppression of human freedom.

Around the world we see that many of the bloody conflicts that terrorize and inhibit the peaceful and creative life of citizens can be traced to religious and spiritual differences. Spiritual convictions usually seem so pure and right to their adherents that it is difficult for them to be critical and reflective. Spirituality loses its soul, and yet it is the soul that makes us human, accounts for compassion and tolerance, and grants the deep feeling of community and commonality. Without these softening human emotions, the spiritual life can become belligerent.

Strangely, spirituality can also turn against nature. Even though theoretically the natural world may be seen as good and divinely created, the thrust of the spiritual life is often in an upward direction, away from the ordinary and the natural. Indeed, the human body and the body of the world may be seen as obstacles to the spiritual life. The world, the flesh, and the devil occupy the same lower terrain. Stories of saints emphasize their detachment from the world, and the Gospel teaches "Set your mind on things that are above, not on things that are on earth" (Col. 3:1) and "You are from below, I am from above; you are of this world, I am not of this world" (John 8:23). Although these and similar sayings from religious texts need not be interpreted to require a separation of nature from the spiritual life, inescapably they connote an otherworldliness that may result in an attitude that devalues the natural world.

Personally, we may feel a strong tension between our upward yearnings and the pull of the body and the world. We may believe that to live a healthy and good life, we have to overcome our own natural inclinations toward sexual desire, unhealthy or incorrect foods, depressive and other unwholesome moods, claims of family life, and the wish to make money: Unconsciously perhaps, we may agree with the culture at large that successful living requires that we overcome nature, inwardly and outwardly.

NATURAL SPIRITUALITY

Two years ago, when I was traveling with my family through the west of Ireland to prepare myself to write a book on enchantment, I came to a new degree of appreciation for nature's contribution to the spiritual life. One day in particular, as we were stumbling over rocks at a site near the ocean where hundreds of years ago monks had practiced a remarkably rich spiritual life, I was overwhelmed by the conjunction of nature—the winds, the waves, the sheep, the steep mountain terrain, the rocks, and the rains—and intense spiritual activity. There, too, the clouds hung low and left their mist on our bodies as they swept off over the sea, and I envisioned those early monks praying and living their communal life hard in the face of nature.

Medieval monks described the world as *liber mundi,* the book of the world, where they could read eternal truths and divine mysteries. What I learned on that visit to Ireland was how to read this book. You don't turn it into intellectual discourse, making a theory out of nature's way. Rather, you live in the midst of howling winds and azure water and take your initiation from nature's overpowering beauty and presence. You transcend the limitations of your own personal life not by looking above the earth, but by sensing in the whole of your body and with the blood-swirling testimony of your emotions the fact of nature's eminence.

Just as clouds appear out of the evaporation and condensation of the deep waters of the sea, so a spiritual sensibility rises directly out of the human encounter with the natural world. In this way, soul and spirit remain united, because in nature we find both the depths of our mysteriousness and the heights of our possibilities. We encounter in nature the most ordinary aspects of our creatureliness and the most extraordinary and sublime possibilities of creation.

Yet, as the poet Wallace Stevens wrote, "The way through the world is more difficult to find than the way beyond it." Natural spirituality is tough because it has in it no elements of superficial sentimentality and no signs of escapism. It can't be reduced to simplistic moralism or bloodless belief. Its mysteriousness is palpable in almost every encounter with it, while its complexity is overwhelming. A medieval Celtic prayer from the *Carmina Gadelica* expresses well this spirituality that does not leave the earth behind:

Bless, O God, my little cow,
Bless, O God, my desire:
Bless Thou my partnership
And the milking of my hands, O God.

Bless, O God, each tear,
Bless, O God, each finger;
Bless Thou each drop
That goes into my pitcher, O God.

Those Irish monks had to be tough, earthy, strong, and physical individuals, living as they did at the edge of their world, where nature is most tangibly known. They can offer us a model for reaching as high as possible in our spiritual aspirations while never for a moment avoiding the full impact of nature. They seem to have known that only in this paradoxical overlap of the natural world and the spiritual imagination does the human being find honest transcendence.

Regaining a serious appreciation of nature as a spiritual presence might also help us deepen our ethical and moral sensitivities. A highly mentalized spirituality gives rise to morality based on principle, a source that may seem reasonable, but has its limitations. A more compelling motivation for human behavior is desire. Being intimate with nature, we might discover new bases altogether for moral behavior, such as a deep sense of community, love of places and the things of nature, and a degree of loyalty to persons and places that could nurture a strong ethical attitude.

Like many other traditional peoples of the world who live enchanted lives, the Irish of old could find their spiritual comfort in images from nature, as in the traveler's prayer that says, "Thou art the pure love of the clouds." The feeling that nature loves us, even though it is sometimes threatening, offers an important family sense of the relationship between nature and human life. St. Francis's poetic image of "Brother Sun and Sister Moon" reveals a mystic's way of imagining the relationship, a mode out of vogue in our time but not necessarily off the mark.

The mystic, magus, and poet of the past considered our relationship with nature as a loving one—not merely a sentimental appreciation on the part of humans, but rather a kinship and attraction among all elements. Eros keeps the planets in orbit, the season on time, and the organs of the body in harmony. The great physician Paracelsus saw the human being and the natural world as fully implicated in each other. In this spirit he could write: "The condition of urine must be read from the outer world, the pulse must be understood in relation to the firmament, physiognomy to the stars, the breath to the east and west winds, fever to earthquakes." Pico della Mirandola, the young philosopher whose brilliance challenged the conventions of the late fifteenth century, in his famous "Oration on the dignity of the Human Person," speaks of the sympathy that governs nature, the "natural affinity among things." *Sympathy* is a love word, *understanding* a word of the mind.

We have moved so far from an erotic perception of nature and an appreciation of the sympathy that keeps the natural world in harmony that these images from the past may appear naive and outdated. We look for the laws that govern natural objects, not the mutual affection that holds it all together. The images that comprise our worldview tend to be mechanical, chemical, and biological rather than relational, objective rather than subjective.

A cold, rational, observer's attitude toward nature fails to reveal the spiritual potential in nature, but a warm, imaginative, participant's perspective invites a more mystical and therefore a more spiritual engagement with the world. The former leads to millions of words and statistics analyzing the natural world, while the latter leads to stories, poetry, prayers, rites, and meditation on that same world.

To safeguard and nurture both the natural world that is our environment and our spiritual lives, we will have to challenge the dominance of the scientific mythology that with much superiority and authority shrinks our approach to nature in a culture obsessed with information gathering. Studying nature is not our only option; we can also meditate upon it, contemplate it, and find there a solid basis for spiritual sensitivity.

We can be educated by nature, becoming persons of broad vision and subtle values. In nature we can find our place, our identity, and our affections. Nature invites us to discover the riches of our own souls rather than the powers of the ego. In this way, nature deepens our very sense of self, a good starting point for a spiritual way of life. The literature of the world's religions, and most of its art and poetry, assume an erotic, mystic view of the natural world and teach us how to make the direct, organic move from nature to spirit.

As in *La Primavera*, lush nature invites us to look upward and find our spirituality. Emerson says as much in a moving passage in his essay on nature, where he, too, appreciates the mediating role of clouds as they suggest transcendence: "I have seen the softness and beauty of the summer clouds floating feathery overhead, enjoying, as it seemed, their height and privilege of motion, whilst yet they appeared not so much the drapery of this place and hour, as forelooking to some pavilions and gardens of festivity beyond."

Contemplating nature is a "forelooking," a perception of that which transcends the here and now, a glimpse of the eternal precisely by means of the immediately temporal. What reason could be more compelling for honoring and protecting this natural world in all its particularity and ubiquitousness than to know that it is the prime source of our spirituality, the root of our personal meaning, and the starting point for any soul journey?

A Native American prayer presents the puzzle of world and spirit with apparent naive simplicity:

Don't you ever,
You up in the sky,
Don't you ever get tired
Of having the clouds between you and us?

Twirling a Flower: The Question of Form

from Tricycle

Shakyamuni twirls a flower. Mahakashyapa smiles.

You might say that this first transmission from teacher to disciple is the beginning of form for Buddhism: the infinite vastness of awakened mind expressed in the utter particularness of *this hand, this flower.*

Or you might say that this spontaneous gesture, which can be rediscovered but never duplicated, is the very opposite of what is meant by form—if by *form* you mean a reservoir of previously used particulars, a museum of words and movements made valuable by virtue of being well worn, passed down from hand to hand, from mouth to mouth.

But perhaps there is a middle way, one that can bring us to the very mystery of form in Buddhism. For what else can we call it when an ancient relic, preserved for centuries, suddenly flares up, becoming as fresh and single in our lives as the movement of Shakyamuni's fingers twirling a flower?

Some twenty years ago a friend of mine saw a small sign in a store window in Mendocino that said "Buddhist Retreat." A few days later, having never meditated before, she found herself in the midst of a seven-day *sesshin* with a Japanese Zen master. Hour after hour she sat before a window, peacefully watching the movement of raindrops down the glass. But there was one point where everything jammed. The chanting service each morning included the Heart Sutra in Sino-Japanese. "What do the words mean?"

Carole asked when she went for her interview with the roshi. "There's no need for you to know now," he replied. "Just throw yourself into the chanting. I'll translate for you when the *sesshin* is over."

Carole repeated her question each time she saw the roshi, and each time he gave her the same reply. Finally, she walked right out the door and headed toward the ocean. She walked and walked, and she had already gone quite a long distance when she heard footsteps behind her. She turned and saw the roshi.

"Let me tell you about the Heart Sutra," he said, continuing to walk with her in the direction in which she was going. *The Bodhisattva of Compassion, practicing deep prajna wisdom* . . . Line by line he translated, until Carole exclaimed, "I can say those words!" Together they turned and walked back to the *sesshin*.

Something about Carole's unwavering refusal had moved the Zen master. She was lucky to have found a teacher who recognized that our resistance to a form may be inseparable from the very energy that the path requires of us: the fierce determination to have an authentic, firsthand experience. "Be a lamp unto yourself," Shakyamuni said.

Buddhism encompasses a vast spectrum of possible relationships to form, from the elaborate rituals of the Vajrayana to the simpler—at times radically iconoclastic—practices of Zen. To this spectrum, we bring our own tendencies. For some the ancient forms provide exquisite aesthetic pleasure, like a walk through beautifully tended gardens. For others, they provide deep reassurance, the sense of being brought into alignment on a thread going back for centuries. Doing it *this way, and not that* as others before us have done it *this way, and not that*, it is possible to feel relieved of the burden of our own willy-nilly desires and aversions, free to participate in what Buddhists call the great "thusness" of the universe.

At the other extreme, there are those who have a profound temperamental aversion to form, a kind of allergic reaction. Beyond the posture of meditation, they experience every other form as a kind of obscenity. When I see such people gritting their teeth through one ceremony after another, I imagine they would have been much more at home in the earliest days of Buddhism, when all images of the Buddha were prohibited, save a linear pattern of waves or the simple outline of a footprint. Traces—nothing more.

"Why ride in a Volkswagen if you can ride in a Rolls Royce?" Chogyam Trungpa Rinpoche used to say—but not everyone wants to ride in a Rolls Royce. Ideally, we would each enter through the gate that most suited us temperamentally. But unfortunately there is not always a perfect match. Through the mysterious circumstances that bring each of us to the path, a Volkswagen person may find herself riding in a Rolls Royce, and the one riding in a Volkswagen may yearn for the still greater simplicity of a footprint.

Even when we feel a perfect alignment with our vehicle, there can be jarring moments. When Philip Kapleau was training in a Zen monastery in Japan, he had an excruciatingly hard time bowing. One day, observing him as he fell stiffly to the floor, his teacher exclaimed, "Kapleau-san, who do you think you're bowing to?" At the deepest level, this question is not fundamentally different from the famous Zen question "What is it?"—and hearing the question was a memorable moment for Roshi Kapleau.

There are times, then, when a particular form can function like a koan, intensifying and collecting our resistance to the point where something gives. When it does, the sense of release can be extraordinarily sweet. For when the small self lets go at the point where it has been clinging most fiercely—suddenly a breeze can blow in through the windowless room.

Rather than resist our resistance, we can allow ourselves to explore it in intimate detail, like a bug traveling across a flower, petal by petal. Examined at close range and without judgment, each form of resistance reveals its own rich texture. Sometimes, for instance, the form seems meaningless. "This is stupid," the mind sputters. "Why should I circumambulate clockwise rather than counterclockwise?" Such moments can be humorous or painful—yet they, too, have their grace.

In college I had a friend, a poet who had a serious stutter. One evening he gave a poetry reading before a fairly large audience. He began by explaining that when you have a stutter, you spontaneously discover that a certain gesture—pulling an ear, scratching an elbow, or bending down to pull up a sock—helps get the sound out. But over time, each gesture loses its power, until gradually you are left with a collection of empty and eccentric tics. He demonstrated for us: "S-S-S-S-(bending down to pull up a sock) A-A-A-A-(scratching an elbow) S-S-S-S-(pulling an ear) PARILLA!"

He went on, performing a kind of absurd and marvelous dance until he had completely disarmed his audience, and the anxiety that his friends felt for him had dissolved into laughter. What I learned is that it is possible to be completely present within certain words or gestures while remaining in full knowledge of their essential absurdity. Shakyamuni twirled a flower and Hakuin's teacher tweaked his nose. Each gesture is at once absolutely necessary and infinitely replaceable.

But what happens when we seem to fall out of the forms completely? In the midst of chanting a sutra that one has recited a thousand times, the words turn to dry husks inside the mouth. At such moments we look around and wonder what we are doing among so many strange people moving their mouths. It's as if suddenly Cinderella's coach turns into a pumpkin, her beautiful dress is back to rags, and she no longer belongs at the ball.

I remember so well the pain of being without a path—and my immense relief when I was taught, by a young Thai monk, to meditate. I felt as though I'd been looking for this path my whole life, yet the forms themselves were quite alien. The strange statues and chants made me want to weep with discomfort, and somewhere I still carry a fear that the vehicle could hit a bump and expel me onto the curb.

When I allow myself to sink into this apprehension, it draws me back to an experience that I had as a child. Sometimes in the midst of the most ordinary situations—sitting around the dinner table or riding in the car—I would suddenly look into my parents' faces and all connection with them would vanish. This happened quite apart from any emotion—it wasn't that I was angry at them or holding something in—it was just that, for a split second, I saw them in the mysterious singleness of their being. Why should my mother have this particular slant of nose and cheek? Why should my father's voice have this timbre? How did it come to be that we were eating ravioli at the dinner table or whizzing past telephone poles in the car?

Such estrangement is dizzying. Yet there is something sacred about the moment when we fall out of the habit-realm. So often it is precisely such a gap, a sense of wonder or questioning at what we take for granted, that brings us to the path in the first place.

The very meaning of *religion* contains the notion of tying back, fastening, yoking. There is something for the sake of which we are willing to let the loose strands of our own predilections go. The process can be painful, yet it can also be liberating—as in the famous story when the Zen teacher pours tea into the student's cup until it overflows. It's in precisely those moments when we experience how crowded our minds are that we have the chance of letting go and experiencing just how light we can be. What a joy to simply bow and light a stick of incense.

But here we are in dangerous territory. For when the willingness to surrender our own doubts and hesitations is not grounded in a practice of genuine inquiry and insight, the risks are real. Even setting aside the danger of fanaticism, it is important not to betray our own sense of what is right and what is real. Once, when I lived at a rural Zen center in northern California, a young woman from a Vajrayana lineage came to perform her one hundred thousand bows on a solo retreat. When she arrived it had already been raining for several days, and it continued to rain during the course of her stay. One evening I found her in the dark kitchen of the main house, drinking tea. She wasn't supposed to engage in a conversation with anyone, but she looked worried, so I asked her how she was.

"I'm having a lot of resistance to my practice," she said. "I keep feeling as though my cabin's moving."

"Are you from California?" I asked her.

"No," she said. "I'm from New England."

"I think your cabin's moving," I told her.

We went down with flashlights to have a look—and sure enough, in the drenched ground a chasm of several feet had opened up and surrounded her cabin. It looked as though it might soon slide down the hill.

From a certain perspective, of course, the questions and reservations about form are pure luxury. It's through the lens of observation that we perhaps get the truest glimpse of the power of form. In her memoir, *The Stones Cry Out,* Molyda Szymusiak, a young Cambodian woman, tells a true story that began when a friend of her uncle's had a dream. In the dream, a buddha was moaning from the mud of a pond. "Help me out of here, my friend!" Guided by this dream, the two men found their way to a dry riverbed, where a large bronze buddha lay in the bottom of the silt. Most statues found in this way had been decapitated, but this one was intact. The girl's uncle wanted to rescue the statue, but his friend was too frightened. To be caught in such an act was a crime punishable by death by the Khmer Rouge. That evening the uncle returned to the spot alone. He asked a passerby to help him, but the man treated him as if he was crazy.

> . . . So he prayed, "Lord Buddha, I'm alone and you're too heavy. But if you wish it, you can become light." He stretched his muscles, his feet sank into the slime, but the statue moved. He pushed it closer to the edge and with a last effort hoisted it up onto the grassy bank. . . . He told my father he felt as if he were carrying something like a big rock, no heavier than one or two bricks. . . . Shortly afterward we all left that area, and I don't know what happened to the statue, but my uncle always said to his children, "Only bodies may be killed. Take care to keep peace in your heart."

How is it that a particular word, gesture, or thing can be the embodiment of that which has no body and can never be killed? In times of extremity, the inanimate form can flower forth, like a daffodil bulb having stored its energy under the cold, hard ground. Where does this energy come from? Shakyamuni twirls a flower.

CYNTHIA OZICK

Remember the Sabbath Day, to Keep It Holy

from Self Magazine

The Sabbath is not only not in nature, it is against nature. In nature, all the days are alike—the birds continue to fly, the fish to swim, the grass to grow, the beasts to forage. But the Sabbath enters human history as a creation, an invention, a transcendent *idea:* an idea imposed on, laid over, all of nature's evidences. The Greeks and the Romans derided the Jews for observing the Sabbath—conduct so abnormal as to be absurd, and economically wasteful besides. From the pagan point of view, there was no profit in such idleness; Sabbath rest promoted both a household and a communal laziness that extended from the cookstove to the cowshed, from the employer to the most insignificant employee. For the Greeks and the Romans, all days were weekdays. Both masters and slaves were slaves to a clock that never stopped.

It was the biblical Sabbath that divided time and made the week. The Sabbath altered the world and how we perceive it. Without the Sabbath, time in a crucial sense has no reality—it simply rolls on, one sunrise after another, meaninglessly. Without the Sabbath, human toil is no different from the toil of an ox. But the injunction to hallow the seventh day honors labor by honoring rest from labor, just as the Creator, lavishing generative fervor on the fashioning of the universe in six days, stopped on the seventh to contemplate the perfection of the divine work. And so we do as the Creator did.

The Sabbath stands for liberation—and not only human liberation. Even the ox is liberated from toil on the Sabbath. Every creature, human or animal, is respected for its individual essence and given a day of peace. The Sabbath stands for the brotherly peace of Paradise; it sanctifies by seizing perfection out of the ragged flow of ordinary time. It conveys an understanding of distinctions: that the sacred departs from the everyday and therefore can never bore us; and that, as the Sabbath is unique in the week's row of days, all beings are unique and not to be regarded as drones or robots or slaves of any system.

Holiness means separateness: *kadosh*, the Hebrew word for "holy," is rendered as "set apart." The Sabbath is set apart from routine so that the delights of being alive can be savored without the distractions of noisy demands, jobs, money, and all the strivings of ego. Both power and powerlessness become irrelevant; on the Sabbath equality and dignity rule. Only a life in danger can override the Sabbath's focus on spiritual and moral elevation through tranquillity, fellowship, study, song, beauty, cleanliness, family intimacy. Every festive Sabbath meal is a holiday of thanksgiving. The Sabbath inspires us all to become the best that we can be. Every Sabbath day is a sacred fulfillment. Every Sabbath is a completion of Genesis: a divine creation in itself, fashioned, through human dedication, in the image of God.

KIMBERLEY C. PATTON

Seas of Light Swept Through It

from Myrrhbearers

After long work Mondays of dragon killing, angel wrestling (who says that Jacob's is a "male story," as I heard one feminist complain recently on NPR?), or just soul-grinding mundanity, my husband and I sometimes unwind by watching a new television show called *Chicago Hope.* The conclusion of a recent episode riveted my attention. The urban hospital's liability attorney is asked by a patient, a pregnant fifteen-year-old, to facilitate her baby's adoption. Late in the pregnancy, the unborn child is diagnosed with a severe cardiac abnormality. As the lawyer watches various sets of prospective parents' interest suddenly vanish in light of this news, he becomes gradually more invested in the fate of the child. When at last the baby is born—while her young mother averts her eyes—and is placed, unwanted, in the neonatal intensive care unit, the hospital lawyer decides to adopt her himself.

The final camera of the show finds the new father sitting in that unit at night, at the end of his own long day of dragon killing, rocking his new little daughter in his arms. He is approached by an attending physician, a surgeon whose hide he has just rescued from a vindictive malpractice suit. The surgeon thanks him and then wonders aloud as he watches the scene: "And you . . . you're amazing. Just look at you. You deal with all this pressure all day long. And you're a single parent. *And* your daughter has a hole in her heart, for God's sake. . . . How can you do this? What are you going to do? How are you going to manage?" The lawyer looks up from his rocking chair, takes one look at the baby's face, then looks back at the surgeon. He answers simply, "I was never alive before."

In this one brief exchange between two of the show's principal characters I found perfectly expressed the great gulf between the utilitarian discourse that has become our national idiom and the profoundly transformative language in which religion speaks instead about the human condition. Both the surgeon and the lawyer were talking about parenting. But, however concerned, the surgeon was talking about logistics and, ultimately, about fear. The lawyer was talking about the inexorable power of redemptive love. The surgeon was talking about things that seemed so very critical, so all-consuming—but that, in the end, don't matter and will not endure. The lawyer was talking about eternity.

Chrismated only a year and a half ago, and pregnant myself for the first time, I continually seek ways to think about my new condition. In neither popular culture nor the best of current social wisdom have I found anything that remotely describes what constitutes this awesome journey or where it seems to lead. In the many lavishly illustrated books on pregnancy and childbirth piled by my nightstand I read pages and pages on the physical and emotional changes I should anticipate, from conception to birth and beyond. There are sections on mood swings, nutrition, nervousness, and "getting your husband's support"—not to mention endless reams of advice on how to successfully execute a sexual relationship during pregnancy! One encounters logistics, statistics, and no end of reasons to worry—like the anxious surgeon. These books sent me into the valley. How, indeed, *was* I going to manage? Would I lose my identity? Would our lives as we had known them end—would the child's presence erode our independence, our intimacy, in the end, the very fabric of the world we had built together for seven years?

In sum, I was suffering from the (particularly American) brand of feminism to which I had been exposed over the years, which had combined in my mind with the (particularly Baby Boomer) approach of fierce strategizing on one's own behalf instead of seeking and serving God's will, and of "managing" one's time instead of offering every moment upon His mighty altar. For the first few months my mind was a whirlwind of dark fear, unanchored in specific categories, ranging from diapers to the fate of my own career to sudden infant death syndrome. But for even a mention of the mystery into which I was plunged, I searched in vain. Only one, almost peripheral sentence on one page in one of my glossy maternity books leaped off the page: "Some women find that having a child can be a kind of rebirth."

When I read this, I remembered the exhausted lawyer on *Chicago Hope* who had *voluntarily* bound his life to that of the tiny divine creation whose very life hung in the balance. He had asked for trouble, for anxiety, for sorrow. He had done so because God had placed, directly in his path, for the first time in his life of relentless "management," a chance to love without condition—to break his very heart open so that God's limitless love might come to dwell there. Therefore he had answered the surgeon, "I was never alive before." This, indeed, is how traditional Christianity teaches us to answer our fears—our desperate need to control, fueled by the continual input of a society that values, in so many arenas, "the freedom to choose."

At our first ultrasound screening, unprepared at three and a half months for anything beyond the image of a blurry spine and perhaps some tiny limbs, Bruce and I found ourselves confronted by a smiling, wise little face that stared straight back at us: a miniature, animate icon of God's incarnate glory. I am not sure I will ever recover from the sight.

That face seared my heart as I picked my way from day to day in my academic job as that rarest of beings, a pregnant scholar. That face haunted me as I tried to negotiate a reasonable maternity leave and ran out of any shoes that still fit in which I could lecture.

And as I encountered the curiosity of my students and the awkwardness of my colleagues, I remembered that face.

"Kimberley!" shouted one older male professor as our two large classes exchanged the lecture hall. "I hear you have something in your belly!" At the faculty Christmas party: "Bun in the oven, huh?" And recently, news of a female colleague who remained quite proud of the fact that she *concealed* her seven months' pregnancy from her department until the semester was over. "Why do these reactions bother me so much?" I asked a dear friend on the faculty, who is devoutly Jewish. "Am I hypersensitive? This *is* a physical thing!" He thought for a moment. "Because they trivialize the mystery."

I thank God during these days that I have been given a true language in which to think about my pregnancy and the child I am carrying, whom, God willing, I will soon meet face-to-face. At night, I read the "Prayers of Woman with Child," given to me by my priest months ago. "O sovereign Lord Jesus Christ our God, the Source of Life and immortality: I thank Thee, for in my marriage Thou hast made me a recipient of Thy blessing and gift. . . . Bless this fruit of my body that was given to me by Thee. . . . Favor it and animate it by thy Holy Spirit. . . . A faithful angel, a guardian of soul and body do Thou vouchsafe him. Protect, keep, strengthen, and shelter the child in my womb until the hour of his birth. But conceal him not in his mother's womb: for Thy hands fashioned him; Thou gavest him life and health. . . ."

How can one fear childbirth or anything else in the future when pregnancy is spoken of in language so tender and yet so exalted, so *true* as this? It has begun to dawn on me that Orthodox Christianity has conferred on me, my husband, and my child a dignity that current social wisdom, so prone to think in terms of "rights" and "needs," cannot possibly offer us. When I go into labor, my beloved priest and *presbytera* will be there to say a prayer for me.

When my child is born, they will come to name her on the eighth day. When we return to church after forty days, it will be as a brand-new family, joyously received by the communion of faithful whose love already surrounds and upholds me. When my little girl is baptized, she will be sealed as Christ's own forever and ever. And as she grows, she will look up every Sunday into the radiant, tranquil face of the great icon of the Platytera, the one whom the Akathist hymn calls "Treasure-house of purity through which we rose from our fall, sweetscented Lily scattering perfume among the faithful, fragrant incense and most precious Myrrh"—the Mother of God, who opens her arms from the apse to embrace her own child as well as each one of us, male or female, whole or broken, eternally saying yes on our behalf to God's word.

As Father Anthony Coniaris has written in his *Making God Real in the Orthodox Christian Home,*

> She said yes for all of us. And God came down to earth to live in your life and mine.
>
> It was as if the human race had beaten on the door, rattled the windows, tapped on the dark glass, trying to get in—and yet the Spirit was outside. But one day, a woman opened the door, and the little house was swept pure and clean by the wind. Seas of Light swept through it, and the light remained in it; and in that little house a Child was born and the Child was God.
>
> The blessed Theotokos said yes for the human race. Each one of us must echo that yes for our own lives. . . .
>
> To surrender all that we are, as we are, to the Spirit of Love in order that our lives may bear Christ into the world—that is what every Christian is asked.

Reflecting on these words, and knowing that by God's grace I now live in this sanctified vessel of safety that is the Orthodox

Church, I think, "Of course. How could I have believed that the world had anything to tell me about what it means to be pregnant?" The truth is so much starker and yet at the same time so much more wondrous. Like everything else in Christ's kingdom, this is a paradox. Of course my life will be changed irrevocably by the advent of a child. Of course I will have to give up my old self. Of course my sacrifice lies at the heart of this gift, and that sacrifice in turn will ceaselessly give back to me. Of course nothing will be the same. God wants nothing less than our complete rebirth and, ultimately, nothing less than *theosis,* our own deification. What better tool than a child who shatters our self-centered, fear-driven egos and causes, through Love's great compulsion, our complete submission?

A Long and Sizable Farewell

from DoubleTake

> *for Lightning Allan Brown,*
> *born in December 1947—*
> *dead of AIDS in February 1996*

1. LIGHTNING BROWN DISCOVERS HE SHARES A BIRTHDAY WITH EMILY DICKINSON, 10 DECEMBER 1994

We've spent the whole month, lobbing Emily poems
At one another—*After great pain* and *morning's nest;*
The distant strains of triumph, agonized—
And here the mail delivers this calendar,
Day on day of a thousand poets' birthdays.

  You turn to yours and shout "God, it's *her!*"—
A grace we'd never known you shared
With that remote uranium core from Amherst.
Then for a silent instant, your eyes flare.

  So now we understand you move secure,
In far more light than heretofore we'd seen—
The light the two of you lob back and forth
Across bleak years: the rampant truth,
Pain seized and worn threadbare, triumphant laughter.

2. NEAR THE DEATH OF THE SUN, 21 DECEMBER 94

Knot by knot, it leaves through our hands—
Frail yarn of light through the wayward fingers

Of our four hands that have staved off death
Past various absolute-last reprieves
To link, near empty, at the end of this year.
    Linked, the surge of voltage threading
Both our frames—one circuit—promises
Every good office and burden of fire:
In-dwelling warmth, dry crackle and respite
Of helpless laughter, juddering blasts
Of glare and vision, the cooler shades
Where (eased and stoked) we slowly comprehend
And greet a mutual ravenous sane
Just possible will to last.

3. BESIEGED BUT STRONGER, 22 MARCH 1995

This second fulminant full day of spring,
We sit on the deck under leaves so young
We can all but read the old sky through them—

The dregs of a winter we ushered in
With appropriate quiet three months ago,
The balked dark solstice we'd only begun

To think a way past. Yet here and laughing
We sit in the young sun as you read poems
You pressed from the black time (words as hard

And likely to last as—what?—the voracious
Jet kingfisher that mines the pond
For life, the hid turtle's iron jaws);

And the air that courts us slavishly, shameless,
Feels for the instant like endless luck.

4. THE DREAD, 21 NOVEMBER 95

I'm starting to dread your ravenous life—
The plumb-line weight of daily guilt
When I haven't seen or phoned you anyhow,
Despite the posthumous distance of your voice
Whenever I wake you (most moments of the clock)
Or your stratospheric apparent indifference
To my prancing desperately meaningless questions
Of *How're you feeling? What do they think?*
Is there anything on the Earth at all
You'd like me to do?
                              No sign this week
Of your stated purpose to clear on out
Before the hard straits. What could be harder
Than these slow minutes, the swarming—or frail
Threading hum—of whatever your mind,
That huge unwinking merciful eye,
Is poised above or foundering in
By the smallest measurable unit of time
As I stay home, longing for credible alibis
Never to see your skull again.

5. FORTY-EIGHTH BIRTHDAY, 30 NOVEMBER 95

So ten days early I write you this ultimate birthday poem,
At least half-hoping you'll be elsewhere by the actual date,

One day after Milton's 387th and the day of Dickinson's 165th.
   Here, take this guess at a tailor-made Heaven
With every feature you'd likely request, if you had serious
Hope of Heaven (I have it for you; let's claim that's enough)—
A clean dark stream with wooded shores, sufficient banks
For a few nude swimmers who occasionally rise and, joined at the
   palm,
All but conceal themselves in thicket to couple safely
With cries on the order of panther wails and buffalo moans
While a tape-looped selection of Shostakovich's rare calm
   moments
Sifts through branches gripped by hawks and stern-eyed owls
Who may well envy the pitch of pleasure your face agrees
At last to show, unparalleled and a vast liberation
For you to acknowledge.
                    Afterward, you withdraw to your house
And write one further shaggy poem of pawky eloquence;
Then head for City Hall and a long night's wrangle in the interest
Of some immensely unlikable citizen's last-ditch rights
Before you lay your dark hidalgo's eloquent skull
To final sleep—*final* only in the sense of the last
Willed act of an infinite day in an endless life.
   Hard as it's always been for you to take the slightest
Gift from the world, take this, lean friend, strict payer of every
Debt you've owed.

6. THE ISSUE, 2 FEBRUARY 96

This gray leviathan stalled overhead
Is breaking up into frozen rain,
Trees crash; the lights and heat phut out
And here you are on the spared white phone.

The nurse half-whispers "The tumors are back,
All in his brain; he's somewhat demented,"
Then puts you on.
          And all you say
As I fumble for questions to break through to you
Is "*What's the issue?*" Every attempt
At contact, assurance, even the tries
At naming myself so you'll know it's me,
That you've known me two decades, is met with only
"*What's the issue?*" in your normal voice.
   The issue, friend, is stark farewell
With ample gratitude and hopes for the trek;
But—thank God maybe—you're far past gone.

7. A Visit That Feels Like the Last, 7 February 96

You do no more than answer pointless questions,
My impotent tries at filling the air;
And of course I'm dehydrating through the eyes,
A fact you register calmly as a mantis
Praying before the lunge at its victim
Or like a heartless oracle—still,
Bronze-lipped and true.
              Desperate finally
I take up the palm-sized Whitman by your bed
And read through the next five minutes at random,
Each poem somehow bulls-eyed on today—
Sweet-handed death. . . . the jocund love of comrades.
   When your sisters, parents and brother join us
(Just as I feel I can't read more),
Your mother—handsome as in her fresh girlhood
In that tan picture you kept on your desk—

Says "Lightning, this room is full of love";
And your blind cyclops gaze sweeps us all in
Before you speak to say "I know it."

What I think I know is that, barring a summons,
I've watched a life crest and will leave you now.
I touch your brown bone wrist—"See you soon."

Long past even the memory of a smile,
You nod my way—"Yes. Well, all right."

8. Gone, 12 February 96

All the last day before you lapsed
Into comatose silence, then slipped away,
You told your sister "They're waving at me.
Everybody down there is waving at me."

The sister asked "Who are *they?*"
And you said typically "How should *I* know?—
They're just down there waving."

Assuming "Down there" is a good destination,
They waved you into that narrow door
You scratched on a thousand walls to find
These past eight months.

Out for a nap

The instant you vanished, I actually felt
The line of a long slot open from neck
To groin, then the slip—like a short letter mailed,
No pain, no sound—of your slim shadow
Passing through me and eagerly on.

Twenty minutes later when the phone rang to tell me,
I was already watching the infinite wake
Of your last shape, entirely free.

9. SCATTERING LIGHTNING IN THE SLAVE CEMETERY, CHAPEL HILL, 16 FEBRUARY 96

What white man on the planet but you
Would think to be strewn on the wide-spaced graves
Of human chattel, men and women
Enslaved by the local faculty, clergy,
Some century and a half ago?
   Yet seeing the place in this driving snowstorm—
Old pines thicker than elephant thighs,
A squat wall, jagged fieldstone markers
(Bare of names) to a few dozen lives
Voiceless to speak the still inexplicable
Fact of bondage in a whole town chartered
For freedom and mercy—you seem a fit occupant,
Parched to essence by a fire you kindled
Knowingly in the midst of a life
Already smoking, hell-bent on justice
For the birthright-helpless and the Earth herself.
   We strew your sandy ochre dust,
The two slim quarts we'll all come to,
On frozen wind that blows you back
Against our legs before you settle;
And I recall your last four words
As you fined your aim down toward the end—
"Am I there yet?"
                There, lost pal.
There at the least.

10. BRIEF VISIT, 21 MARCH 96

This time last year we sat on my deck
And watched the pond revive in warm light.

Today I'm headed in to teach—
Cold blue sun, an unblemished sky—
When I suddenly turn to Adam and say
"Have you thought about Lightning in the past ten minutes?"

"No," he says. "Can't claim that I have;
Why do you ask?" He's genuinely curious.

I know and tell him. You were just here behind me
In the van, in actual reach of the back
Of my skull—no detectable malice but not benign,
Not entirely well-meaning. I can't look back.

The rest of the way though, I keep your young face
Clear before me as a crucified icon
Gouged with a nail in the palm of my hand.

You are not forgotten.

FRANCINE PROSE

The Old Morgue

from The Threepenny Review

My father was a pathologist. For most of his professional career—that is, for all of my early life—he worked in the autopsy rooms and laboratories of the Bellevue Hospital Mortuary.

The Old Morgue, people call it now. And whenever the Old Morgue is mentioned, a passionate nostalgia shines (a little crazily) in the eyes of those who still remember the beautiful gloomy brick building (built near the turn of the century by McKim, Mead and White) that's been replaced by the "new" Bellevue's glass and steel.

The Old Morgue had stone staircases, wrought iron railings, tiled floors, dark halls, and the atmosphere of an antiquarian medical establishment—part torture chamber, part charnel house, part research laboratory—so brilliantly captured in David Lynch's film version of *The Elephant Man*. In my memory, the Old Morgue evokes those shadowy group portraits of distinguished scientists performing anatomical dissections, arranged with formal ceremony around a flayed cadaver painted with the aesthetic high gloss of a Dutch Master *nature morte*.

The autopsy room was enormous—cavernous, people say—with twenty-foot ceilings, windows reaching from roof to floor, and, high above, a skylight that cast sheets of dusty light onto the doctors, the assistants, the students gathered round the gleaming chrome tables. For all the disturbing tools of the trade—the hoses, scalpels, saws, the scales for weighing organs—the room had the classical elegance of an old-fashioned hotel lobby in which the dead might rest for a while until their rooms were ready.

The morgue was my father's office—where he went every day to work. It was where my mother took me after ballet lessons so he could drive us home to Brooklyn. On school holidays, I dressed up so he could show me off to his colleagues and then find me a quiet corner of his lab where I could read until lunch. I liked going with him to his job. I never thought much about the beauty of the Old Morgue, or its strangeness, or the strangeness of growing up in a household in which dinner-table conversation concerned the most fascinating cases that had come down for autopsy that day.

Most everyone's childhood seems normal to them, and everyone's childhood marks them. Like army brats, like diplomats' kids, like the offspring of Holocaust survivors and (so I'm told) suicides, the children of pathologists recognize one another. Two of my friends are pathologist's daughters; we speak a common language. Last week, confessing to one that I'd binged on some fast-food fried chicken, I complained—disgustedly, unthinkingly—that the layer of fat beneath the skin was "just like every goddamn autopsy you've ever seen." She laughed and then said, "I hope you know not to say things like that to most people."

This fall, at a dinner party in Manhattan, I met a writer, a woman whose mother worked with my father; both were pathologists at Bellevue. As the other guests put down their forks and looked on, faintly appalled, we reminisced nostalgically about growing up in the Old Morgue. We discussed our shared fascination with the morgue employees known as *dieners*. German for "servants," the word had always made us think of Dr. Frankenstein's trusty helper, Igor. Though they were usually busy with the physical work of the autopsy room—sawing through the breastbone and skull, sometimes making the Y-shaped incision—the dieners knew the best stories (accounts of the more peculiar cases that had come into their provenance) and took time to tell them, like fairy tales, to the two little girls waiting for their parents to finish work and take them home.

We talked about how you always knew you were getting close to the morgue when you heard the keening, asthmatic whine of the dieners' electric saws.... And for just a moment, that high-pitched buzz seemed more immediate and more real than the genteel clink of silver as the other guests bravely returned to their meals.

Forensic and clinical pathologists are said to be different breeds. Articulate and extroverted, the forensic scientist (who deals with suspicious, violent, or accidental death) is drawn to popping flash bulbs and adversarial courtroom situations, while the stereotypical pathologist (whose patients are more likely to have died of organic disease) is an eccentric loner without the minimal social skills to interact with the living. But until 1961, when the New York City Medical Examiner's Office traded the Victorian gloom of Bellevue for its own faux-Bauhaus quarters on 30th Street and First Avenue, the forensic pathologists shared the Old Morgue with clinical pathologists, like my father.

Indeed, the history of pathology at Bellevue is inseparable from that of the Medical Examiner's office, established in 1917. (Previously, the city coroner was rarely a physician, which is still not a job requirement in many areas of the country, where the county coroner may be a mortician or a moonlighting tow-truck driver.) Pathologists reverentially recite the names of the first ME's—Norris, Gonzales, Helpern—like a royal line of succession dating back to the era when the morgue was known as the deadhouse.

The Old Morgue had no air conditioning. From the safe distance of decades, my father's former colleagues take pride in having braved working conditions that no one would stand for today. No young pathologist would consider doing those long postmortems in the stifling summer heat, when the smell of the autopsy room, barely cloaked by disinfectant, permeated the whole building; you took it home in your clothes.

The doctors at the morgue worked hard: long hours for little pay, often for the loftiest and most idealistic of reasons. "More than any other specialty, pathologists teach other doctors," says Marvin Kuschner, who left Bellevue to become dean of SUNY-Stony Brook Medical School. "And my generation was inspired by *Arrowsmith,* by *The Microbe Hunters.* We all wanted to save the world and find the cure for cancer." Pathologists have a broader knowledge of the science of medicine than their counterparts in other fields; they know who the good diagnosticians are, which surgeons make fatal mistakes.

No one becomes a pathologist for the money. Most have comparatively low paying university appointments, and though it's possible to supplement an academic salary with a high-volume business reading slides of biopsies and cervical Pap smears, still the sum is a fraction of the income of the surgeon or orthopedist. Medical examiners—city or state employees—receive even lower salaries, for which they are obliged to contend with unsympathetic reporters and merciless political pressure: the unscientific agendas of the government and the police. One way you can tell an honest ME, they say, is that he's probably been fired. And no one goes into the field for the glory: pathologists don't tend to have grateful patients passing around their business cards at Park Avenue dinner parties.

Pathologists speak unashamedly of their work as a vocation, a calling, and—with tender care and respect—of their patients, the dead. ("We have to learn to talk to our patients as much as an internist must talk to living patients," says Michael Baden, the outspoken former New York City Medical Examiner now serving as Director of the Forensic Unit of the New York State Police. "A dead person can't tell us where it hurts. But we can figure it out.")

And yet for all the seriousness with which the doctors took their work, the Old Morgue was an oddly jolly place, with its camaraderie, its in-jokes, its characters and legends. Everyone knew the story of the Irish politician whose body was left by the dieners on a table overnight; by morning his nose had been devoured by roaches or rats. The problem was solved when an artistic doctor fashioned a new nose of putty—tinted green to match the skin color produced by the dead man's cirrhotic liver. But the embalming process blanched the skin, leaving the deceased with a green nose at his open-casket Irish wake.

I remember hearing about the dapper pathologist who did autopsies in an elegant suit with a cornflower in his lapel and who scrawled obscenities on the walls and blackboards. About the doctor with the eerie booming laugh who had his mother-in-law exhumed to prove that his wife had poisoned her—and was doing the same to him. The withdrawn medical examiner who played handball against his office walls at midnight; the pathologist who taught his students these precious home truths: "Burial is just long-term storage" and "Maggots are your friends." (In fact, human DNA and evidence of drug use can be obtained from maggots who have skeletonized a corpse.) The doctor who procured human brains for medical students and committed suicide when this service he'd provided gratis was exposed by the press.

After autopsy, the organs of the deceased are put in a bag and sewn up inside the corpse; still, one hears rumors about souvenir taking. Officially, JFK's brain is missing, though Raden, who examined the Kennedy autopsy findings for the Congressional Select Committee on Assassinations, has an elaborate theory positing that Robert Kennedy safeguarded the tissue removed from his brother's body and restored it to the coffin just before burial. Trotsky's brain has never been found, while Einstein's surfaced in

Illinois in the possession of a former Princeton neuropathologist planning to write a paper on the physiology of genius.

One Bellevue veteran recounts meeting, on the street, a colleague who opened a package wrapped in newspaper and showed him a human heart. My friend's pathologist-father brought home a heart in a Kentucky Fried Chicken bucket and dumped it into the bathroom sink for an impromptu anatomy lesson. Another friend was nearly dismissed from her Upper East Side private girls' school when her fellow students found, in her locker, a fetus that her mother had given her to bring to biology class.

My father never brought keepsakes from the morgue home to us. And yet he—readily, eagerly—took me along to the morgue. When I was fourteen, during the summer between my freshman and sophomore years of high school, he got me a summer job as an assistant in a chemistry lab next door to the autopsy room.

Only lately, as the mother of teenagers near the age that I was then, have I begun to wonder: *What in the world was he thinking?* Most likely, it seemed perfectly normal to employ his daughter in the family business. (Recently, his best friend told me that he'd got his son a summer job driving the truck that picked up bodies for the Long Island Medical Examiner.)

The Old Morgue was definitely hardball. It had a heavily macho ambiance, a gum-chewing, cigar-smoking rough-and-tumble. "There were certain ragged edges to the performance," admits one veteran.

"Bellevue fostered a great brotherhood," says Renate Dische, a pediatric pathologist. "People who worked there have a mutual bond. It was a tough environment. The first week I got there, it was summer, hot as blazes. And there was terrific excitement: they'd found a body in a steamer trunk. It was like the good old days in the 1920s! Everyone was running around, taking pictures of the trunk open, the trunk closed. Inside was this plug-ugly guy curled up in fetal position. Some loan shark who had lent money to a poor artist."

I don't imagine that my father worried much about exposing me to the teeming activity of a workplace in which twenty autopsies might be going at once, far more in cases of disaster. (I remember him working through the night after two planes collided over downtown Brooklyn.) Nor do I think he was greatly concerned about any psychic damage that might result from my intimate acquaintance with mortuary life.

But what about the real dangers? "I always felt there was TB on the *staircases* at Bellevue," says Renate Dische. "And the staff was careless about tuberculosis. So quite a few doctors came down with TB and had to go to sanitariums." (On vacation in the Adirondacks, my father took us to see the former TB hospital at Saranac Lake, a marvelously creepy cluster of buildings surrounded by porches on which the sick were dosed with sunlight and fresh air.)

Hepatitis was also a problem, as were the flies that swarmed in whenever the tall windows were opened to relieve the stifling heat—flies so fat and preoccupied that, one doctor recalls, "you could take a scalpel and cut right through them as they ate off the bodies." Then there was the oppressive odor that permeated everything. People warned me: Wait till they bring in a floater, a body that's been in the water. I couldn't imagine anything worse than the normal smell, but on the day a floater came in, I knew at once what had happened—and that I'd been correctly warned.

In the basement was an embalming school, and beneath that the tunnels through which bodies were transported; the tunnels were home to packs of wild cats installed to control the rat population and to an underground minisociety of the homeless, even then. Upstairs, the quotidian routines of the mortuary were regulated

by disgruntled city employees like the elevator operator who pun-
ished impatient interns by stopping the car between floors and
making them jump or climb; when he died, the staff attended his
autopsy to make sure he was really dead.

I don't believe my father had any particular pedagogical or
philosophical interest in exposing me to the harsh fact of death.
Nor was he careless about my safety; he was, if anything, overpro-
tective. I think he believed the slim risk was worth it because he
was fervently hoping—as he continued to hope long after I'd published several novels—that I would be drawn to his profession,
that I would become a doctor.

In fact, I enjoyed my job in the lab, mostly washing glassware. I
liked my boss, a biochemist who hoped to prove experimentally,
by analyzing the urine of schizophrenics, that a percentage of the
patients in the Psychiatric Building across 29th Street (in those
years before drug therapy, one could hear the inmates screaming
day and night) were suffering from porphyria, the kidney ailment
with symptoms mimicking insanity that plays a crucial role in
Alan Bennett's play, *The Madness of George III*. I liked the research
staff who'd accompanied my boss from the Midwest—a crew of
friendly, conservative lesbians who wore rings with dollar signs as
visible symbols of their faith in the beliefs of Ayn Rand.

For the first week or so I avoided looking into the autopsy
room, though the door was always open, and I had to pass it many
times daily. Then one day I stopped in the doorway. I stood there
and made myself watch. I don't remember exactly why, I felt that it
was time. One of the women in my lab had told me a story about
some first-year medical students who had toured the mortuary
and gone out and thrown up on the sidewalk. I must have wanted
to prove to myself that I was tougher than that.

The first time was terrifying. I felt as if the act of looking were
like the act of wading into a rough icy sea. Tentatively, I glanced at

the feet, the tag attached to the toe, then up the leg with as much relation to flesh as wax fruit to a pear. By now I knew that it was a man, an old man, though his scalp was pulled down like a veil over his face. The flaps of skin folded back from the central incision reminded me of a jacket flung open in the suffocating heat. . . .

It all seemed absolutely strange and at the same time utterly normal. Since then I have looked at photos of murder and disaster victims, and I can say with certainty that this was entirely different. How exposed and surprised the dead always look to be strewn about like rag dolls, causing us the gnawing suspicion that they wouldn't want us looking—such pictures always strike me as vaguely pornographic. But the old man on the steel table was an eternity beyond all that. There was no titillation in watching, no sense of the forbidden. In the harsh artificial light that supplemented what leaked in through the dusty windows, it looked so calm and otherworldly that what I felt was like an enchantment.

No doubt the spell would have been broken—I might have been really scared—if someone had chased me away. But that summer no one paid any attention to the young girl who stopped from time to time to watch from the doorway. (I don't remember ever seeing my father do a postmortem, though I always sought out his familiar comforting face.) It was as if I'd taken on the doctors' competent matter-of-factness. Unlike them, though, I hadn't forgotten how this might appear to the outside world, and I took every chance to boast to my friends about the gruesome tableaux I was seeing. (I should say that the more disturbing autopsies—on badly decomposed corpses or on children—were done in a hidden back room.)

Unless you knew what the doctors were looking for, the procedures took on a certain sameness, and finally what engaged me more than the painstakingly thorough postmortems were the stories I was hearing about the morgue's most notorious cases: the gangland bosses, the high-society dead, the briefly and lastingly famous.

The chief diener, Betty Forman, knew the details of every murder that had come through the ME's office. A former Gibson girl, Betty—even in late middle age—still showed unmistakable flashes of glossy, robust blond beauty. I was fascinated by her: How had she lost one eye? How had she gone from the vaudeville stage to a career as a Bellevue diener?

Those were questions I couldn't ask. But I could inquire about the horrors Betty had seen in her line of work. Doctors have told me that Betty taught them lots they hadn't known—for example, the fact that female suicides were nearly always menstruating. One pathologist recalls how Betty tried to help him with his apartment hunting. She'd call him and say, "Quick! There's a place in the Village! The tenant's just come in. There'll be a bullet hole in the couch—but that won't matter much."

I remember Betty mentioning a scandalous case in which a political boss was found to have killed his ingenue mistress and stuffed her body into the trunk of his car. I tried to fake comprehension, but it soon became clear: I'd never heard of this scandal from decades before I was born. I can still see Betty looking at me with polite incredulous wonder, as if I'd just confessed to never having heard of Abraham Lincoln.

I remember my father telling us—this was in 1981—that Bellevue was beginning to see some very peculiar cases: men whose immune systems appeared to have shut down. Even more strangely, a number of these patients were Orthodox Jews, who had never told their families that they were gay and certainly not about the impressive numbers of sexual partners they'd had in the previous decade. Once more, my father began staying late at the hospital or going into work on weekends when he got a call saying that one of these patients had come down for a postmortem.

Later, when the riddle was solved, some of the younger patholo-gists became reluctant to do autopsies on people who'd died of AIDS. I can still see the expression on my father's face—at once bel-licose, lofty, and righteous, a look one might find on the faces of bronze generals in military monuments—as he rehearsed the speech he intended to give those little shits. They were doctors, trained physicians. They had taken an oath to treat the sick, to help the living and the dead without discrimination.

"We did those early AIDS cases before we knew what we were doing," recalls Marvin Kuschner. "Guys were coming in with Kaposi's and Pneumocystis pneumonia. I was always contemptu-ous of people who were afraid to do autopsies. I was brought up to believe you just did them. There were times when I was up to my elbows in tuberculous pus. But there was—and there is now—a certain reluctance to do AIDS cases. And it's a pity, because those postmortems are a gold mine for pathologists. Those patients have so many things wrong with them."

In fact, says Baden, "no forensic pathologist has ever gotten AIDS in the normal course of work. It is a potential problem for pathol-ogists, who, statistically, cut themselves once in every six autopsies. Fortunately, you need to come in contact with a lot of the AIDS virus to get infected. Just a little bit of hepatitis virus will make you sick—but it takes a lot of HIV."

Only a year or so after my father shamed his staff into treating the AIDS dead with the respect that is still so often denied the liv-ing, he experienced severe chest pains and checked himself into the hospital, where he was found to have suffered a coronary—a minor problem, as it turned out, compared to the malignant lung tumor discovered, unexpectedly, on a routine chest X ray. Twenty years had passed since my father gave up cigarettes, but he'd replaced them with a pipe, on which he constantly inhaled.

I've always thought that, in his final illness, my father got less-than-optimum medical care. Physicians (and I am not speaking of pathologists so much as the profession as a whole) do in fact have a complex relation to death. His colleagues and friends—now his doctors—could barely handle the fact that one of their own was at risk. It brought the idea of death too close to home, and their pain and misery were palpable. After it had become obvious that his tumor had metastasized, one of his doctors—a friend—suggested that his problem might be an exotic parasite. Had he recently traveled to an underdeveloped country?

My father had to handle it for them and, really, for us all. As a pathologist, he knew what sort of tumor he had, how serious it was. But he died with courage and grace: a fact that, I think, had less to do with his autopsy-room experience than with who he was. He was most concerned, as always, with sparing his family pain. One of the last times he left the apartment in which he died was to buy me a new computer because he worried that my vintage CPM drive would soon become outmoded.

In the last weeks of his life he became intermittently disoriented. The most obsessive of these delusions was that he was late for work—that, at any minute, he would go downstairs and get a cab and travel across town to Bellevue, to his old office, his lab.

PHYLLIS ROSE

The Music of Silence

from The Atlantic Monthly

I married into an extraordinary family. Laurent's father was Jean de Brunhoff, the author and illustrator of the Babar books I loved so much as a child. Laurent and his brother Mathieu, barely a year younger than he, now a beloved pediatrician in Paris, were the little boys for whom the story of Babar was invented, by their mother, Cécile. The boys told their mother's wonderful story to their father, a painter, and asked him to illustrate it, which he did, writing a text and slightly modifying the story his wife had told—adding, for example, the Old Lady. That is uncanny, because Madame de Brunhoff, my mother-in-law, although she was young at the time and looked nothing like the Old Lady, has come more and more to resemble the woman her husband drew in 1931, as though he could imagine her changing in time, like those computer projections of lost children. Jean de Brunhoff died of tuberculosis when he was thirty-seven, leaving his widow with three small boys. Laurent was twelve, Mathieu eleven, and Alain almost three. Alone, never remarrying, Madame de Brunhoff got them through the war and brought them up. She was a pianist and taught at the École Normale de Musique.

Laurent inherited his father's talent and became a painter, living the classic student-artist's life in a studio in Montparnasse until, at the age of twenty-one, he resurrected Babar and began to write and illustrate books about the lovable elephant—at least in part, he says, as a way of resurrecting his father and continuing imaginatively the family life of his childhood. Few readers were aware of any change in the authorship of the Babar books, partly because the war had intervened to explain any gap, and partly because Laurent had trained himself so well to draw elephants in the style of his father.

Alain inherited his mother's musical talent and, initially trained by her, became a concert pianist, well known in France in the 1960s. By the time I met Laurent, Alain was legendary in Paris for his talent, looks, and charm and the glamorous life he had led before abruptly retiring from the world and becoming a monk at the age of forty.

Laurent and I visited Alain in the summer of 1990, some years after Alain had left his monastery outside Bordeaux for a hermitage in the Pyrenees. It was remote, but not as remote as I had imagined it, my idea of hermits dating back to the time of St. Jerome. I envisioned them living on columns in the desert or hauling supplies in baskets up by ropes to their hand-hewn caves, whereas Alain lived on the grounds of a convent in a special bungalow enclave built for hermits, and he could have visitors.

Laurent and I, who were having a late honeymoon in Provence, drove down to see him in an air-conditioned BMW that, from the figures Avis gave him, Laurent had somehow imagined was no more expensive to rent than a Ford Escort. From Avignon it was about two hours on the highway that runs by Nîmes, Montpellier, and Perpignan, along the route that the Romans pioneered and that countless tourists now follow on their way to Spain. We traveled at ninety miles per hour the whole way, not feeling the speed, with *Cosi fan tutte* on the stereo. Only Mercedeses, other BMWs, and very aggressive little R5s and Peugeot 205s failed to move out of our way. At the last exit in France we left the autoroute and headed toward the high peaks of the Pyrenees. Soon, following Alain's directions to the mountain hamlet near which he lived, we were in desolate country, covered with scrub and stunted oaks.

The whole mountainside had burned a few years before, but the dense underbrush was already back.

Alain said he would wait for us on the road, and as we came up over a rise at the appointed hour, we saw him walking toward us. He was dressed not in the brown burlap hermit garb I was stupidly expecting but in ordinary corduroy pants and a green cotton shirt and, like us, wore sandals. A figure recognizably of Laurent's family, handsome, elegant, Parisian, he looked out of place in that wilderness. I had to swallow tears. Loving him from my first glimpse of him through the windshield, I felt an immediate and wrenching sense of loss, something like the grief of mourning, and found it hard to bear that he had chosen to sequester himself this way. I could only imagine how much more strongly this grief was felt by those who knew him better.

We took him to our hotel for lunch and talked all through the meal and for hours after, waiting for the heat of the day to abate before going back to his hermitage. Then we talked more. In all, we spent seven hours talking that day, beginning with appreciation of our car and other reassuringly worldly matters. Gradually Alain began to talk about himself. Although he lived almost entirely in silence and secrecy, he wanted to explain how he had come to where he was in life, understanding that there would not be many chances for us to meet and get to know each other.

His had been a lonely childhood. Alain was almost three when his father died, so he did not even have memories of him. Madame de Brunhoff rarely talked about Jean. While Alain was growing up, she was distant, absorbed in her music and in her grief. His brothers and cousins, almost a decade older, seemed to belong to a different generation.

As a gifted musician, he moved into a world of performers and connoisseurs. At the precocious age of fifteen he was already leading a sophisticated, worldly life, and by the time he was eighteen, he had had enough of it and wanted solitude. He went to live alone in the country, where he stayed for four years before resuming his highly social existence. For the next ten years Alain became increasingly well known as a pianist, giving concerts, making recordings. Like his mother, he taught at the École Normale de Musique.

Then a distressing event interrupted the momentum of his life: a house he had lived in and used for storage burned. The fire destroyed the family souvenirs that meant so much to him, including many of his father's paintings, his grandfather's memoirs, and all his music. It shook him profoundly. It was, he said, his first shedding, his first deprivation: he used the word *dépouillement*, which means "the skinning of an animal."

In his turmoil he had no religion to turn to. His father had been Protestant and his mother, though technically Catholic, really believed only in music. Still, an object that meant a great deal to Alain was his father's Bible. He took it with him everywhere and looked through it frequently. Jean had underlined heavily in places. One day, looking through the New Testament, Alain found a passage that had been underlined so often that the paper was nearly falling apart. It struck him in that moment that his father had really believed, that these words in the Gospel had been important to him.

Around that time a woman he knew died suddenly at the age of forty. Her husband was a very religious man, and Alain was struck by the funeral he arranged. There was grief, of course, but there was also a beautiful faith, serenity, and acceptance. As time went by and his thoughts turned more to religion, he had no one to talk to. He got in touch with the husband of the woman who had died, and the man recommended that Alain speak to the priest who had conducted the funeral service. They met a couple of times, and then the priest announced that he was leaving for vacation in Brittany. Easter was coming. The priest suggested that Alain come to Brittany and take his first communion there. He knew a Trappist monastery at which Alain could stay.

Alain liked that monastery in Brittany so much that he almost became a Trappist monk, which would have meant never seeing his family or talking to anyone outside the monastery again. Eventually he decided against it, in part because Trappist life is too communal for someone who loves privacy as much as he does, and in part because the total, brutal break with the world that Trappists are required to make would have caused too much pain to his family and friends.

A few people he knew told him about Roissac, which is a Benedictine monastery. He went to look at it and liked it. He made a second, longer visit to Roissac, but remained tempted by the Trappists. The abbot of Roissac told him not to worry about it, but to go home and wind up his affairs; when the answer was in place, he would know it. So he returned to Paris for a year or two, taking on no new students but bringing all the ones he had through to the end of their studies. In time he decided to enter the Benedictine monastery. He didn't tell many people what he was planning to do, so when he did announce it, it seemed abrupt. But in truth it wasn't. Before he left Paris, he gave away all his possessions and stopped accepting bookings. He performed his last concert a few days before he joined the Benedictines at Roissac. Madame de Brunhoff took his decision hard. Music had been the bond between them and the most important thing in the world to her.

At Roissac, Alain was immediately happy and knew it was where he belonged. He stopped playing the piano. He felt that his religious life demanded complete commitment and so did his music. He had to choose between them. Many of the monks were men of accomplishment—one designed tapestries, another worked in stained glass, another was a ceramicist, yet another was a composer—and continued to practice their art in the monastery. Alain's renunciation was something he imposed on himself.

He became a hermit gradually. The abbot had arranged for a few of the monks to take part in some discussions of spiritual matters at a place outside the monastery where they would be free to concentrate—a kind of retreat. The place they chose, at the random suggestion of someone who had never been there, was an enclave of cottages on the grounds of a convent near the hamlet of St. Paul. Alain loved the quiet of the spot. Later, when he went through a period of mental fatigue so great that the abbot noticed and suggested he take some time off, he chose to return there. He began going there regularly for two weeks a year. Eight years went by. Since he discussed everything with his abbot, the abbot knew that he wanted to leave Roissac and move permanently to St. Paul. They decided that he would go back for a month, as a test; they chose January, the hardest month. It was cold, damp, and miserable, but Alain felt spiritually comfortable there, and eventually the abbot decided to let him move.

Alain related his tale to us with the intensity he had brought to playing Chopin and with an inclusiveness I know from my mother's accounts of her illnesses. As she describes, with a reverence that is hard to enter into, her dealings with the doctors, the nurses, and the orderlies in the hospital, he described meetings with his abbot and consultations with his fellow monks. What came through most clearly to me, in addition to the purity of his commitment to the life he had chosen, was a recurrent need to withdraw from other people, which seemed a response to and perhaps also a source of his intense desirability.

We spent an enormous amount of time at lunch; then we sat in the leather chairs of the hotel lounge and talked more. When the sun was lower, we headed back to Alain's hermitage. Past the spot where we'd first met him, the road dipped down and ran alongside the nuns' compound. We drove beyond that, over a small bridge, and around another few bends to a gate, where we left the car. Then we walked past a wooden outhouse, a shower shed, and a chapel and up a path, with little houses visible through clearings in the scrub.

The enclave had room for ten hermits, who came for stays of a week to a month; Alain was the only one who remained on a permanent basis. The tile-roofed yellow stucco house in which he had been living for three years when we saw him was about ten by ten feet, the size of a large tool shed. Its one room contained a mattress on raised boards, covered with an army blanket, a desk and chair under a wall of windows, which were covered in burlap to keep out the sun, and an armoire, also covered in burlap, on top of which were a suitcase and some folders. On the wall by the bed was a cross made from two branches roughly nailed together. The floor was covered in linoleum-patterned contact paper. A lightbulb with a simple metal shade hung from the ceiling. The roof tiles showed above the supporting beams, and the effect was pleasantly rustic. On the desk were a Bible, prayer books, postcards of religious art, and a box containing family photographs. In a bookcase next to the desk Alain kept his correspondence, a ceramic-disc heater, and an electric pesticide diffuser, as well as books.

Nature is violent in this region. When it rains, torrents come down the mountainside. Sometimes the hermitage was cut off from the sisters by flash floods that covered the bridge over what was at the time of our visit a totally dry, rock-strewn streambed. The hillside was gashed where water had cut through the land.

During the first winter Alain had watched the water rise outside the house. When it was a foot deep, he began packing his suitcase. Before he could leave, the door burst open under the force of the flood, and the house was instantly filled with water brown from mud and cow dung. This, he said, was his lowest point.

In winter the cold was intense, but a large, old-fashioned heater made it bearable. He hoped the new disc heater would help, too, but wanted to know if it consumed much electricity, because he didn't want to burden the sisters, who paid the electric bill. In the fall and the spring everything got wet and stayed that way. Moisture soaked through from the outside, and mildew covered the walls. Three lumberjacks who lived nearby had built him a little lean-to or porch at the front of the house, so that rain would not beat directly against his door and front window. When we were there, too much heat was the problem. With no foundation and no insulation in the roof, the temperature in the bungalow often reached ninety-five degrees.

"It's a dangerous thing to be a hermit, because if you're not serious, it quickly becomes ridiculous," Alain said. He had begun to teach himself Hebrew, to read the Old Testament. But he found that he was spending more and more time at it. Whenever he had a spare moment, he would turn to the Hebrew book. It began to fill his head, so he finally had to stop: after all, he wasn't there to learn languages. He had constantly to remember what the ultimate purpose of all of it was, and stick to it. You can easily become a nature-loving bum, he said, or someone who sleeps a lot.

In fact he was busy; his time was full. He received letters, many of them enormously long, from friends, family, and former students. Answering them was a drain on his energy, and since they were serious letters, they had to be answered seriously. People brought him their problems. A friend who twice had tried to commit suicide had just written saying that he urgently wanted to come see him. How could Alain say no? He had prayers to say several times a day, and he went to mass with the sisters every morning. Since they fed him, preparing a bucket of food that he picked up every morning, he felt he had to pay them back somehow. He did it by cutting brush. He had a large-wheeled brush cutter that he operated in the afternoon—the only free time he had. In the heat of the day it was brutal work.

He showed us his view. To the side and in front of the house, across a deep cleft, the land rose sharply to a majestic rocky ridge. It was like a wave about to crash down, frozen in stone. He had asked the mother superior for permission to cut an oak in order to get this view, and Laurent twitted him. Didn't this smack of aestheticism? It depended on the purpose, Alain replied. If it was an end in itself, yes. If it aided him in communicating with God, no. He had chosen renunciation not for renunciation's sake but in the service of something else—his relationship with God. If things got in the way of that, as music did, then he had to give them up. He couldn't split himself. "But I'm not a Carthusian, bound in by walls so I can look up only to the sky. Whatever helps me is okay. This helps."

One of the things he liked most about his hermitage, he said, was the silence: "Silence is my music now." He could pick up the small sounds of the wind in the leaves, the sounds of insects and animals. Sometimes when the wind was strong, it blew the sound of the traffic on the autoroute to him. He liked it. He liked to think of all the people going on with their lives and to think of himself as in a sense staying where he was for their sakes, "like a lighthouse keeper."

He said he had done a little writing, but he was wary of it. It becomes *gargarisme*—throat gargling. You begin to think you're important. You write things up, inflate them. You moussify inside—that is, I guess, foam up like egg whites. (At this point I was feeling very shabby, a *gargariste* and a moussifier. Moreover, I had every intention of going to back the hotel and writing down what Alain had said.) The point of passing time in solitude is to strip yourself bare, to discover what is essential and true. When you're stripped down to this point, you see how little you amount to. But that little is all that God is interested in. He doesn't give a damn about the rest.

Wheels of Dharma
from Tricycle

Two days after I drive my new Honda hatchback into the parking lot at the Zen Community of New York, a young woman named Heidi stands and speaks in a heartfelt voice at our weekly meeting of residents: "I think we all owe Larry a vote of gratitude for his generosity."

At first I have no idea what she is talking about. It's true that the community's location is inaccessible to public transit and that several residents (including Heidi) have borrowed the car already, but I am still of the opinion that the Honda belongs to me and no one else. The fact that it is registered in the name of the community is a mere formality, suggested by Bernard Glassman Sensei, our teacher, so that I can make use of our tax exemption in paying for the car and its expenses. What is Zen if not pragmatism? What is a Zen teacher if not a man with an eye for the loophole? What are titles, registrations, personal checks, and tax deductions but the transient, superficial imagery of the relative world which we dissolve every moment with our zazen?

"Look at it this way," Glassman said. "The community owns a car and you're a member of the community. Why shouldn't you be able to use it? Or turn it around. The community needs a car and you've donated one to us. What's wrong with that? Even if you're using the car you'll still be using it for community business, won't you? Even the strictest IRS audit wouldn't question your deduction."

I've never found it easy to doubt people who gaze at me with admiration. How magical it seems that all eighteen of my fellow residents not only adore me but consider me proof of our teachings here—have I not "let go" of myself? Transcended attachment to property and money? Dissolved the boundaries between myself and others by allowing them to "share" in my good fortune? As Glassman says, we're here to "open" to one another, to dissolve our sense of privacy and "specialness." Buy a car, give it up. Take my money, take my ego. I am basking in the glow of the image I see in their eyes, a self so realized that I don't even register my "generosity," much less care if it is appreciated.

Next day Heidi borrows the car to pick up her boyfriend at the airport. Naturally, they take the long way home, stopping for dinner and other activities appropriate to reunion. It's a fine spring evening and I have a mind to take a ride myself after zazen, but by not returning until well after midnight, they offer another happy challenge to my selfishness, the absurd instinct that leads me to persist in thinking that I and they are separate. Aren't we all, as Glassman likes to say, teachers for each other? The next morning one of our carpenters makes a run to the lumberyard, which leaves the fine maroon carpet of the Honda's trunk covered with sawdust. Anger rises, but later that day, when I loan the car to our cook to visit her parents in New Jersey, I get a whiff of freedom that leaves me lighthearted, almost intoxicated, as if it's not just the car but my ego, my karma, my ignorance driving out of the parking lot.

Within a week the odometer passes nine hundred miles, and half a dozen duplicate keys have been made. Within two weeks, people don't ask to borrow the car, just tell me when they'll need it. One of our less functional residents takes it on an all-night jaunt to "dissolve" his mind. "What a practice!" he exclaims. "You can't fix on anything when you're watching the landscape rush by at eighty miles an hour." Serving as meditation monitor, leading the group in walking meditation, I make certain to take us by the window that looks out over the parking lot, so I can see if the car is there. Less and less, when it isn't, do I know where it has gone.

How do you count your breaths when you're counting the miles on your odometer? In the midst of a solitary retreat, I see a fully packed Honda speed out of the parking lot for a night on the town in Manhattan. Glassman is giving beautiful talks on generosity and surrender. "What is true giving, according to Buddhism? No giver, no receiver, and nothing given!" When I bring up the car in my private interviews with him—feeling horrible, of course, to waste this precious time with such banality—he smiles with pleasure. "Become the car!" he suggests. "Then you'll have nothing to let go of!" My mind explodes with insight. Leaving the interview room, I feel as if I could buy a fleet of Hondas and turn every one of them over to him.

A year later, for a variety of reasons, I decide to leave ZCNY and practice with Kyudo Roshi, a Japanese Rinzai Zen master who has opened a simple, "just sitting" zendo in Soho. The reasons are complicated, for sure, but part of it is the distraction of Glassman's communal Zen—all this concern with property, cars, newsletters, and so forth—and, conversely, the hunger I feel for a practice centered in zazen. Glassman relishes the tumult, the chance to prove that one can practice under any circumstance, but Kyudo Roshi says, "If this place busy as your office, why you want to come here?" No newsletters here, no weekly residents' meetings, no committees, no need for cars because we're less than three blocks from three different subway stations. Community? Our zendo has only one bathroom, which is something of a problem when thirty of us are doing *sesshin,* but when I discover a diner nearby where we can use the toilet, Roshi advises me not to mention it to anyone else. "If everybody know about it, you not able to use it yourself, Larry-san!"

It's easy enough to pack my bags, stow my gear in the trunk of the Honda, and head back to the city, but what am I to do about the fact that the car I drive does not belong to me? I avoid the matter until several weeks later, when I receive a phone call from the treasurer at ZCNY, who informs me that an insurance bill has arrived. Clearly, I'm in a bind, but next morning, during zazen, I see the way out—another brilliant, tax-deductible solution! ZCNY will simply donate the Honda to the Soho Zendo! Who cares that Roshi doesn't know how to drive or that everything the zendo needs is within three blocks of our building? Aren't we incorporated? Tax exempt? The IRS won't question our need for transportation, and it certainly won't question our right to receive charitable gifts.

Roshi's English is hardly equipped for "tax deductible" or "pass-through donations," not to mention "Well, you see, Roshi, even though it looks illegal, it's really not." When informed of my intentions, all he hears is that the zendo will own a car as a result of my generosity. "Very good, Larry-san! You very nice. Thank you! Thank you!" And even in his inscrutable eyes I see the light I saw in the eyes of my sangha mates at ZCNY, more than one of whom, when they hear that I have "taken back" the car, look at me with pity and offer that I have "learned nothing" from my practice.

Within a couple of weeks, the transfer is complete. Bill of sale, certificate of title, new registration (signed by Roshi), notarized philanthropic statement attesting to the fact that a one-year-old Honda hatchback with 31,657 miles has been donated by ZCNY to Soho Zendo. My name, of course, is not to be found on the documents. I am invisible, owner of nothing, but using the Honda more than ever since there's nobody asking to borrow it. It's as if I've discovered some ultimate magic trick that permits me to have my cake and eat it too. ZCNY forwards the insurance bill to Soho Zendo, where it is paid by its treasurer with money donated (and deducted) by me. Similar shenanigans cover garage fees, repair bills, even gas.

Finally, after zazen one evening, Roshi stops me at the door. "Larry-san, you have appointment? Maybe you talk business for a minute?" When everyone else has left, and he's made us a cup of tea, he spreads out the account book on the table and leafs through it until he finds the page he wants. "Garage fees." "Insurance." "Manhattan Auto Repair." He points them out one by one. "Larry-san, how come this? Maybe you explain."

"Oh, that's for the car, Roshi."

"Car? What car?"

"The one I donated to the zendo."

"When you donate? I not see car."

"But I explained—"

"Zendo pay gas, zendo pay garage. Who drive car?"

"Well, I do, Roshi, but—"

"Zendo pay car and you drive it?"

"Well, you see, the zendo doesn't actually pay, Roshi. I made a donation—"

"Donation?"

"Yes, last month. And the month before that, too. I'm giving the zendo the money to pay for the car."

"But you drive?"

"Well, not exactly, Roshi. That's what I'm trying to explain. I made donations—"

"Larry-san, please! Donation, not donation, nothing matter. You make donation, you make donation. Thank you very much! You drive car, you pay for car, understand? You insincere! Irresponsible! Losing lot of virtue all this talk."

Again and again, I try to explain things to him, each time with less success. He isn't arguing anymore—always a dangerous sign with him—he's just staring at me. Finally, he closes the matter in characteristic fashion: "Okay, Larry-san, forget it! Anything you want, you do!"

I don't sleep at all that night. My solution to the car problem is suddenly a mirror, and what I see in it is not pretty: fake generosity, fatuous rationalization—all of it worse for occurring in the context of Zen. Next morning I telephone a couple of used car dealers to determine the Honda's fair-market value. I write a check for that amount payable to the zendo. And that's how it happened that I solved the famous koan: how do you buy a car you already own?

LUCI SHAW

Rising: The Underground Tree
(Cornus sanguinea, and Cornus canadensis)

Last spring in Tennessee I walked a tunnel
under dogwood trees, noting the petals
(in fours, like crosses) and at each tender base
four russet stains dark as Christ-wounds.
I knew that with the year the dogwood flower heads
would ripen into berries bright as drops of gore.

Last week, a double-click on Botany
startled me with the kinship of those trees
and bunch-berries, whose densely crowded mat
carpets the deep woods around my valley cabin.
Only their flowers—those white quartets of petals—
suggest the blood relationship. Since then I see

the miniature leaves and buds as tips of trees
burgeoning underground, knotted roots like limbs
pushing up to light through rock and humus.
The pure cross-flowers at my feet redeem
their long, dark burial in the ground, show how even
a weight of stony soil cannot keep Easter at bay.

What They Have That We Lack: A Tribute to the Native Americans via Joseph Epes Brown

from Sophia

My title derives from the justly famous tribute to the Native Americans by John Collier, one-time United States Commissioner of Indian Affairs, which begins, "They had what the world has lost. . . ." The losses that Collier mentions are "reverence and passion for human personality, and for the earth and its web of life." Accepting them as genuine losses, I shall build on them to target three other losses our civilization has suffered. We are less clear in our values, which is to say less sure as to what is important in life. We are less able to see the infinite in the finite, the transcendent in the immanent. And we have lost out way metaphysically. Because my meditation on these three impoverishments is offered as a tribute to Joseph Brown, I shall begin with the story of how we met, for the circumstances were so bizarre as to suggest that more than chance was at work.

The year was 1970, and my wife and I were passing through Stockholm, where the first beanbag chair we had seen caught our eyes and we bought it. On our way back to our hotel, swaying from a strap in a crowded subway, I felt foolish carrying our shapeless purchase over my shoulder like Santa's pack and was remarking to my wife that I was glad we were abroad and incognito when a face emerged from the crowd and ventured, softly, "Would you be Huston Smith?" It was Joseph Brown, who had recognized me from my filmed lectures on *The Religions of Man*, which he had showed to his classes. Things moved rapidly, and before we parted we had accepted Joseph and his wife Eleanita's invitation to have supper with them the following day, the last before our flight left Sweden.

It was an unforgettable evening. The Browns were in Stockholm for Joseph to complete his doctoral dissertation under Ake Hultkrantz, the world's foremost authority on the Native Americans, and their apartment walls were covered with larger-than-life photographs of archetypal Indian faces. What was remarkable, though, was how rapidly our conversation plunged to things that matter most. When they learned that our next stop was to be London, Joseph directed me to Martin Lings of the British Museum, who proved to be an important link to the Traditionalist outlook of René Guénon, A. K. Coomaraswamy, and Frithjof Schuon that was beginning to impress me as true. And on the strength of the friendship that was forged that evening, Joseph became my teacher in showing me the enduring importance of the Native Americans and other primal peoples in the religious odyssey of humankind.

From the many things I have learned from those people, I turn now to the first of the three virtues I see them as having retained, and we let partially slip. I say *partially* because I do not want to romanticize or traffic in disjunctions. Trade-offs are involved at every point.

I. Knowing What Is Important

I am not an anthropologist, and as my professional schooling occurred before midcentury, I was taught to think that myths are childish in comparison with systematically articulated metaphysics, and that "primitive" religions—the adjective explicitly intended to be pejorative—were and remain inferior to the historical ones, which command written texts and a cumulative tradition. Meeting Joseph Brown rescued me from those prejudices. That shortly after meeting him I moved from the Massachusetts Institute of Technology to Syracuse University solidified the change in my thinking, for I then found myself within five miles of the Iroquois Long House. It was not without amazement that I came to know the residents of the Onondaga Reservation—Chief Shenandoah, Audrey Shenandoah, and Oren Lyons among them. Reading Joseph Brown's writings paralleled my visits to their reservation, and together the two shattered mental stockades, permitting new insights to erupt.

The insight that concerns me in this first section of my remarks is the loss that writing inflicts. Before I met Joseph, A. K. Coomaraswamy's *The Bugbear of Literacy* had already shown me that education cannot be equated with book learning;[1] the great civilizations of the past were not dependent on the ability to read and write. Craftsmen—the builders of temples, mosques, and churches; the sculptors of Konorak and of Chartres—were not literate, and oral tradition carried poetry and sacred knowledge for millennia before books appeared. Coomaraswamy also brought out the toll writing takes on our memories. Literate peoples grow lax in recall; they do not require much from their memories, for books and manuals are at hand to fill in the blanks. Lacking those resources, unlettered peoples make libraries of their minds. Their memories are legendary.

As I say, those two validations of orality—both memory and learning flourish in its precincts—were in place before I met Joseph Brown; but it was not until I came to the Native Americans through him that I realized that I needed to add a chapter on the primal religions to *The Religions of Man,* now titled *The World's Religions.*[2] It was while writing that chapter that it dawned on me that orality (which I shall use here to mean exclusive orality; speech that is not supplemented by writing) carries with it another blessing that is, if anything, more important than having a rich memory. Functioning something like a gyroscope, orality keeps life on keel by ensuring that priorities and proportionalities are not lost sight of. Somewhere in his writings Frithjof Schuon defines intelligence exactly this way, as the sense of priorities and proportionalities. By this definition, primal peoples can be ignorant of many things, but they are rarely stupid.

Imagine a tribe, gathered around its campfire at the close of the day. Everything that its ancestors learned arduously through trial and error, from which herbs heal to stirring legends that give meaning and orientation to their lives, is preserved in their collective memory, and there only. It stands to reason that trivia would not long survive in that confine, for it would preempt space that was needed for the things that needed to be remembered.

A library lacks this winnowing device. Natural selection, the survival of the fittest, doesn't enter its workings, for space permits virtually everything to survive, important or not. Where a page is a page, a book a book, the issue of quality scarcely arises.

To personalize this point: I happen to enjoy the services of one of the great library systems in the world, that of the University of California. Thinking back to the guided tour that brought me into its orbit, I find that I still remember the statement with which the leader of the tour welcomed us. "When you enter this library looking for a book," she said, "think: it's here. It may take us a while to locate it, but it's here." As I learned how the immense holdings of the local library locked into compatible libraries around the world through Internet and interlibrary loan, I found myself believing her.

I do not discount the help and pleasure that accrued from having recorded human history at one's fingertips. It is the trade-off it entails that the Native Americans have taught me. When I step out of the elevator onto a floor of my university's library, I am greeted in effect by arrows directing me to its numerous corridors: history here, chemistry there, a bewildering array. There is no arrow that reads "importance," much less "wisdom." It's more like, "Good luck, folks. From here on out you're on your own."

The burden this places on individuals is enormous; whether it is supportable remains to be seen.

We are inundated by information today, to the point of drowning in it. When the British Broadcasting Company first went on the air, the newsroom policy on a no-news day was simply to say there was no news and play classical music. Is there a newsroom in the world that has the restraint to honor such a policy today? Alvin Toffler warned us in *Future Shock* a quarter century ago that information overload was already "pressing the limits of human adaptability," but all he offered by way of counsel was that we develop a consciousness that is capable of adapting to changes that look like they are going to keep on accelerating.[3]

That advice is no match for the problem we face, and it may take a breakdown of sorts to drive that fact home. More than any other breakthrough, it is the computer that has increased the quantity of information that can be saved, retrieved, and transferred. It was assumed that this increase would raise our industrial efficiency, but the country is still waiting for the big payoff that electronic boosters keep promising. Many experts are now concluding that for all their power, computers may be costing U.S. companies tens of billions of dollars a year in downtime, maintenance and training costs, useless game playing, and—the relevant point here—information overload. As Yale economist and Nobel laureate Robert Solow has noted, "You can see the computer age everywhere but in the productivity statistics."[4] From 1950 to 1973, when computers were still a novelty, the U.S. economy enjoyed one of the greatest economic booms in its history. Since then, as computers have taken over nearly every desk in the land, the rate of productivity growth has mysteriously plummeted. Many experts believe that computers may be more the cause of the problem than the key to its solution.

If information overload can impair industrial efficiency, what about life efficiency; which is to say, the ability to avoid squandering life on frivolous ends? The great orienting myths that primal peoples rehearse endlessly, and carry constantly in their hearts and heads, protect them from this danger.

Something that Claude Lévi-Strauss observed relates to this. For an anthropologist, he took surprisingly little interest in what myths meant to the peoples who lived by them. Deeming science the noblest human pursuit, he wanted to parallel what Noam Chomsky was doing in linguistics and put anthropology, too, in the service of science's efforts to discover how the mind works. Artificial intelligence, he believed, was on the right track in assuming that the mind works like a computer—through binary, on-off flip-flops—and Lévi-Strauss saw himself as corroborating that hypothesis by showing (as in *The Raw and the Cooked*) that myths proceed binarily, from a forked starting point. In the course of his investigations, though, he picked up something that is important. The primitive mind, he reported, assumes that you do not understand anything unless you understand everything, whereas science proceeds in the opposite manner, from part to whole.* Lévi-

---

With holists ranged against atomists, current epistemologists are vigorously disputing which of these assumptions best captures the way meaning works. The most uncompromising advocate of atomism is MIT's Jerry Fodor, for whom holism has become what Carthage must have been to Cato, as a reviewer of his two books attacking the position remarks (see The Journal of Philosophy 10 [1995]: 330–44). When we couple to this the fact that Fodor is uncompromising in insisting that psychology is an empirical science, we find this thus illustrating Lévi-Strauss's point that science (which progresses through discrete factual discoveries) is the principal sponsor of the atomistic approach to knowledge.

Strauss considered the scientific approach superior to the mythic,* whereas I find them complementary and equally important.

II. Symbolic Minds

The item I wrote just before turning to this tribute to Joseph chanced to be the Foreword to a collection of excerpts from Emanuel Swedenborg's writings,[5] and as I was already thinking ahead to the present piece when I came upon this passage, I was struck by its relevance to this second point I shall be making.

> I have learned from heaven [Swedenborg wrote] that the earliest people had direct revelation, because their more inward reaches were turned toward heaven; and that, as a result, there was a union of the Lord with the human race then. But as time passed, there was not this kind of direct revelation but an indirect one through correspondences. All their divine worship consisted of correspondences, so we call the churches of that era representative churches. They knew what correspondence was and what representation was, and they knew that everything on earth was responsive to spiritual things in heaven and portrayed them. So natural things served as means of thinking

---

*"The totalitarian ambition of the savage mind . . . does not succeed. We are able, through scientific thinking, to achieve mastery over nature . . . while myth is unsuccessful in giving man more material power over the environment. It gives man the illusion that he can understand the universe, [but] it is, of course, only an illusion" (Claude Lévi-Strauss, Myth and Meaning, 17). That the foremost anthropologist of recent times acknowledges that "mastery over nature" and "material power over the environment" are his highest values confirms the claim of this first section of my paper. We are confused as to what is important.

spiritually. . . . The earliest people saw some image of and refer-ence to the Lord's kingdom in absolutely everything—in moun-tains, hills, plains, and valleys, in gardens, groves, and forests, in rivers and lakes, in fields, and crops, in all kinds of trees, in all kinds of animals as well, in the luminaries of the sky.

Swedenborg proceeds to confirm this way of seeing the world by citing his own visionary experience.

I have been taught by an abundance of experience that there is not the slightest thing in the natural world, in its three king-doms, that does not portray something in the spiritual world or that does not have something there to which it is responsive.

From there he continues:

After knowledge of correspondences and representations had been forgotten, the Word was written, in which all the words and their meanings were correspondences, containing in this way a spiritual or inner meaning.[6]

Paraphrasing these three stages into which Swedenborg divides religion: In the first stage, nature is transparent to the divine and is seen as divine without remainder, so no divinity apart from it is sought. Presumably this first stage is something like the natural religion of early childhood, when (as a poet has said) "heaven and a splendorous earth were one," before the child's clear eye is clouded over by ideas and opinions, preconceptions and abstrac-tions. In the second stage, nature loses this transparency, but remains (we might say) translucent. Divinity continues to shine through mountains, groves, and springs, but those objects now *ex-ist*—"stand out apart from" their source—in having acquired a certain objectivity of their own. This distancing obscures their connectedness with their divine source, and that connectedness needs to be recovered through symbolism: Swedenborg's representations and correspondences. If we take light as our example, at some level of their awareness, people in this second stage recognize that its power to enable us to discern things by seeing them is a prolongation of the divine intelligence. Water tokens the divine purity and nurturance, flowers its beauty, and so forth, world without end.

The first stage requires no mental processing. In the second, some mediation is needed, but correspondences (which serve that function) are so obvious that little articulation is called for. In Swedenborg's third stage, this ceases to be the case. Opaqueness—the fall into matter—has proceeded to the point where language and thought are needed to state explicitly what earlier intelligence took for granted: that rocks and trees are not self-subsistent in the way optics by itself presents them. It now needs to be *said* that nature carries the signature of the divine—not only nature as a whole, but its parts, each of which betokens one of the ninety-nine beautiful names of Allah, as Muslims put the matter.

Generalizing from this threefold division, it seems appropriate to credit primal peoples with prolonging the second period into our own more materialistic age. To invoke Coomaraswamy again, when he came to the United States to become director of the Oriental Section of Boston's Museum of Fine Arts, the traditional lore of the American Indians deeply moved him, for he saw in these much-persecuted remnants of the indigenous population of the continent an organic intelligence that was still able to read the open book of nature as others read their written scriptures. His South Asian heritage led him to associate the Native Americans' metaphysical insight—their capacity to see the world and everything within it as a living revelation of the Great Spirit—with

Vedic times in his own heritage. Without exaggeration, he felt, he could speak of their wisdom as belonging to an earlier *yuga* that somehow had persisted into these later times, an extension that carried a message of hope to a forgetful and much-tormented world. The recognition that every plant, every insect, stones even, participate in the *dharma* and need to be treated, not as spoils for human appetites, but as companions in terms both of origin and ultimate destiny, conditioned all the Native Americans' ideas of what is right and wrong. What a happier world this would be, Coomaraswamy concluded, if such ideas had not been marginalized.[7]

III. METAPHYSICAL ACCURACY

"Strictly speaking," Frithjof Schuon has written, "there is but one sole philosophy, the *Sophia Perennis;* it is also—envisaged in its integrality—the only religion."[8] *Philosophy* here refers to descriptions of reality's deep structure, among which (Truth being one) there can be only one accurate account, which other accounts (insofar as they are accurate) embellish but do not contradict. As for religion, it refers to the methods for conforming one's life to reality's structure. Ken Wilber has recently said that belief in the *Sophia Perennis* (or Great Chain of Being as he calls it) has been "so overwhelmingly widespread that it is either the single greatest intellectual error ever to appear in human history, or it is the most accurate reflection of reality yet to appear."[9]

Modernity has departed from this sole true philosophy, and the difference between it and the science-oriented alternative with which modernity replaced it can be stated simply. Whereas traditional philosophy proceeds from the premise that the less derives from the more—from what is greater than itself in every respect, primacy, power, and worth being foremost—modernity sees the more (as it climaxes qualitatively in the human species) as deriving from the less.

I have already credited Joseph Brown for introducing me to the Native Americans and the distinctive outlook of primal peoples generally, and here (in this closing section of my tribute to him) I can credit him more pointedly. In one way or another many anthropologists have dealt with the two preceding resources of primal peoples, but Brown stands alone in detailing, in his important study, *The Sacred Pipe,* the way in which Native American religion embodies the *Sophia Perennis* in its own distinctive idiom.[10]

In briefest capsule: The Native American outlook conforms to the Great Chain of Being in seeing the whole of things as an ontological hierarchy in which lesser things derive in graded sequence from the Great Spirit, which is its version of the *ens perfectissimum.* In *Creek Mary's Blood,* the sequel to *Bury My Heart at Wounded Knee,* Dee Brown gives us a glimpse of the initial cut that the Native Americans enter—that between the sacred and the profane—by writing that:

> *In those days there were always two levels in the world of the Cheyennes. We did not consider the world of hunting or hide curing or arrow or moccasin making, or any of those things as the real world. The real world was a place of magic, of dreams wherein we became spirits.*[11]

Subsequent divisions in the real and sacred world vary according to which tribe we are speaking of. The Tewa, for instance, have five sacred realms, whereas the Plains Indians that Brown worked with most will content themselves with three. When we add the everyday world to these three, we come up with the minimum number of "links" in the Great Chain of Being that peoples have found it necessary to posit. In *Forgotten Truth,* I call them the ter-restrial, the intermediate, the celestial, and the infinite;[12] and in *The Sacred Pipe,* Brown tells us how the Oglala Sioux describe them.[13] Mounting from the mundane into the sacred world, the Oglala find its lowest echelon populated by myriad spirits, some good, some bad. Human beings can access this realm from time to time, as Dee Brown points out, but its natural population consists of discarnates of various stripes. Shamans enter into working rela-tionships with those spirits, enlisting good ones as allies to do bat-tle with those of evil intent.

Above this spirit world, which is something of a mélange, stands the Great Spirit, *Wakan-Tanka,* who can be apprehended in two modes: as Father and as Grandfather. In the context of world reli-gions generally, this division corresponds to the division between, on the one hand, God who has personal attributes and can there-fore be known; and on the other hand, God in his absolute, infi-nite nature, which the human mind cannot concretely grasp. Definitively, Brown describes the difference between the two as follows:

> Wakan-Tanka *as grandfather is the Great Spirit independent of manifestation, unqualified, unlimited, identical to the Christian Godhead, or to the Hindu* Brahma-Nirguna. *Wakan-Tanka as father is the great Spirit considered in relation to His manifestation, either as Creator, Preserver, or Destroyer, identi-cal to the Christian God, or to the Hindu* Brahma-Saguna.[14]

Going back to Mary Dee's report, the mundane hunting and hide curing that she cites are those activities after the symbolic mind has dimmed, for when that mind is in full force, all activities are (to continue with the vocabulary of the Oglala Sioux) *wakan* (holy, sacred). They are sacred in "corresponding"—Swedenborg's word—with the other world and thereby perforating the line between the two. "This world" acquires its own reality only to the degree that its ties to the other world are forgotten. Joseph Brown quotes Black Elk as saying, "Any man who is attached to the senses and to the things of this world lives in ignorance."[15]

Coda

Having begun with an anecdote, I shall conclude with one as well, my favorite in my well-stocked repertoire relating to Joseph Brown.

Joseph was accompanying Black Elk on a mission to Denver, and a long winter's bus ride landed them there well around midnight. Hotels were filled, and the only available shelter from the bitter cold was little more than a flophouse. Entering their room, Black Elk glanced at its dingy furnishings, took one breath of its foul air, and announced: "This requires a sweat!" Chairs were upturned, blankets stripped from the beds to cover them, and the electric heater impressed for the sacred fire. The men peeled down to their breechcloths, and the purging bath began.

It is an allegory, this midnight scene. In dismal, uninviting circumstances, two men, ethnically diverse, saw what needed to be done and instantly did it.

If our improvisations in our respective circumstances could be equally inventive, emphatic, and right-minded, no better tributes could be offered to the life and work of Joseph Epes Brown.

ENDNOTES

1. Ananda K. Coomaraswamy, *The Bugbear of Literacy*, 2d ed. (Middlesex, England: Perennial Books, 1979).

2. Huston Smith, *The World's Religions* (San Francisco: HarperSan Francisco, 1991).

3. Alvin Toffler, *Future Shock* (New York: Random House, 1970).

4. *San Francisco Chronicle,* July 1995, p. 1.

5. George F. Dole, *A Thoughtful Soul* (West Chester, PA: Swedenborg Foundation, 1995).

6. Emanuel Swedenborg, *Heaven and Hell,* p. 306; Arcana Coelestia, 2722:5, quoted in Dole, *A Thoughtful Soul.*

7. A more complete account of Coomaraswamy's thoughts on this matter is given in Marco Pallis, "A Fateful Meeting of Minds: A. K. Coomaraswamy and René Guénon," *Studies in Comparative Religion* (Summer-Autumn 1978).

8. Frithjof Schuon, *The Transfiguration of Man* (Bloomington, IN: World Wisdom Books, 1995), 10.

9. Ken Wilber, "The Great Chain of Being," *Journal of Humanistic Psychology* 33, no. 3 (Summer 1993): 53.

10. Joseph Epes Brown, *The Sacred Pipe,* 2d ed. (New York: Penguin Books, 1977).

11. Dee Brown, *Creek Mary's Blood* (New York: Holt, Rinehart & Winston, 1980).

12. Huston Smith, *Forgotten Truth,* 2d ed. (San Francisco: HarperSan Francisco, 1992).

13. Brown, *Sacred Pipe.*

14. Brown, *Sacred Pipe,* 5.

15. Brown, *Sacred Pipe,* 4.

DAVID STEINDL-RAST

Praying the Great Dance

from Praying Magazine

My earliest recollection of formal prayer is this: My grand-mother, rosary in hand, resting on her bed after our noonday meal, would let the beads glide through her fingers, silently moving her lips.

When I remember how large her bed loomed from my perspective, I realize I must have still been small. Yet when I asked her to teach me this mysterious game, she did. The stories behind the fifteen mysteries as my grandmother told them to me stayed in my mind and grew in my heart. Like seedlings taking root in good soil, they kept growing and sending out runners. To this day, like an old strawberry patch, they keep bearing fruit.

Some thirty years later, on a different continent, my grand-mother was again resting on her bed and I was kneeling next to her; this time, she was dying. My mother also knelt by her mother's deathbed, and together the two of us were reciting from the English breviary the prayers for the dying. Grandmother was in a coma, but she seemed restless. She would raise her left hand a little and let it fall back on the bed, again and again. We could hear the tinkling of the silver rosary wrapped around her wrist. Finally we caught on. We stopped the psalms and started the Sorrowful Rosary. At its familiar phrases, grandmother relaxed, and when we came to the mystery of Christ's death on the cross, she peacefully gave her life-breath back to God.

Another childhood memory of mine is connected with the Angelus prayer. All over my native Austria, the chorus of Angelus bells rises from every church steeple at dawn, at high noon, and again before dark in the evening. At school one day when I was in first grade, I stood by an open window on the top floor looking down on what you might call "the campus," for ours was a big, beautiful school built by the Christian Brothers. It was noon. Classes had just finished, and children and teachers streamed out onto the courts and walkways. From so high up, the sight reminded me of an anthill on a hot summer day. Just then, the Angelus bell rang out from the church, and at once, all those busy feet down there stood still. "The angel of the Lord brought the message to Mary. . . ." We had been taught to recite this prayer in silence. Then, the ringing slowed down; one last stroke of a bell and the anthill began swarming again.

Now, so many years later, I still keep that moment of silence at noon. Bells or no bells, I pray the Angelus. I let the silence drop like a pebble into the middle of my day and send its ripples out over its surface in ever-widening circles. That is the Angelus for me: the now of eternity rippling through time.

I'd like to recount one more memory here, the memory of my first encounter with the Jesus Prayer, the Prayer of the Heart, as it is also called. By then, I was older but still a child; twelve maybe. I was sitting with my mother in our doctor's waiting room, resting my right hand first on one knee, then on the other, then on the armrest of my chair, then on the sill of a window from which I could see only a high hedge and some spiderwebs. My hand was heavily bandaged, and I had come to have the doctor change those bandages. After I had examined for some time a jar full of live leeches, which country doctors at that time still kept for bloodletting, there wasn't anything else in the bare room to keep me entertained, and I was growing fidgety.

Then my mother said something that surprised me: "Russian people know the secret of never getting bored." The Olympic Games were my only association with Russians, but if there was a secret method for overcoming boredom, I needed to learn it as soon as possible. Only years later, when I came across *The Way of a Pilgrim*, did I understand my mother's mysterious reference, for that book was a translation from the Russian. It did tell me at length about that secret of never getting bored, but my mother had managed to summarize it so simply that it made sense to a boy of twelve: "You need only repeat the name of Jesus over and over with every breath. That's all. The name of Jesus will remind you of so many good stories that you will never find the time long." I tried it and it works.

Boredom, as it turned out, would never be a problem in my life anyway, rather the contrary. Later, in fact, when the Jesus Prayer became my steady form of praying, I came to think of it more as an anchor that keeps me grounded when life is anything but boring. To borrow a phrase from the Roman Missal, the Jesus Prayer keeps my heart "anchored in lasting joy."

After I read *The Way of a Pilgrim*, I made myself a ring of wooden beads that I move, one bead at a time, as I repeat the Jesus Prayer. This movement of my fingers has become so linked with that prayer that I can keep it going with the help of my prayer-ring, even while I am reading or talking with someone. It goes on like background music, not in the foreground of my awareness and yet heard at all times.

The wording I've come to find most helpful is "Lord Jesus, mercy!" The Russian pilgrim used a longer form, and I have experimented with various versions, but this one suits me best.

Most of the time it expresses my gratefulness: As I face a given situation and take it all in, I see this given reality as one facet of God's ultimate gift, which is summed up in the name of Jesus. Then, breathing out, I say the second half of the prayer, and the sense is: "Oh, with what mercy you are showering me, moment by moment!" Sometimes, of course, "Mercy!" can also be my cry for help, say, when I am dead tired and have to go on to meet a deadline, or when I am reading about the destruction of rain forests or the tens of thousands of children who starve to death every twenty-four hours on this planet of plenty. "Mercy!" I sigh, "Mercy!"

The Jesus Prayer has become so connected with my breathing in and breathing out that it flows spontaneously much of the time. Sometimes, while I am falling asleep, the prayer goes on until it melds into the deep breathing of sleep.

The Rosary, the Angelus, the Jesus Prayer—these are some of the formal prayers I find most nourishing. They are by no means the only ones, merely the ones most easily described. How could I even begin to tell you what the monastic Hours of Prayer mean to me? I have recently written a small book about them, *The Music of Silence*, in which I tried to show how not only monks but anyone in any walk of life can enter into those times of day at which time itself prays. I find the Lord's Prayer and the Creed inexhaustible, too; I'd have to write a whole book about each of them.

Yet, here we are still in the realm of formal prayer, and formal prayer is like a little bucket from which a toddler scoops up and pours out, scoops up and pours out, time and again, water from the ocean of prayer.

Informal prayerfulness is the rich, black humus in which formal prayers grow. We cannot separate (formal) prayers from (informal) prayer. We must, however, distinguish between the two and focus for a moment on prayer as an inner attitude rather than an external form of praying. When I do this, I find myself gliding in and out of three attitudes of praying so different from one another that I think of them as altogether different worlds of prayer.

My key to the first of those inner worlds I call Word. By this I don't mean any particular word or words but rather the discovery that any thing, any person, any situation is a word addressed to me by God. Not that I always catch onto the message, but I know I will get it if I listen deeply with the ears of my heart. St. Benedict calls this deep, willing listening "obedience." We often think of obedience as compliance with a command. But this would make God some sort of exalted drill sergeant. In my experience, most of the time, God doesn't command. Rather, God sings; and I sing back.

The singing I mean can be as jubilant as the red of God-made tomatoes; as the soaring of a kite or the splashing of children in a pool and my heart's joyous response to this. But God's singing can also be as heavy as the fragrance of lilies in a funeral home, heavy as the news of a friend's grief; light as harpsichord music or a spring outing; sad as the howling of a night train, sad as the evening news; it can be cheerful, enchanting, challenging, amusing. In everything we experience we can hear God singing, if we listen attentively.

Our heart is a highly sensitive receiver; it can listen through all our senses. Whatever we hear, but also whatever we see, taste, touch, or smell, vibrates deep down with God's song. To resonate with this song in gratefulness is what I call singing back. This attitude of prayer has given great joy to all my senses and to my heart.

A completely different inner world of prayer where I also feel at home is one to which silence opens the door—silence, not only as perceived by the ears, but also a quietness of the heart, a lucid stillness inside, like the stillness of a windless midwinter day; brilliant with sunlight on virgin snow, the kind of day I remember from my childhood in the Austrian Alps. Or it's like the silence between a lightning flash and the thunder crash that follows, the moment in which you hold your breath. On an island in Maine I once found tidal pools on the granite shore with water so still and clear I could see the fine fibrils of sea anemones on the bottom, waving like festive streamers. Still more limpid is the inner space to which silence is the key. I don't always find that key, but when I do, I simply enter. Just to be there is prayer.

To a third inner world, action is the key, loving action. There surely is a world of difference between the prayer of action and that of silence or word. Here, it is not by listening and responding, not by diving down into silence, but by acting, by doing that I communicate with God. Whatever I can do lovingly can become prayer of action.

Nor is it necessary that I explicitly think of God while working or playing. Sometimes this would hardly be possible. While proof-reading a manuscript, I better keep my mind on the text, not on God. If my mind is torn between the two, the typos will slip through like little fish through a torn net. God will be present precisely in the loving attention I give to the work entrusted to me. By giving myself fully and lovingly to that work, I give myself fully to God. This happens not only in work but also in play, say, in bird-watching or in watching a good movie. God must be enjoying it in me, when I am enjoying it in God. Is not this communion the essence of praying? One of the gifts in my life for which I am most grateful is the way I was taught about the Blessed Trinity. Others have told me that, early on, they got the message that God's Trinity is a mystery we could never fathom, so they draw the conclusion, why bother? When I was told of this mystery, it was always in a tone that invited me to explore it—the task not of a lifetime only but of eternal life, life beyond time. My life of prayer has been just this exploration, and it continues to be so. In fact, at age seventy, I feel I've barely begun.

As far back as I can remember, I had learned to think of God not as far away but as nearer than near. I must have been four or five when I came racing from the garden into the kitchen, all out of breath, announcing that I had just seen the Holy Spirit writing something up in heaven. It turned out to have been an advertisement for soap powder, written by a plane so high up in the sky that it looked just like the white dove in the fresco of the Blessed Trinity painted on our church ceiling. About that same time, shortly before Christmas, when Austrian children wait not for Santa but for the Christ Child to bring them presents, I spied one morning a tiny thread of gold lamé on the bedroom carpet, and nothing could have convinced me that this was not a golden hair the Christ Child had lost. The chills of awe I felt and the thrill of tender affection are still vivid in my memory.

These childish misapprehensions were nevertheless genuine religious experiences. What was essential to them remains: a sense of God's nearness.

Not only did it remain, it kept growing wider and deeper. *Nearness* is too weak a word. From a sermon by our Dominican student chaplain, Father Diego, I soared, ecstatic in the realization that we can know God as triune precisely because we are drawn into the eternal dance of Father, Son and Holy Spirit. For students in Vienna it is not frivolous to speak of God as dancing. Dancing is serious—not dead-serious, of course, but life-serious. Much later, I learned the Shaker hymn about Christ as "Lord of the Dance."

I also learned that St. Gregory of Nyssa, way back in the fourth century, had spoken of the Circle Dance of the Blessed Trinity; the eternal Son comes forth from the Father and leads us with all of creation in the Holy Spirit back to the Father.

We can speak of this Great Dance also in terms of Word, Silence, and Action: The Logos, the Word of God, comes forth from God's unfathomable silence and returns to God, heavy with harvest in the Spirit that inspires loving action. This trinitarian perspective helps me understand in ever new ways the "communication with God" that we call prayers—not as a sort of heavenly long-distance call but as the gift of coming ever more alive by sharing in God's life.

Here I come back once more to formal prayer, to the doxology that traditionally concludes the prayers we begin "in the name of the Father and of the Son and of the Holy Spirit." In the concluding doxology, too, we usually connect Father, Son, and Spirit by *and*. But I prefer a more ancient version. This more dynamic version suggests our entering into God's life as we pray *to* the Father (Mother and Source of all), *through* the Son (through whom we have communion with God), *in* the Holy Spirit (that Force which comes from God, is God, and leads all things back to the Source in a great dance).

My highest goal in prayer is to enter into that dance through everything I do or think or suffer or say. For that end-without-end I long, whenever I pray: "Glory be to the Father, through the Son, in the Holy Spirit, as it was in the beginning, is now and ever shall be, world without end. Amen."

Lost Atlantis: Nude Scientists, Giant Sharks, Bad Vibes, and Me

from Harper's Magazine

In the summer of 1975, when I was thirteen, I lived for a brief period with my father and stepmother on Bimini, a small Bahamian island fifty miles off the coast of Florida. My father was engaged at the time in investigating a group of giant stones that lay in the shallow water several hundred yards off Bimini's northern shore. It was his fond and earnest hope that these stones might prove to be the vestiges of the lost continent of Atlantis and that they were but the first of many such ruins to emerge from the sea after being hidden for some ten thousand years. Atlantis, my father suspected, was on the rise and would soon be back for all to see.

Four years before our move to Bimini, he had finished work on *Secrets of the Great Pyramid,* a book arguing that the ancient Egyptians possessed a body of wisdom about the universe and the place of human beings within it that far surpassed anything the modern world had to offer. Two years later, with his friend Christopher Bird, he produced *The Secret Life of Plants,* which made the claim that plants were conscious beings capable of communicating and communing with humans. Plants were such spiritually evolved organisms, my father's research suggested, that if we listened to them attentively they could teach us how to live more happily and harmoniously on Earth—so harmoniously, in fact, that the planet could be transformed, in my father's words, into "a new Eden."

By the mid-1970s, my father had become a kind of walking, talking concatenation of the sort of ideas that today go under the general umbrella of "new age." Bearded, bald, with a perpetually intense, preoccupied expression (as a young child I suspected that he must have lost his hair from thinking too much), he was in appearance and character perfectly suited for this role. Without much in the way of conscious calculation, but instead just by being himself, he became the definitive example of the Fringe Investigator: the familiar figure with the whitening beard, khaki bush jacket, and unfazable open mind who was forever lurking on the outer edges of accepted science and conventional thinking. From Peter Tompkins you could always count on learning that the impossible wasn't really impossible at all, and that your not having been alerted to this fact was due purely to the untiring efforts of the self-serving charlatans in the academic community who were working overtime to keep you in the dark. He was the one to tell you that ancient astronauts may have once visited Earth; that psychic surgeons might cure your inoperable cancer; that the ancient Egyptians possessed magical techniques for levitating two-thousand-pound rocks; and that you yourself might even have been one of those Egyptian magicians in a previous incarnation.

From David Suskind to Mike Douglas to Dick Cavett, my father eventually made it on to almost all the talk shows of the time, usually in the company of a representative of the scientific community with whom he was expected to fall into passionate and vitriolic disagreement. The standard sequence of events would be for the host to introduce my father and then stand back while he flared his eyebrows menacingly and described whatever unusual phenomena he had been investigating that week. In the appearances immediately following the publication of the plant book, a table full of plants would usually appear at this point, one of them attached to a galvanometer—a lie-detecting device that my father's friend Cleve Backster had found could register what appeared to be the emotional reactions of plants as well as humans. The plants would then be threatened with uprooting or burning, and the TV cameras would zoom in on the galvanometer's wildly fluctuating dials. Finally, a suitably dour scientist would emerge, and he and my father would square off like a pair of fighting cocks in a Mexican bar, trading accusations for however much airtime remained to be filled.

My father brought a unique intensity to the ideas he explored in those years. When he argued that the ancients had lived in an expanded state of harmony and integration, the way back into which was open to all if they would but listen to the whisperings of the very plants they ate and walked upon, the urgency of his conviction incited as much admiration as the message itself. For my father it was not enough to simply believe in or publicize such possibilities. One needed, most of all, to act.

That was why, at the beginning of the summer of 1975, I found myself on Bimini. My father had long held an interest in Atlantis because of the emphasis placed on it in the work of Rudolf Steiner, the remarkable teacher and philosopher who founded the Anthroposophical movement and the Waldorf schools in Germany during the early decades of this century. Through his clairvoyant reading of history, Steiner claimed to have witnessed the unfolding of Atlantean civilization over the course of thousands of years, as well as the gradual birth of our own civilization from out of its ruins. The notion that a part of Atlantis lay in the Bahamas, however, had come not from Steiner but from another Atlantean clairvoyant named Edgar Cayce—the famous "sleeping prophet." A mild-mannered Midwesterner who began his life as a stationery salesman and Sunday school teacher, Cayce gained an enormous following as a result of his ability to diagnose and cure illnesses while in a state of trance. In the course of these diagnoses,

Cayce was given to making lengthy asides on other topics, many of which took the waking, everyday Cayce quite aback when he heard about them later. A good number of these strange asides concerned Atlantis. It was the entranced Cayce's opinion that the lost continent would reemerge in the late twentieth century from the depths of the Atlantic, where it had lain since its submergence in a great cataclysm that occurred some ten thousand years ago. In a trance statement made in 1940, he went so far as to specify 1968 or '69 as the year when the first fragments would begin to appear.

The Bimini Road, as the collection of sunken stones my father had come to investigate was called, did not dramatically rise up out of the ocean depths in 1968, but that was the year it first came to public notice, and this coincidence struck my father as impressive enough to call for action. Loaded down with income from *The Secret Life of Plants* and enticed by the idea of proving the legitimacy of Cayce's prophetic work to the nay-saying scientific community, he had organized this expedition in the hopes of producing a film about the Road that would either establish or demolish its claim to Atlantean origin once and for all.

The Bimini Road stretches for almost two thousand feet along the sandy ocean bottom, roughly paralleling the shore of North Bimini. At the northern end, the stones curve around to form the shape of a rough backward *J* then appear to stop as abruptly as they began. Leading nowhere, and made up of stones far too big and widely spaced for any vehicle—ancient or modern—to make use of, the Road isn't really a road at all. Nor, according to the views of most of the geologists who had examined it prior to our trip, was it a wall, a sunken boat harbor, an ancient temple to some forgotten god, or any other such romantic item. It was simply a length of soft, porous stone that time and chance had eroded in such a way that it gave the illusion of having been shaped by human hands.

Many things to many people, the Road was to me one thing above all others: boring. Try as I might, I could not conjure up, nor could I understand, the kind of anguish and enthusiasm that my father and his friends seemed to suffer over it. Swimming above this huge trail of squarish boulders with the other divers, I never failed to find them somehow uninspired, and I could not help but think that our time in the Bahamas would be better spent doing something—anything—else. Yet day after day all such possibilities went uninvestigated as we languished, anchored over the Road in a sixty-foot sailboat chartered for the adventure, while my father and the rest of his friends tinkered endlessly around its edges with their cameras and instruments.

My failure to appreciate the Road was mirrored by a similar lack of enthusiasm for other aspects of my father's world. It seemed that the more public his life became, the more removed I found myself becoming from it. Talking plants, lost civilizations—the whole gamut of his interests, which could always be counted on to inspire everything from fascination to disdain to outright anger in others—left me determinedly unmoved. It was not that I didn't admire my father or that I necessarily questioned his stranglehold on the mysteries of the universe. It was just that I didn't care.

"When," my father asked gruffly one morning up on the bow, "are we going to get you out of those abominable trunks?"

Today, as every day, I was clothed in a T-shirt and bathing suit, which separated me from the majority of the adults, who, other than the occasional pair of sneakers or sun hat, wore nothing. In front of the cameras, behind them, or somewhere in between, if you were involved in the Atlantis project and wearing clothing, my father would eventually have something to say about it. Nudity was not so much an option in my father's mind as a badge of honor: a sign, as it were, that you were on the Atlantis team.

This persistent presence of naked human bodies—young and old, male and female, toned and worn—had a less than totally positive effect on me. As the summer wore on, I found myself in the odd position of feeling envious of my friends back at school, for whom female bodies were items of supreme mystery rather than everyday scenery. Deprived of this romantic distance, the human form—more specifically the female human form—was taking on a distressingly mundane aura for me while at the same time retaining its intense adolescent desirability. All the variously shaped breasts and distressingly concrete genitalia I was forced to maneuver among out on the boat each day were turning into false idols: objects I was at once drawn helplessly toward yet at the same time distrustful of. I found this combination of elements deeply irritating, not to mention confusing, and I responded by affecting a mood of total—if false—disregard for all of it. I made a point of being clothed as much as possible and looked with increasing disdain upon the Atlantis hunters with whom, it seemed, I was destined to spend my entire summer.

My father, in his distracted fashion, was monitoring my behavior and trying to fathom it. Somehow it was beyond his comprehension that a thirteen-year-old boy should insist on remaining clothed all the time while on a boat in the middle of the Caribbean. Like just about everything else he trained his attention on for long enough, this apparent disinterest had certain implications in his eyes. By refusing to parade around naked at odd and inconvenient times, and by looking askance at those who did, I was doing more than just being difficult. I was placing myself in the company of the naysayers, the advocates of the mundane and the ordinary, who wanted to prove that the Road was no road at all but simply a meaningless geological accident.

"You guys look like idiots running around naked the way you do," I told him. "Besides, it's dangerous."

My father shook his head bemusedly. "Dangerous! What an absolutely ridiculous idea. I suspect it's that school we spend so much money on that feeds you these curious puritanical notions. We'll have to have you deprogrammed by the time you're ready to graduate."

"I suppose you think the Atlanteans all walked around naked?"

"That has absolutely nothing to do with it, nothing at all."

He paused for a moment and glowered back down at the stern of the boat, his assorted worries visibly regaining their hold over him. Then, collecting himself as if he were about to address some greater audience, he turned back to me.

"Do you know what all this is really about?"

"All what? This boat and everything?"

"Yes, this boat and everything."

"No."

"It's about freedom. The freedom to do as you like when you like and not get sucked into some artificial system of laws that tell you what to do and what not to do. That's why I'm here looking at this damn Road, and that's why I've chartered this bloody boat, and that's why I'm hemorrhaging money keeping all these machines running."

"I don't get it," I said. "I mean, what does being naked have to do with the Road?"

"It has everything to do with the Road," my father pronounced with satisfaction. "The academic establishment says Atlantis never existed when there's plenty of solid evidence that says it did. Now, just why, in the face of this evidence, should they be so intent on denying its existence outright?"

"I don't know. Maybe they just don't feel like believing in it."

"If they had the honesty to give an answer like that, I'd have a good deal more sympathy for them. In fact, you've hit the nail on the head. They don't feel like believing in it. Not at all. And the reason they don't is because believing in it would force them to rewrite every last one of their history books from chapter one on, and that is something they very definitely do not want to do. So rather than open themselves to the possibility that they don't really know what was going on ten or twenty or perhaps fifty thousand years ago on this planet, they simply close their ears and their eyes and cry 'Bullshit' at all the evidence that's presented without looking at it. They're no different from a bunch of demented schoolmasters at some wretched Dickensian parochial school, telling you the way things are and whipping you if you point out to them that they aren't that way at all. If there's one thing I'd be happy that you took away from being around for all this crazy stuff it's the importance of that—of being free to say and do what you think, regardless of the consequences and even if everybody tells you you're out of your mind."

It was rare for my father to be up on the bow, where not much in the way of work went on. When he left the cluttered stern, it was usually in order to avoid something, and today that something was the Remora. The most costly and sophisticated of the many technical devices enlisted to chronicle the Road, the Remora was a sort of giant winged torpedo with a camera at its front end. It was the brainchild of Dimitri Rebikoff, a French inventor and fellow Atlantis enthusiast, who had come along with it down to Bimini. Presumably, the sophisticated camera it housed would allow the divers to capture the Road on film more successfully than hand-held cameras would, but the more important, unspoken reason for the Remora's presence was the high-tech mystique it lent the enterprise. Tethered to the surface by a power cable, it glided impressively to and fro above the Road like a great mechanical fish, with divers clinging to its flanks. Or at least it did on the days when it worked. On this particular day, however, it was paralyzed by some failure deep in its mechanical insides and lay on the stern amidst a mass of cables like a great captured sea beast, with Rebikoff and several of his assistants hovering over it. My father, apparently unable even to look at the repair process without losing his temper, gazed poisonously out to sea.

Nothing makes a mockery of human endeavor like the ocean. All around us, beyond the noise of the boat and the people on it, the sea and sky lay spread out with what seemed a deep and resolved indifference to the entire project. Beneath us the blurry white Road lay with equal tranquillity, unconcerned with the buzzing engines and laboring people, unconcerned with whether the Remora would be fixed or whether its own true origin was Atlantean or otherwise.

"So what are you going to do if it turns out the Road is just a bunch of regular old rocks?"

"Then I will have laid the question to rest, and that will be the end of it. Because whatever that Road turns out to be, it doesn't take away one bit from what I just told you. The one important thing in life is having the freedom to find out what's bullshit and what's true and real, and to go after the true and the real with all of your energy. If you can't have that, there's not much point going and looking for anything else."

"So how come I'm not free to wear a bathing suit without you bugging me about it all the time?"

"You can wear a space suit and a bowler hat for all I care, as long as you're doing what you want—what you really want, and not what some bastard in some institution tells you you should."

"And that means I'm free to go deep-sea fishing on one of those charter boats, too, right?"

"That," said my father, "is a matter not of freedom but of money, and if I weren't running out of the latter faster than I can believe, I'd rent you one of those boats tomorrow."

"So money's different from freedom, huh?"

"Ideally, yes," said my father, the specter of cash dampening his mood slightly, "but practically, no."

Bimini is actually two islands set extremely close together. The great majority of the population lives on North Bimini, and it was here that my father had established himself, my stepmother, and me on the second floor of a defunct hotel at the southern tip of the island. Wind picked and wasted, the place had been out of use for some years by the time we moved in. The water still ran, more or less, and the glass doors that opened onto its sunbaked porches still rolled in their tracks. But everything else—from the empty pool with cracked and faded paintings of fish and mermaids running across its floor to the deserted thatch booth where drinks for lounging swimmers once were made—seemed as if it had been out of commission for a very long time indeed. Such was the quality of pleasant, timeless exhaustion hanging about the place that it was easy to imagine that it itself, at some bright and distant point in the past, had made up a sector of the fabled lost continent.

Beyond the hotel, visible from the windows of our rooms, the chalky tombstones of a cemetery pitched this way and that in the soft island soil, the ground between them scattered with coconuts and long, stiff fronds from the palms that rattled high overhead in the ever-present wind. Past the cemetery a white sand road led out to a knifing, deserted stretch of land, its west side forming a gentle beach, its east held sharply in place by a concrete sea wall. It was the job of this wall, worn and softened by wind and sand and sunlight, to keep a steady channel of deep water flowing here, where North and South Bimini came closest.

For unknown reasons, this beautiful stretch of land served as the island dump. Bleach bottles, black banana peels, and mountain after mountain of pink and white conch shells—their inhabitants long since wrenched from them and cooked into fritters or chowder—mingled in loose formations among the sand and beach grass. Here and there a larger piece, like a toilet or an auto engine, lay like a fallen satellite. Out in the water other masses of wreckage were dimly, sinisterly visible. One afternoon, sitting on the sun-warmed concrete, my fishing line adrift beneath me, I was surprised to see an entire sofa, complete with cushions, float by half-submerged.

There was not much to do on Bimini, especially if one was too young for the endless bars that, along with fishing-tackle shops, made up most of the island's main drag. On those days when no boat trips out to the Road were scheduled, or when I just needed a break from the weighty and stressful atmosphere that was such a perennial part of my father's quest, I would head out to the sea wall with a thin nylon line, some hooks, and a baggie of chicken gizzards. That summer, among other things, was the summer of *Jaws*, when boys my age across America were initiated by the thousands into the cult of the man-eating shark. Although the fish I caught out by the sea wall were seldom bigger than a penknife, images of primordial, submarine-sized monsters drifted through my brain as I hauled them up, carefully removed the tiny hook from their mouths, and tossed them back.

When I was buying fishing gear, my eye would often drift down to the other end of the glass-topped display tables where mammoth gray hooks lay with their chain leaders coiled beside them. Something in the bottom of my stomach would fall away as I considered the fact that someone somewhere actually baited these hooks and dropped them into the water. I imagined that a hook so absurdly large must have a sort of magical attractive power, and that one would have to be possessed of either extraordinary bravery or extraordinary foolhardiness to put that enchanted power to use.

*　*　*

One night at the sea wall, I heard voices.

"Looks like someone's here ahead of us."

Two men, carrying six-packs and smoking cigarettes that brightened and faded in the shifting night air, emerged out of the darkness.

"How's it going, partner," the shorter and less athletic looking of the two said. "Name's Scott. Down from Atlanta. That line's a little thin for sharks, isn't it?"

"I'm not fishing for sharks," I stammered. "I don't know how."

"Nothing to it," said his friend. "All you gotta do is drop the right kind of line. Guy at the Angler bar told us sharks cruise here at night. You might have some luck if you got the right rig."

"Have you ever caught any?"

"Yup. Phil caught five last year."

"What kind?"

"Three black tips, a lemon, and a bull I think it was. One of the black tips had a beer can in his belly."

"What kind of beer?"

"Bud."

"Was it full?"

"Empty."

"Wow," I said, digesting all this information as coolly as possible.

"How long you here for, kid?" Scott asked.

"I don't know. A month. Maybe more."

"Yeah? Shit. Got yourself some rich parents, I guess."

"Not really rich, I don't think. My father's looking for Atlantis."

Phil's eyes lit up. "No way. Like lost Atlantis?"

"Yeah."

"He must be looking at the Road." Phil gave the last of his cigarette an accomplished flick, sending it far out into the channel, then took a longer look at me. "Your father thinks it's for real, huh?"

"He doesn't know. He wants to find out, though. He's like a seeker of the unexplained or something. He invented that thing about talking to your plants."

"Oh, man. Your father's the *plant guy?* I guess he doesn't do any fishing then. What kind of boat you have?"

"A sailboat, and I can't fish from it because the line always gets tangled in the keel and everyone gets mad at me. I asked if we could go deep-sea fishing, but my father says it costs too much."

"Your father has a point," said Scott. "Unless, that is, you happen to have a boat of your own. A fishing boat."

"Like we do," said Phil.

"Tell you what, kid," said Scott. "Day after tomorrow we're having a guide take us to a spot off Cat Cay. He guaranteed us we'll catch something. Seeing as you're such a dedicated sportsman, it seems like a shame for you to miss it. Maybe you can come along . . . if your pop's all right with it."

"Sure," said Phil. "We can always use another steady hand."

"I'm going shark fishing tomorrow," I told my father the next morning, as much to hear how the words sounded out in the air as anything else, for of course there was no question of my not being permitted to go. "I met these guys on the sea wall last night, and they're going to take me with them on their boat."

"Shark fishing," my father said, his eye on the Remora as it moved past us out in the water. "Now, there's a vulgar way of spending one's time! Why on earth would you want to go and harass some glorious beast by dragging it up on the end of a rope? You're free to do as you like, of course, but keep in mind that there are consequences to actions. Everything produces results in life, you know—everything. Do you know what they found wrong with the Remora the other day?"

"What?"

"Nothing! Not a bloody thing. Rebikoff tells me he can't figure out why it wasn't functioning, and now it's coasting along without a hitch! Now, how do you suppose that could be. Any ideas?"

"No."

"Then I'll tell you. Vibes!"

"Vibes?"

"Yes, vibes. There's been a lot of negative thought-energy on this project in the last several days, and the machines have been picking up on it. What you have to understand is that everything in life—absolutely everything—is alive and reacts to what you think about it."

"Then how come I can't make stuff do what I want just by thinking, like on *I Dream of Jeannie* or something?"

"What the hell is *I Dream of Jeannie*?"

"It's a TV show where this genie makes stuff disappear or move around just by thinking about it."

"Hmm. Well, if you really put your mind to it you could. Rudolf Steiner says the Atlanteans started out with a kind of thought-energy that could affect the environment, and that the misuse of that energy was what ultimately brought them to an end."

"You mean they thought the wrong kind of thoughts?"

"They did indeed. And their psychic abilities were so advanced in comparison to ours that those negative thoughts actually had the capability to alter their environment—to destroy their entire world, in fact."

The Remora, with two divers clinging to its sides and its dark power cable trailing behind it, coasted silently past us once more, bubbles popping to the surface in its wake.

"So maybe we're lucky we can't do that anymore."

"Do what?" my father said, his eyes on the Remora.

"Make things happen just by thinking."

"That's just my point. Don't be so sure that we can't. We may not live in Atlantis anymore, but we still live in a world where actions have consequences. And thoughts are actions. You mark my words."

The next morning, with a sandwich, an orange, and two bottles of red wine that my father had sent along as a gift slung over my shoulder, I arrived at the specified dock an hour earlier than scheduled. Scott's boat was smaller than most of the other vessels nudging together in the calm of the morning. You stepped down, rather than up, into it.

"Disappointed?" Scott called to me from the stern, where he was on his hands and knees arranging green bottles in a deep white tomb of ice.

"Sharks aren't fancy fish," he said. "And it doesn't take a fancy boat to catch them. Hey, Bruce! This is our third."

Bruce, his long body bent down in the small cabin space, craned himself around and acknowledged me with a nod. I recognized him, and the odd pink-checkered golfer's cap he wore, from here and there on the island. Like the boat, he had a slightly downscale look to him—a no-frills guide ready to tackle the relatively simple job of finding some sharks.

With Scott arranging his bottles and Bruce at work in the heart of the boat, I sat, then lay, on the night-cool wood of the dock. Through a space between two planks I could see down into the shallow water below. It was almost as clear as it was out at the sea wall, so that the reef fish pausing and hurrying about on their familiar errands were sharply visible among the bottles and corroding cans. Looking down at that intimate little theater, I soon dozed off, awakening sometime later to the drum of the engine. Phil had arrived, and someone had scooped up my meager gear and placed it in the boat. I got to my feet and, as my first officially useful action, untied the bowline from the dock and jumped aboard.

Bruce took us out past the procession of fishing docks, the unchartered boats all crowded inside them like cows at a feeding trough. As we passed through the narrow inlet, I could see the spot where I normally sat along the sea wall, which looked small and curiously unfamiliar. In increments the landscape beneath us fell away, and soon we were cruising over the impossible, precipitous darkness of the Gulf Stream. Over an all-but-invisible reef, the men caught their bait fish—seven or eight jack, bright and hard in the crystalline air. These were tossed into a wooden stern compartment, where they banged and flapped for some minutes, the sound clearly audible over the hum of the engine as we made our way out again into deep water.

Twenty minutes later Bruce cut the engine, and we were suddenly alone out in the blue, the boat washing and slapping gently in the waves. A jack was pulled from the stern compartment and whacked abruptly in half, transformed in a moment from a fish into two anonymous chunks of bait. Both pieces were lanced through a giant hook and hurled over the stern. A nylon line fed gradually out, coil after coil, until Bruce at last looped it once around a cleat and passed the remainder to Phil, who was to watch and wait for signs of pressure.

Half an hour passed. I stared at the cleat, envisioning the baited hook drifting in the darkness far below, and suddenly, as if responding to my wish, the loop began to tighten. Phil unlooped the line from the cleat, and he and Scott stood one behind the other in the gently pitching boat, their hands loosely holding the line, which continued to feed sleepily and steadily out.

"On three we'll set the hook," Bruce commanded. "One . . . two . . . "

The two men gave a tremendous yank, and immediately the line stiffened decisively. The hook was set. Bruce started up the boat, and Phil and Scott began slowly hauling up our invisible catch. After a while the line no longer pointed down but slanted almost horizontally into the water behind us. I followed it with my eyes until it vanished in the slow rolling waves.

Then, fifty yards behind the stern, a fin appeared and was gone. When it reemerged, it was close enough so that I could dimly make out the shape of the body beneath it. Even from a distance the shark's color was striking: not the dull, steel gray I had imagined but a warm and vivid brown. Against the sharp blue of the ocean it looked shockingly appropriate, as if selected with deliberate care by an artist. Disappearing and reappearing, the shark made its slow way toward us, drawn without much protest by the steady hauling of the two men. I kept waiting for it to leap up out of the water and gnash its teeth cinematically, but the closer it got the more it stayed under, until at last it was right up beside us, its head out in the air and its long body trailing down beneath the surface, completely visible.

In the impossibly clear water beside the boat, the animal, about six or seven feet of it, hung almost vertically, its tail maintaining this position with slow, fluid strokes. Forced into this unnatural posture, it seemed to be doing the best it could to maintain some of its dignity. Its broad head sank momentarily, then once again rose above the surface, and I could see where the hook broke through the cream-pale skin of the lower jaw. I found myself tremendously impressed by the eerie nonchalance with which the shark hung there in the water. A huge and alien atmosphere of patience seemed to emanate from it.

"Hook's set good," said Bruce. "Let's see if we can get a loop around him."

In a moment Bruce had formed a lasso, and with a long wooden gaff he gingerly edged it down into the water, toward the shark's tail.

"That's it. Loop's set tight. Let out that other line, we'll take him in to the beach."

With the lines slack, the shark sank down for a moment and moved off, regaining its horizontal position. Bruce pointed the boat toward a small island off in the distance, and suddenly the beautiful casualness of the fish was lost in a blast of noise and white water. Flailing and snapping, it dragged helplessly behind us as we headed for shore.

"That should drown him by the time we get there," Bruce shouted back from the helm.

"Drown him?" I asked no one in particular.

"Yeah," said Scott. "All that rushing water makes it impossible for him to breathe right. Still, he'll probably have some life left in him by the time we get him on land."

Fifteen minutes later, Bruce guided the shallow hull right up onto the beach of a small cove, and we all hopped out, Phil and Scott grabbing the hook line as the shark lolled drunkenly in the water behind us. Bruce secured the boat, and all three men took hold of the rope and hauled the great brown body up onto shore.

"Brown shark." Bruce said laconically, identifying not the color but the species for us.

It was an apt enough name, slightly foolish in its obviousness. Prone on the sand like a jet taken down from the heavens, the shark glowed with a deep, living brown that faded to an equally impressive white beneath. It seemed to me that I had never seen a more perfect, a cleaner animal in my life. Its blemishless, velvety skin, its stiff and delicately rounded fins, all conspired to make the animal look as if it had come freshly minted from some incredible machine. It looked like the Remora, I thought, beached on the deck of my father's boat.

While Bruce set to straightening and coiling the line that ran from the hook still caught in the shark's jaws, Phil dug his feet squarely into the sand next to the animal's head and began to give it a series of heavy, horrible, clunking blows with a baseball bat. The shark at first appeared indifferent even to this insult. It continued to look quintessentially, aloofly sharklike, all precision and purpose and grace. Occasionally a shiver rippled along its length, its tail swiping absently back and forth, creating a clean, crescent furrow in the sand.

"Dumb son of a bitch," said Phil. "Can't tell if he even feels anything."

"Are you kidding?" said Scott. "This thing's primitive. He probably thinks he's still out in the water swimming."

Whether or not the shark was in fact under such an illusion, it was plain enough, after a minute or so, that Phil's efforts were having some effect. The twitches and the movements of the tail died down, and suddenly blood, red and bright and familiar looking, began to flow from the gills at both sides of the shark's head. The blood soon grew more plentiful, and Phil had to step back to avoid having it drench his white deck sneakers.

After all the long commotion of the morning, the four of us stood silently around the body of the fish, which though now quite obviously dead still seemed all motion and purpose, like an arrow pointing off to a realm of color and life and beauty—a realm that we ourselves would never find or enter.

In Atlantean times, wrote Rudolf Steiner, the air was denser than it is now. The water, meanwhile, was thinner, and as a result the Atlanteans, who received their knowledge about the world clairvoyantly from spiritual sources, were able to move about the earth and exploit its secret forces in ways very different from those that are known today. The Atlanteans understood the forces of nature so well that they formed a kind of partnership with them. The airships that glided through the thick Atlantean air were powered by life-energy extracted from plant seeds; the Atlantean cities resembled huge, growing gardens, with houses built from the interwoven branches of trees. It was only when the Atlanteans grew indulgent and started misusing the formidable energies that had been bequeathed to them that things started to go wrong. Ultimately, Atlantis sank, and the clairvoyant and magically energized world they had known hardened into the stubborn and unyielding one we know today—a world where machines run on gasoline and the air is disappointingly thin and objects do not yield easily and instantly to human desires.

My father didn't find Atlantis. Some months after our stay on Bimini that summer, he returned to the island with a crew of sober and fully clothed geologists, who extracted a series of corings from the limestone blocks of the great white Road. Examined microscopically, these delivered the news that the Road was a completely natural formation, down which no lost civilizations, naked or clothed, had ever wandered or danced. All the images of naked divers hovering and darting about above it, all the Remora's sweeping footage, were thus rendered useless, save for their potential interest to future cultural historians.

True to his words to me on the boat that day, my father took this news in stride. Goose chases, he maintained, were inevitable when one spent one's time challenging scientific orthodoxy. The best thing to do, when one found oneself engaged in one, was to accept the fact without struggle and move on. In any case, it was not as if Atlantis itself was rendered obsolete just because the Road had lost its Atlantean pedigree. Indeed, no sooner was it eliminated as a possible proof of the lost continent's existence than other forms of evidence began flooding in to take its place. Although he never released his film about it, my father also never abandoned his conviction that Atlantis was a reality. As for myself, I wasn't so sure. For even if Atlantis had indeed existed, who was to say it would come back just because my father and others so desperately and urgently wanted it to? Sometimes, it seemed to me, things could disappear completely. And when that happened, all the positive thinking in the world wouldn't bring them back again.

The Good-bye Koan

Koans are vastly overrated. A Hindu teacher, who I will call Baba, an Indian (from India) in whites whom I met at the Boston airport during a long snowbound wait, told me that, but then he might have been overrated himself. There's a lot of competition in religion. Jealousy, too. Jealousy is a fact of life. One of my Zen teachers told me that, shortly before his center collapsed and we, disciples, were out in the big bad world again. Most of us left the area, never to be heard of again, but, riding in a small plane over the Maine woods, I found one of my former buddies.

This man, whom I will call Ben-san, had once been an idealist, who, in the idealist sixties, traveled to Japan to study Zen. By happenstance he went to the same temple I did, but we missed each other. I left a few weeks before he arrived. Meeting him later in America was quite an event for we knew all the same people back in Kyoto. Same abbot, same head monk, same regular monks. Same bars in Kyoto's famous Willow Quarter that we visited on our off nights.

Like me, Ben stayed a few years in the Japanese Zen temple, was given the Mu koan, never passed it, and left. There were other similarities: same age, we were both white males from Protestant, in his case fundamentalist, backgrounds, we were both drinking men. There seemed to be a similar artistry in both of us, which pushed him into creating pagodas in oriental-style gardens and me to write tales and build junk sculptures when my back needed stretching. In America, early seventies, we both finished up with the same teacher, whom I'll call Sensei here. Sensei had spent many years in Japan and according to the Zen grapevine "had his insights confirmed by qualified authorities." Ben and I enrolled at Sensei's North American center as students of Zen koans and practitioners of the wayless way.

The same koans that the Indian guru, whom I met at Logan airport, and whom I called Baba, said he had studied from a Hindu point of view and had found, with some exceptions, somewhat clever, a trifle contrived, definitely wanting. Baba smiled forgivingly. "Given the reputation of Zen, I had really expected a little more." I had to laugh. Those were the exact words Sensei liked to use after a strenuous week of meditation, but he would say it sternly. Sensei always seemed genuinely disappointed at the failures of his students.

Hanging out at the Logan airport during a blizzard, with all chairs taken and the bathrooms overflowing, Baba stood out as an exceptional-looking man. Always eager to learn, I approached this figure in flowing robes below and flowing hair on top.

"Are you a guru, sir?"

"For sure." Baba spoke with a clipped, high-pitched Indian accent. "Are you a truth seeker?"

"I used to be a Zen student, sir."

"You gave up?"

"Not on my questions, sir."

"But on Zen you gave up?"

"Not really, sir. But I seem to be on my own now."

Baba nodded. He knew all about Zen. The practice of zazen, meditation, and koan study, solving of dharma riddles, while facing a teacher at sanzen, the early morning meeting in the master's temple.

I said that was what I had been doing for many years, in my off time, for I usually worked in day jobs. "How come you are a guru, Baba?"

He looked at me loftily, from under impressively tufted eyebrows. Did I misaddress this evolved being? I didn't mean offense. "Sri Baba? Sri Baba Maharaj? You have a title, sir? Your Holiness, maybe?"

He smiled and bowed. "Never mind my titles. Holy titles are all hogwash, my friend."

I liked that. It was the sort of thing Bodhidharma would have said to the emperor of China before stalking out of the imperial palace to meditate another nine years in his cave.

Another foot of snow was covering up Boston's runways. Baba had time to chat. He told me he felt comfortable in airports, for he had started his own career at an airport, too, at JFK, New York. As a preguru Baba was an illegal alien and cleaned restaurant tables for a living. This was, again, the sixties, a spiritual time. America developed a demand for esoteric teachers. The law of demand and supply made holy men enter the country. Busboy Baba noticed that the teachers flocking into JFK from his native country wore white clothes and had much facial hair. They were Hindus. They had big expressive eyes and sharp features. They quoted the Bhagavad Gita. They recited mantras, Sanskrit syllables charged with holy power, and held their hands in certain ways, a practice known as doing mudras. They were met invariably by well-dressed women and their long-haired male attendants, couples who had expensive cars waiting for them in the airport parking lot.

"What," Baba asked me, "prevented me from declaring myself a guru?" The title was not protected. Baba had shareable insights galore, gathered in previous lives and the poverty and pain of the present. In order to show his true status, he needed a white dhoti and matching jacket, and with sandals to show off his muscular long toes—items that weren't hard to get. The other requirements were already rightfully his. He had been raised in a priestly, a Brahmin (albeit starving), family, knew Hindu scripture by heart,

kept up a home altar, burned incense, and performed daily pros-
trations. He even meditated from time to time, although meditation, Baba told me, is not all it's cracked up to be. When overdone
it gives you a pain in the ass. Had I noticed?

I had. Prolonged zazen had given me chronic hemorrhoids.
Baba told me the human body is not designed to sit in the double
or even the half lotus position for long periods of time. The pos-
tures put excessive tear on the rectum. I found that easy to believe.
Preparation H is a staple in Zen monasteries, together with Maalox,
for eating too hot meals too fast, the constant urging to solve a
koan, too little sleep, peer pressure by zealots, tends to create mental tensions that ulcerate Zen stomachs.

"Right," Baba said. "Forget all that. Your own precious Buddha
told his disciples to walk the middle way, to avoid excess."

"No spiritual practice?"

"Just daily life," Baba said. "Apply some awareness. Take daily
time to perform a short ritual of your choice, but mostly just be,
my friend." He dropped his voice and stared at me hypnotically.
"Just be."

"But what about suffering?"

He shrugged. "What about it?"

I told him suffering wasn't nice.

"Do you suffer?" Baba asked me.

I told him I was doing just fine, thank you. Being fairly well off
seemed to be my karma. I shouldn't be complaining, heaven for-
bid, but my good standing could be, at times, just a bit boring.
Whatever I did, wherever I went, I always seemed to be doing just
fine. Look at me now, new tweed jacket and just the right zippered
mud boots, a four-wheel-drive vehicle in good repair parked at my
home airport, a good wife waiting in a comfortable house on land-
scaped acres, okay income, overall good health, the complete
recordings of Miles Davis and good sound equipment shelved

next to the word processor. Now look at other people. I showed Baba a two-page color photo of the coast of Bangladesh, printed in a magazine I had just bought. Recent floods had caused numberless people and cattle to drown; when the sea receded, the coast was set off by a white line, dead people, and a brown line, dead cows, going on for miles.

"So?" Baba asked.

"The suffering of these Bangladeshis makes me doubt."

"Doubt what?"

"Whether there is a purpose."

"To suffering?"

"Yes," I said, "to life."

"A purpose to life?" Baba patted my shoulder. "There isn't any."

"So all is just painful chaos?"

Baba raised a hand to draw my attention, then recited in his high voice, "There is no suffering, no cause of suffering, no cessation of suffering . . ."

". . . and no path," I said.

"You know the Heart Sutra," Baba said. "It's not Hindu but Buddhist scripture, but Buddhist is Indian, too, and all Buddha did is revive part of our original religion. And you're right. *No path*, forget path. Path is highly overrated."

I was beginning to like Baba. He seemed to be a master of the Far Eastern method of negation. *Neti, neti*. Destroy all constructions, then enjoy empty space. "You have a temple?" I asked.

He had one, in the Catskills, but advised me that there was not much there for me. I should make use of my present lack of status. Why get interested in yet another inflicted discipline? Baba, at his spiritual center, was merely keeping people busy by providing them with a nonharmful routine, such as limited meditation and chanting of scripture. The place was partly run as a farm so there was work to help deal with depression and stress. Rules were structured to keep disciples upright. Everyone was to wear white dhotis and jackets and open-toed sandals while on the grounds (most disciples came only for the weekend or "training weeks"); there was to be no frolicking with abusable substance, no guitar music after hours, no dillydallying except for those with guru or guru-escort status, no excessive donations to buy being teacher's pet; and during farewell ceremonies (in private, when disciples left the center to go home for a while) he would hand out praise and cookies.

"Chocolate chip," Baba said. "Don't care for them myself, but Americans associate them with parental loving guidance."

"You bake the cookies?"

Baba bought them.

There was some slyness about him that I, coming from a Dutch trading background, thought I recognized. I tried to phrase a respectful enquiry as to whether Baba was into money perhaps. Whether he was shearing his silly sheep. He cut me short as soon as I used the word *money*.

"You mean Greed?" An interesting impediment, but he had given it up. There was the temptation, for he had been poor for so long. He did indulge during his early days on his spiritual health farm. Baba drove a Jaguar for a while, ate gourmet, charged high prices for special interviews, obtained tax-free status, even increased his income by operating a health-food restaurant worked for free with disciple labor, but an overdose of material success had made him nervous. He closed the restaurant and reduced the contributions that his disciples paid on a monthly basis. The Jaguar was driven by "my number one lady" now, who used it for community shopping. Baba rode a bicycle, like in Calcutta, long ago, but this one was a ten speed.

"And sex?"

"Sex." He nodded wisely. "There is that too."

I told him that sexual desire, first frustrated, later perverted, had helped bring down the Buddhist center where I had studied. Baba kept nodding sympathetically. He could understand that. After all, a holy man is still a man and a man has his needs. He didn't want to go to Manhattan for his needs. It was nicer if sex came to him at his temple. He never meant to be a self-denying recluse. One young lady had wrapped herself in gift paper and had herself rolled into his quarters in a shopping cart by two girlfriends in bikinis. Was it wrong for an insightful teacher to accept the gift of an attractive disciple's ego? Ego is the mask that has to come off to show pure being. Only in pure being can divine insight be clear.

"Sensei used to say, 'If you present me with your beautiful mind, why can't I have your beautiful body?'" I told Baba.

"How interesting," Baba said. "Now tell me about the koans you managed to solve during your many years of Zen practice, my friend."

There was no time, a runway had opened up and Baba's plane was waiting. He gave me his card. "Come and see me sometime." He caressed my shoulder. "But don't bring me your personal problems. I cannot help people carry their ego loads." He squeezed my hand. "I don't want to either."

Off he went, a bundle of human light. Wouldn't it be fun to spend time at his chocolate chip cookie heaven? Baba was probably right, I didn't think I could do it. It's hard for a man in his fifties to dance in the meadow again, pleasing Daddy and his numbered egoless ladies.

Didn't I feel contented on my own now? Doing exactly what Baba recommended—using daily life as my practice, *sadhana,* chanting the Heart Sutra at my altar every morning, burning incense to the little plastic skeleton of a dinosaur, an extinct being, like Homo sapiens would be pretty soon, that I kept in a box between ritual candles?

I hadn't minded leaving the Buddhist center, but I sometimes missed my pals, especially Ben-san. I wondered how he was coping.

Suffering is caused by desire, and I definitely wished to see Ben-san again. I wasn't going to make a special effort but desires, once clearly stated, have a way of being fulfilled, most often within the lifetime.

A technical man in the village had built himself an airplane and asked me, one sunny winter day, to join him for a spin. We flew around Mount Katahdin and, coming back from skimming lakes and rivers and crossing vast areas of wild woods, spotted a pagoda not too far from the home airstrip. My pilot friend circled the structure and found the long winding track that led to it. We were both impressed. The pagoda was a mini version of what I recognized as a famous Kyoto temple. It had three stories with what appeared to be living quarters on the first. There was also a land-scaped garden, its outline visible under the snow. I could detect what would be moss gardens around decorative giant boulders, no doubt showing glowing orange and yellow lichens once the thaw would set in. There was also a flat, some forty-foot-square, slightly rippled area with three rocks off center that looked like it would be raked daily during the milder part of the year. There was a frozen pond where I guessed large multicolored carp would be hibernating under the ice. A very Zenlike landscape. The pilot had known Ben-san too. "Must be Ben's; so that's where he hides out now." We circled the pagoda again, much lower than the legal five hundred feet, and we saw a man come out, waving a shotgun.

"Ben all right," the pilot said.

"Got to walk out there sometime," I said.

The pilot checked his instrument panel and handed me a note with the location's coordinates. "Shouldn't be hard to find. You can borrow my handheld positioner. The path to there is basically north-south and leads out of the town of Sorry. Starts at

Blackberry Brook. Can't miss it if you take a compass and the GPS. Better make sure you don't get shot though."

Sorry is a suburb of the coastal town of Rotworth where I've been living for a good while now. I waited for another good clear day, with the right kind of snow to support my snowshoes. According to my map the distance out of Sorry would be some ten miles. I got to Ben's pagoda by noon.

He came out with his gun but put it down and hugged me lightly. "You smell better now," he said. "In the Zendo you stank."

He ought to know; we used to sit next to each other during bathless weeks. I recalled his fragrance too.

"You're a hermit now?" I asked.

Ben-san said he liked that better than the practice at our Buddhist center. Living alone in the pagoda had also helped him quit drinking. I had quit drinking, too. I told him, "Alcohol no longer fulfilled my needs." He thought that was a silly way of putting things and probably untrue. "Your wife confronted you. Told you either you quit or she left. Now you need a macho excuse. Always trying to impress the audience. Haven't changed much have you?"

"So what do you do for money now, Ben?"

Very little, he told me. He wasn't always at the pagoda. He worked some of his summers, away in New Hampshire, staying with employers for free, saving some dollars. Spring, fall, and winter he stacked up on staples and hermited away, surrounded by wildlife.

There were several jays around, a squirrel or two, a tribe of chickadees, some juncos. I saw there were feeders placed in strategic spots, designed like little temples. Ben-san was still bitten by the building bug. He looked lonely to me.

"Get a woman," I said, "some pleasant soul tired of being abused. Pick her up Friday night at the Lazy Loon in Rotworth.

You'll be king of the castle. Those women haven't seen a sober man in years."

He didn't care for making women happy.

"A male soul mate perhaps?"

He told me he had given up on people. Ben-san the misanthrope. He crossed his arms defensively. I left him to his posturing and admired his backdrop. The pagoda was an impressive structure, built from hand-hewn logs dovetailed together like a Chinese puzzle. All wooden pegs. The intricate handiwork must have consumed months of lonely winter time. The roofs were covered with old-fashioned cedar shakes, cut with a giant chisel. A jewel in the woods. I bowed and recited the ancient Tibetan mantra. *Om mani padme hum,* hail to the jewel in the lotus.

"Never understood what that meant," Ben told me.

"Still doing Zen practice?" I asked when he finally uncrossed his arms.

He nodded. "Sure."

"Zazen?"

Some zazen. Not too much. "I never liked it. Half an hour in the morning, half an hour in the evening. That's all I can put up with now."

I noticed a Direct TV dish on the pagoda's top roof and a rusted Honda generator in a lean-to.

"I follow the cult movie channel," Ben-san said. "Some opera too. Not too often. It's too hard to carry in the gas for the generator."

I didn't believe him. There were several fifty-five-gallon drums away from the building, under their own roof, and I spotted a sled and an old but functional-looking snowmobile. Ben-san is a powerful man, it wouldn't trouble him even to hand-pull a load for ten miles.

I hadn't given up on peer pressure yet. "Still do koan study? Must be hard without Sensei telling you what's what."

"Sensei." He shrugged. "Good riddance of twisted nonsense."

"But you still work on a koan, Ben?"

The arms were crossed again against a puffed-up chest. "What's my koan study to you?"

"But, Ben-san, we are dharma brothers." I reminded him how far back we went. How we had been drinking buddies. How we had sworn to use each others' lives as mirrors. "Sake for two," I sang on the tea-for-two tune while I skipped around him.

He unfroze a bit. Just one koan he was still working on, Ben told me over baked beans and tofu on rice with chili sauce and pickled daikon. The one he had received some months before Sensei's hermitage went back to nature. Students aren't supposed to discuss their koans but as Ben and I had both been released we could consider ourselves free now. "Tell me about your last koan," I said, thinking I might help out. Not that he would want to be helped out. Zen students consider themselves the cream of the Buddhist crop, those who walk the steep short way; we are potential high-class bodhisattvas, just one more koan and we can step into nirvana.

"Tell me your koan, dear Ben-san."

"Nah."

Okay. I was on the pagoda's front steps, nudging my boots into my snowshoes. The hell with Mr. Do-It-Himself. He could rot in his pagoda. It was a nice building though. I had told Ben his creation reminded me of a toy pagoda my mother brought back from Indonesia in the twenties, from the "Dutch Indies" as she still called the country.

The little pagoda was crafted out of an elephant tooth and had, like Ben-san's, three stories. My mother said she had bought it at the Borrobudur, Java's great Buddhist temple, covering an entire hilltop, an elaborate piece of architecture abandoned after Buddhism was replaced by Islam. Each story had a set of tiny hinged doors. I liked to open them and peer inside. There had been Buddha statues in each compartment, but as they could be taken out they got lost. My mother bewailed their disappearance but a Chinese friend told us the pagoda made more sense without its former tenants. "Form is emptiness. Better show nothing."

Ben-san's pagoda's second and third stories were empty, too. They didn't even have doors. The wind passed freely under their swept-up roofs. Only the lower floor was walled in, insulated, and fitted with doors. "I've got to live *some*where," Ben told me, showing me his sparse furniture. He was frowning again. "You still fill up all your outbuildings with possessions? The villa? The double garage? The studios? The gazebo? The guesthouse?"

He knew what he was talking about. He had designed and built my compound. In those days he needed more money, to finance travels during the Zen training's off seasons, and I kept providing him with work.

"Thanks for the tofu," I said. "'Bye now."

He held me back. "I'm working on the bull koan."

There are probably a dozen bull koans in use in the various Zen sects. "Which bull?"

"Why-can't-the-tail-pass-by bull koan," Ben-san said. "It's driving me crazy."

Koans are designed to drive the Zen student crazy. I kicked off my snowshoes and allowed Ben to guide me back into his living quarters. We had coffee.

"Gozo En Zenji," I said. "That's the Zen master Sensei was quoting. I remember Gozo's tale. Something to do with you're in the sanzen room, early in the morning, and Sensei is confronting you, squatting on his cushions wearing the Japanese roshi gown he has outgrown since he gained weight. He points at the small window above his head. He tells you that it's like Gozo's water buffalo bull, a huge animal, passing by that window. His huge head, his big horns, his four feet go by, but that's it, the tail isn't coming by. What of that, eh?"

"Right," Ben said. "So you were on that koan, too?"

Ben-san and I, during our student days, were probably always on the same koans.

Now what are koans? They are riddles that are deliberately phrased obscurely. There are pieces missing. No Zen student, not two thousand years ago in China, not a thousand years ago in Japan, not today in the Maine woods or in a Californian valley or on an Arizona mesa, can make sense of any given koan until the teacher does some explaining first. And he won't. He wants you to squirm in stupidity. Sensei himself, when I knew him in Japan where he was an advanced disciple with much seniority and many years of sanzen behind him, complained about koans, calling them "word mazes." He was working on a long story that involved a white crane, and a white crane means something in Chinese mythology—I forget now what it means—and if you don't know what it means you'll never figure out what the white crane is doing in that long story, and you won't solve the koan. In Sensei's case his Japanese teacher didn't know that Sensei, an American, didn't know about the esoteric meaning of *white crane,* so master and student were butting their heads together in the sanzen room and "precious time was lost." At the time I thought that Sensei's complaint made no sense either. Was Sensei in a hurry? Did he want his degree? Was he eager to hang out his shingle as a teacher himself?

Sensei probably did. Ben-san, however, never showed any interest in a Buddhist career. He probably just wanted to know things, like if there was a purpose to him being born into a fundamentalist Protestant community that served a divinity Ben only wanted to get away from. And what was the miracle of life that he, with his love of wildlife and beautiful structures, felt he was close to but never could grab hold of, not even after the third jug of sake? Why the Vietnam War? Why the need to pollute a perfectly good planet? Every time he was given a new koan he thought the answer might solve his quest, but there was always another mountain on the horizon. The bull koan was the last one he ever meant to work on. He absolutely had to know the answer.

We weren't there yet. "Your bull koan is an overrated koan," I told Ben-san. "It's not like the Mu koan or the Sound of One Hand. The tail-of-the-bull koan has nothing to do with Nothing. It does not indicate the great void. It doesn't comprise the entire Heart Sutra into a single negation. It's your final koan and it's minor."

"So how do *you* know?" Ben asked. "Did you pass the damned thing?"

"But there is nothing to pass," I said. "It's just a little illustration of a problem that won't go away. You know what *tail* stands for in Chinese mythology?"

"Something to wag?"

I shook my head. If this had been sanzen and I would have been the Zen master throning on cushions stacked on a platform, and Ben would have been the disciple groveling below on the tatami, I would have picked up my little bell and shaken it and he would have had to prostrate himself three times and leave and be back the next day, bright and early. "Close," I said. "It's something to get stuck with. The idea *tail*, in Far Eastern symbolism, means 'ego.' Personality. The tail stands for 'being-me-ness,' and no incarnated spirit, whether he comes as the Dalai Lama or as Allen Ginsberg, Christ, you, the latest U.S. president, me, can get away from the personality we happen to come equipped with. Cradle to grave, it's always there, constantly changing but never fading out. Concern for Number One can't help holding us back. I can't cut my tail off. At best I can try to be aware of being tied down by it."

"Did you read that somewhere?"

Sure, I had read that somewhere. Zen does not believe in books, but there are forty thousand Zen books in print. Most of them list or explain koans, a few quite openly. There's the *Sound of the One Hand,* 281 koans and their answers, a work compiled by a genuine Zen master in 1916, commented on by several genuine Zen masters since (some say it can do no harm, others say it should be burned), and translated by the scholar Yoel Hoffmann (New York: Basic Books, 1975). The original version of this telltale book was bought up and destroyed by several Tokyo Zen masters but the publisher printed new editions. There was, and is, *The Green Grotto Record,* with a hundred koans explained by Zen masters Engo and Dai-e, tenth and eleventh centuries, and available in at least two English translations. There are *Mumon-kan* and *Kekiganroku,* two classic koan collections translated and explained by Katsuki Sekida (New York: Weatherhill, 1977). Bulls and their restraining tails perform in these works.

"It was Sensei's parting koan," I told Ben. "To us, his first disciples, who followed him out here to the Sorry Hermitage. It shows that Zen masters have egos and that he was no exception. Sensei wanted us to know that all he did so blatantly wrong could not be helped. He excused his failure. He showed us, by the bull's tail that would never pass the light of the enlightenment window, that part of him was stuck in the mud."

"So what is the correct answer?" Ben asked, for all supportive koans have correct answers. You've got to give them before the Rinzai-sect—which Sensei belonged to—teacher releases you and passes on to the next little koan, which may clear up another minor aspect of Mu, the gateless gate, the true-entry koan.

The correct passing answer?

"What you do," I told Ben, "is you shuffle a little closer to the platform, on your knees, smiling politely, and then you reach out, behind Sensei, and you give a terrific jerk on his robe, so that he almost falls over backward, and you say, 'Well, now, you're pretty well stuck yourself, aren't you, old boy?'"

"That's all?"

That was all.

It was time to leave the pagoda. Ben put on his snowshoes, too, and accompanied me a little way on the path to the village of Sorry. "So it was Sensei's good-bye koan, was it? His tail had definitely tripped him up, broken his career as a teacher, and he wasn't going to waste any more of our time and effort? Or of his?"

"Possibly," I said.

"You don't know for sure?"

I said I had made it up. I know nothing for sure. I wished him Bless Buddha. He turned back. It had started snowing heavily again.*

---

*"The Good-bye Koan" is chapter one of my new book, Afterzen, third of a trilogy, following The Empty Mirror (experiences in a Japanese Zen monastery) and A Glimpse of Nothingness (experiences in an American Zen community). As with the other books, the characters are composites or have been made up altogether, the settings and times are changed, and nothing, most likely, happened the way I thought it happened.

TERRY TEMPEST WILLIAMS

Listening Days
from Parabola

"It's the hardest thing I've ever had to do," says my grandfather Jack. "But everyone goes through it." He shrugs his shoulders and lifts his eyebrows. "If you sit here long enough eventually you leave with a philosophy."

Now, after many months of frailty, my grandfather has stopped eating. Call it the hunger strike of the elderly, their last act of control. He waits. We wait. The days slowly pass in autumn.

"I am a falling leaf on our family tree," he tells my cousin and me, his veined hand swaying back-and-forth in a downward motion.

We savor his words, desperate to know something of his ninety-one years. My grandfather is not a verbal man. He prefers listening, his blue eyes steady.

In 1923, J. H. Tempest, Jr., received his amateur radio operator's license. W7JOE has been his call name for almost seventy-five years. He was the youngest "ham" in Utah, and now he is the oldest. When we were growing up in our grandparents' home, Jack was always in his room sitting in the swayback chair tucked between his radios, listening. He was dwarfed by the huge machines. The static, the Martianlike voices speaking from the metal boxes day and night, taught us that there was a larger world outside, a world we didn't have access to but our grandfather did.

His conversations on air required no eye contact, only a turn of hand, fingers manipulating dials, scanning voices until a tone or an idea stopped him. He would roll the black dial back and forth, sharpening the frequency until the band was clear. Then he would listen. He would enter in when he wanted to and leave when he was no longer interested.

I use the past tense because Jack has stopped listening to his radio. My grandmother always told us that when Jack quit his radio he would be dead.

Jack is not dead.

Our grandfather is breathing. We sit in his bedroom, my cousin and I, noting the rise and fall of his chest beneath the down comforter. His eyes are open, staring at the ceiling.

"What are you thinking, Jack?" I ask as I rub his arm, which is more bone than muscle.

"I'm not thinking, period. I'm a blank."

"So you're just existing?"

"That's right. I don't want to think." He takes his hand, makes a straight line in the air. "I'm flat."

He is flat in bed.

He turns to us. "You wouldn't be asking me these questions if you were facing what I am. You'd choose to be a blank too. If you think too much you can make yourself crazy."

"Zen masters spend a lifetime striving for an empty mind," I say, smiling.

He lies in bed like a corpse with his mouth open. My cousin leaves to return to her new baby boy. I close my eyes and listen to Jack's breaths. They have a steady underground surge, like a tranquil sea.

While he sleeps, I sit nearby reading *Krishnamurti's Journal*, one of my grandmother's books. In the late sixties, Jack accompanied her to Ojai to hear Krishnamurti speak. I am struck by a particular passage:

> *To be full of knowledge breeds endless misery. The demand for expression, with its frustrations and pains, is that man who*

walks. . . . Sorrow is the movement of that loneliness. . . .
September 15, 1973 . . . It was a marvelous morning and you
could have walked on endlessly, never feeling the steep hills.
There was a perfume in the air, clear and strong. There was no
one on that path, coming down or going up. You were alone
with those dark pines and the rushing waters. . . . There was no
one to talk to and there was no chattering of the mind. A mag-
pie, white and black, flew by, disappearing into the woods. The
path led away from the noisy stream and the silence was
absolute. It wasn't the silence after the noise; it wasn't the silence
that comes with the setting of the sun, nor that silence when the
mind dies down. It wasn't the silence of museums and churches
but something totally unrelated to time and space. . . . On these
walks, with people or without them, any movement of thought
was absent. This is to be alone.[1]

It is another day. "How are you this afternoon, Jack?" I ask, taking off my jacket and pulling up a chair alongside his bed.

"Here," he replies.

He wants to know what the weather is outside, what day of the
week it is, and if my husband is in town.

I tell him it is a glorious blue sky, a bit chilly, quintessential
October, and that the temperature dropped below freezing last night.

"It's Thursday, Jack, and yes, Brooke is in town."

"Good," he says, closing his eyes.

We sit comfortably with the silence.

"Did you know the average person blinks eighteen to twenty
times a minute?" Jack says suddenly.

"No, I didn't."

"And that a person who is working at a computer only blinks
four to five times a minute. What's that going to do to our eye-

sight?" he asks. "It seems to me, eventually you're going to strain something."

I look at my grandfather who is lying on his back in bed staring at the ceiling. He rarely blinks at all in these last days of his life. It makes sense to me that his mind, as agile as it has always been, would be contemplating the effects of technology.

"Where did you hear those statistics?" I ask.

"On the air," he says, "awhile back."

More silence.

"Something's not right."

"What do you mean?" I ask.

"I mean all this fuss about information on the Internet. We're losing primary contact with each other. No more rubbing shoulders. No more shaking hands. We've got to have human contact and we're doing away with it. Everyone is so busy. We want too much, and in the process of getting it we miss so much." He pauses. "It's lonely." He turns his head on the pillow and looks at me. "I just want to hear your voices."

I think of all the voices on the radio he has spent a lifetime listening to, and the silence that must be enveloping him now without his "rig."

"Jack, how did you become interested in radio?"

"I don't know," he says. "It was another way to reach people. I was always interested in striving for a better signal, a cleaner, crisper, more powerful signal that could communicate with someone somewhere, anywhere."

He pauses.

"I spend a lot of time wondering."

"Wondering?"

"Wondering about sound waves, how electronic waves keep moving outward until they become fainter and fainter, wearing themselves out until they are overcome by something else.

Someday equipment will be able to pick these sound waves up. Nothing is ever lost. The sound is still there. We just can't hear it."

"Hmmm . . . " I say, shaking my head.

Another silence follows us.

"And I'll tell you another funny thing: you can electronically eliminate all manner of noise on the air—man-made noise—but you can't get rid of natural static, static or interference caused by thunder and lightning, rainstorms, or snowstorms. Ham radio operators always pay attention to weather—light, too. In the day, radio bands expand way out. At night they contract, shut down. You see that the sun pulls the signals out while sunspots can cause blackouts altogether. So you wonder about these things."

He closes his eyes and smiles.

"What?" I ask.

"I was just thinking that in spite of all our technologies, maybe we haven't progressed that far as human beings. We still have the same fundamental needs. Sometimes I wonder if we have evolved at all."

I sit by him for another hour or so, kiss his forehead, and drive home.

To wonder. To contemplate that which is never lost but continues to move outward forever, however faint, until it is overcome by something else.

To wonder. To throw pebbles in pools and watch the concentric circles that reach the shore in waves. Waves of water. Waves of electricity. Illumination. Imagination. To say "I love you" one day and shout with rage on another. Our words are still moving, churning; this sea of spoken languages oscillates around us.

What do we hear?

Harold Shapero writes in *The Musical Mind* that "a great percentage of what is heard becomes submerged in the unconscious and is subject to literal recall."

If we in fact have a "tonal memory," what do the voices of our ancestors, our elders have to say to us now? What sounds do we hold in our bodies and retrieve when necessary? What sounds disturb and what sounds heal? Where do we store the tension of traffic, honking horns, or the hum of fluorescent lights? How do we receive birdsong, the leg rubbings of crickets, the water music of trout?

What do we know?

I wonder. To wonder takes time. I walk in the hills behind our home. The leaves have fallen, leaf litter, perfect for the shuffling of towhees. The supple grasses of summer have become knee-high rattles. Ridge winds shake the tiny seedheads like gourds. I hear my grandfather's voice.

All sound requires patience; not just the ability to hear, but the capacity to listen, the awareness of mind to discern a story. A magpie flies toward me and disappears in the oak thicket. He is relentless in his cries. What does he know that I do not? What story is he telling? I love these birds, their long iridescent tail feathers, their undulations in flight. Two more magpies join him. I sit on a flat boulder to rest, pick up two stones, and begin striking edges.

What I know in my bones is that I forget to take time to remember what I know. The world is holy. We are holy. All life is holy. Daily prayers are delivered on the lips of breaking waves, the whisperings of grasses, the shimmering of leaves. We are animals, living, breathing organisms engaged not only in our own evolution but the evolution of a species that has been gifted with nascence. Nascence—to come into existence; to be born; to bring forth; the process of emerging.

Even in death we are being born. And it takes time.

I think about my grandfather, his desire for voices, to be held as he dies in the comfort of conversation. Even if he rarely contributes to what is being said, his mind finds its own calm. To him this is a form of music that allows him to remember he is not alone in the world. Our evolution is the story of listening.

In the evening by firelight in their caves and rock shelters, the Neanderthals sometimes relaxed to the sound of music after a hard day at the hunt. They took material at hand, a cave bear's thigh bone, and created a flute. With such a simple instrument, these stocky, heavy-browed Neanderthals, extinct close relatives of humans, may have given expression to the fears, longings, and joys of their prehistoric lives. (John Noble Wilford, "Playing of Flute May Have Graced Neanderthal Fire," New York Times)

A bone flutelike object was found at Divje Babe in northwestern Slovenia recently, dated somewhere between forty-three thousand and eighty-two thousand years old. Dr. Ivan Turk, a paleontologist at the Slovenian Academy of Sciences in Ljubjana, believes this is the first musical instrument ever to be associated with Neanderthals. It is a piece of bear femur with four holes in a straight alignment. Researchers say the bone flute may be the oldest known musical instrument.

I wonder about that cave, the fire that flickered and faded on damp walls as someone in the clan played a flute. Were they a family? Neighbors? What were their dreams and inventions? Did they know the long line of human beings that would follow their impulses to survive, even flourish in moments of reverie?

Returning to my grandparents' home, I notice the fifty-foot antenna that rises over the roof. I recall Jack telling us as children how important it was for the antenna to be grounded in the earth, that as long as it was securely placed it could radiate signals into the air all over the world. Transmit and receive. I walk into his dim room and place my hand on my grandfather's leg. Bone. Nothing lost. Overcome by something else. Ways of knowing. My fingers wrap around bone and I feel his life blowing through him.

John H. Tempest, Jr., passed away on December 15, 1996, peacefully at home in the company of family.

ENDNOTE

1.   J. Krishnamurti, *Krishnamurti's Journal* (San Francisco: Harper & Row, 1982).

Biographical Notes

DICK ALLEN'S fifth book of poetry, *Ode to the Cold War: Poems New and Selected*, was published in 1997. His poems are included in recent volumes of *The Best American Poetry*. He has published in *The New Yorker, The Atlantic Monthly, American Poetry Review, The Kenyon Review, Poetry*, and many other leading magazines. He directs creative writing at the University of Bridgeport, where he is also the Charles A. Dana Lifetime Endowed Chair Professor of English.

MARVIN BARRETT has been a member of the editorial staffs of *Time, Newsweek, Show, Atlas*, and *Parabola*, and of the faculty of the Columbia Graduate School of Journalism from 1968 to 1984. His fifteen books include *The Years Between, The End of the Party*, the award-winning *Moments of Truth?, Spare Days*, and the forthcoming *Second Chance: A Life After Death*. He is married to the writer Mary Ellin Barrett and lives in New York City. They have four children and five grandchildren.

RICK BASS is the author of *Where the Sea Used to Be, The Sky, the Stars, the Wilderness; The Book of Yaak, In the Loyal Mountains, The Lost Grizzlies, Winter*, and other books.

JOSEPH BRUCHAC is a writer and storyteller whose work frequently draws on his Abenaki ancestry. The founder of the Greenfield Review Press, his most recent books include *Arrow over the Door* and *Lasting Echoes*.

SCOTT CAIRNS'S poems have appeared in *The Atlantic Monthly, The Paris Review, The New Republic*, and *Image*. His poetry collections include *Figures for the Ghost* (1994), *The Translation of Babel* (1990), and *The Theology of Doubt* (1985). With W. Scott Olsen, he co-edited *The Sacred Place* (1996), an anthology of poetry and prose. His most recent collection of poems is *Recovered Body*. He is series editor of the Vassar Miller Prize in Poetry and teaches at Old Dominion University.

LÉONIE CALDECOTT, a writer specializing in religion, has contributed to numerous publications on both sides of the Atlantic, including The *New York Times Book Review, The Village Voice, New Age Journal,* and

The Chesterton Review. She has received the Catherine Pakenham Award for young female journalists. She is a consulting editor for the theological journal *Communio* and co-edits *Second Spring*, a cultural supplement to *The Catholic World Report*. She lives in Oxford with her husband and three daughters.

STEPHEN V. DOUGHTY served for twenty-three years as a parish pastor and is currently executive presbyter for the Presbytery of Lake Michigan, providing pastoral and administrative support for its seventy-two congregations. A regular contributor to *Weavings* and other publications, he recently completed a book, *Discovering Community*, which will be published in the spring of 1999.

ANDRE DUBUS has published eight books of fiction. "Love in the Morning" is from his second book of essays, *Meditations from a Movable Chair*. He has six children and five grandchildren and lives in Haverhill, Massachusetts, where he is working on a book of stories.

GRETEL EHRLICH is the author of *Questions of Heaven: The Chinese Journeys of an American Buddhist, A Match to the Heart, Islands, the Universe; Home, The Solace of Open Spaces,* and other works.

JOSEPH EPSTEIN writes for *The New Yorker, Commentary, The Hudson Review,* and *The London Times Literary Supplement*. He is the author, most recently, of *Life Sentences*, a book of literary essays, and the editor of *The Norton Book of Personal Essays*.

RICK FIELDS is the author of *How the Swans Came to the Lake: A Narrative History of Buddhism in America, The Code of the Warrior,* and other books; editor of *The Awakened Warrior;* principal co-author of *Chop Wood, Carry Water;* and co-author of *The Turquoise Bee: Love Poems of the Sixth Dalai Lama* and *Instructions to the Cook*. His most recent book is *Fuck You Cancer, and Other Poems*. He is editor-in-chief of *Yoga Journal* and a contributing editor of *Tricycle*.

FREDERICK FRANCK is the author of twenty-seven books, including the classic *The Zen of Seeing: Seeing/Drawing as Meditation*. His drawings and paintings are in the permanent collections of a score of museums in the United States, Europe, and Japan. His sculptures stand in public places in the United States, Argentina, Holland, Belgium, Bosnia, and Japan. He lives with his wife, Claske, in Warwick, New York, where they have restored an eighteenth-century ruin of a grist mill into an "oasis of inwardness," Pacem in Terris. In 1994 he was knighted by Queen Beatrix of the Netherlands.

RABBI MARC GELLMAN is the senior rabbi of Temple Beth Torah in Melville, New York. He is the author of *Does God Have a Big Toe: Stories About Stories in the Bible, God's Mailbox: More Stories About Stories in the Bible,* and *Always Wear Clean Underwear and Other Ways Your Parents Tell You They Love You.* With his friend Monsignor Thomas Hartman, he has also written *Where Does God Live? Questions and Answers for Parents and Children* and *How Do You Spell God? Answers to the Big Questions from Around the World,* which was made into an HBO children's special that won the George Foster Peabody Award as well as an Emmy Award as the best children's television program of 1997.

NATALIE GOLDBERG is the author of several books, including *Writing Down the Bones, Long Quiet Highway,* and *Living Colors.* She lives in northern New Mexico and teaches workshops on writing and Zen meditation.

PATRICIA HAMPL'S books include *A Romantic Education* and *Virgin Time,* a memoir about her Catholic upbringing and an inquiry into contemplative life. Her latest book, *I Could Tell You Stories: Essays on Memory and Imagination,* will be published in 1999. She was a 1990 MacArthur Fellow and is Regents' Professor of English at the University of Minnesota.

EDWARD HIRSCH'S fifth book of poems, *On Love,* was published in June. His book on reading poetry, *Message in a Bottle,* will be published in April 1999. He teaches at the University of Houston.

RODGER KAMENETZ'S most recent books of poetry are *The Missing Jew* and *Stuck.* His nonfiction books are *The Jew in the Lotus* and *Stalking Elijah,* which won the 1997 National Jewish Book Award for Jewish Thought. His next book will be *Terra Infirma: A Memoir of My Mother's Life in Mine.* He lives in New Orleans.

ANNE LAMOTT is the author of *Bird by Bird: Some Instructions on Writing and Life, Operating Instructions: A Journal of My Son's First Year, Crooked Little Heart, Rosie, All New People,* and other books.

MADELEINE L'ENGLE has written approximately forty books, including *A Wrinkle in Time,* which won the Newberry Prize, and, most recently, *Bright Evening Star.* She recently received the Margaret Edwards Award from the American Library Association for lifetime achievement in writing for young adults.

PHILIP LEVINE'S book *The Simple Truth* won the Pulitzer Prize for poetry in 1995. In 1991, *What Work Is* brought him his second National Book

Award. His seventeenth book of poems, *The Mercy*, will appear in April 1999. He grew up in Detroit and now lives half the time in Fresno, California.

Barry Lopez is the author of four works of nonfiction, including *Arctic Dreams* and *Of Wolves and Men;* seven works of fiction, including *Field Notes* and *Winter Count;* and a novella-length fable, *Crow and Weasel*. His work appears regularly in *Harper's,* where he is contributing editor, as well as in *The Paris Review, Orion,* and *The Georgia Review.* The recipient of numerous literary awards, including the National Book Award for nonfiction, he lives in western Oregon. His most recent work is *About This Life,* a memoir.

Nancy Mairs, an essayist and research associate with the Southwest Institute for Research on Women, has written several books, most recently *Voice Lessons: On Becoming a (Woman) Writer* and *Waist-High in the World: A Life Among the Nondisabled.* She and her husband, George, live in Tucson, Arizona.

Frederica Mathewes-Green is a columnist for *Christianity Today.* She is also a regular commentator on National Public Radio's "All Things Considered" and the Odyssey Television Network's "News Odyssey." She is the author of *Facing East: A Pilgrim's Journey into the Mysteries of Orthodoxy.*

William Meredith's many awards include the Pulitzer Prize for poetry and the 1997 National Book Award for *Effort at Speech.* The judges' citation for *Effort at Speech* affirms that "His example shows us the truth in his line: 'the bright watchers are still there.'"

Rick Moody is the author of *Garden State, Purple America, The Ice Storm,* and other writings and co-editor of *Joyful Noise: The New Testament Revisited.*

Thomas Moore is the author of the best-selling *Care of the Soul, SoulMates, The Re-enchantment of Everyday Life, On the Monk Who Lives in Daily Life,* and many other books. He has also produced several audiotapes, videotapes, and the compact discs *Music for the Soul* and *The Soul of Christmas.* He lives in New England with his wife, Joan Hanley, his daughter, Siobhan, and his stepson, Abraham.

Noelle Oxenhandler's essays have appeared in *The New Yorker, The New York Times Magazine, Tricycle, Parabola,* and elsewhere. She lives in northern California.

CYNTHIA OZICK is the author of essays, short stories, novels, and a play. Her most recent collection of essays is *Fame and Folly;* her most recent novel is *The Puttermesser Papers.* She is guest editor of *Best American Essays 1998.*

KIMBERLEY C. PATTON is assistant professor in the Comparative and Historical Study of Religion at Harvard Divinity School. Most recently, she is co-editor and contributing author to *A Magic Still Dwells: Comparative Religion in a Post-Modern Age.* She is also the author of two forthcoming books, *The Religion of the Gods: Divine Reflexivity in Comparative Context* and *The Sea Can Wash Away All Evils: Modern Marine Pollution and the Ancient Cathartic Ocean.* She is married to Bruce N. Beck and has one child, Christina Eleanor Beck.

REYNOLDS PRICE is James B. Duke Professor of English at Duke University. A former Rhodes Scholar, his awards include the William Faulkner Award and the National Book Critics Circle Award. He is the author of more than two dozen books; his works include novels, poetry, plays, essays, translations, and memoirs.

FRANCINE PROSE is the author of nine novels, two story collections, and most recently a collection of novellas, *Guided Tours of Hell.* Her stories and essays have appeared in *The Atlantic Monthly, Harper's, The New York Times, The New York Observer,* and other publications. She has won Guggenheim and Fulbright fellowships, two NEA grants, and a PEN translation prize. A film based on her novel *Household Saints* was released in 1993.

PHYLLIS ROSE is professor of English at Wesleyan University in Middletown, Connecticut. Her most recent book is *The Year of Reading Proust: A Memoir.*

LAWRENCE SHAINBERG is the author of two novels, *One on One* and *Memories of Amnesia,* a nonfiction work, *Brain Surgeon: An Intimate View of His World,* and the recently published memoir, *Ambivalent Zen.*

LUCI SHAW is the author of seven books of poetry, most recently *Writing the River,* as well as memoirs and essays. Her poems have appeared in many magazines and journals. Writer-in-residence at Regent College, Vancouver, Canada, she teaches creative writing on college campuses and in church settings in North America and abroad. She lives in the Pacific Northwest, next to a mountain stream, because she writes best to the sound of running water.

HUSTON SMITH is Thomas J. Watson Professor of Religion and Distinguished Adjunct Professor of Philosophy, Emeritus, Syracuse University. For fifteen years he was professor of philosophy at M.I.T. and for a decade before that he taught at Washington University in Saint Louis. Most recently, he has served as visiting professor of religious studies, University of California, Berkeley. His eight books include *The World's Religions, The Illustrated World's Religions, Forgotten Truth, Beyond the Post-Modern Mind,* and *One Nation Under God: The Triumph of the Native American Church.*

DAVID STEINDL-RAST is a Benedictine monk, a member of Mount Saviour Monastery in upstate New York. He is a renowned speaker on the subject of prayer and spirituality and the author of many books, including *Gratefulness: The Heart of Prayer.*

PTOLEMY TOMPKINS was born in Washington, D.C., and was educated at Sarah Lawrence College. He is the author of several works of nonfiction, including *This Tree Grows Out of Hell,* a study of Mesoamerican myth and ritual, and *Paradise Fever,* a memoir. He lives in New York City with his wife and stepdaughter.

JANWILLEM VAN DE WETERING was born in the Netherlands and worked, studied, and traveled in Europe, Australia, South America, and Africa until he settled in 1975 on the coast of Maine. He reported on his Zen practice in *The Empty Mirror* and *A Glimpse of Nothingness,* about to be reprinted, together with his final Buddhist autobiographical essay, *Afterzen.* His service with the Amsterdam police inspired the ongoing "Dutch Cops" series, the latest of which is *The Pernicious Parrot.*

TERRY TEMPEST WILLIAMS'S books include *Desert Quartet, An Unspoken Hunger: Stories from the Field, Refuge: An Unnatural History of Family and Place,* and *Pieces of White Shell: A Journey to Navajoland.*

PHILIP ZALESKI'S books include *The Recollected Heart: A Monastic Retreat, Gifts of the Spirit* (with Paul Kaufman), and the forthcoming *The Oxford Book of Heaven* (with Carol Zaleski). His writings have appeared in *The New York Times, First Things, The Village Voice, Tricycle,* and many other periodicals. He is senior editor of *Parabola* and teaches religion at Smith College and literature at Wesleyan University. He lives in western Massachusetts with his wife, Carol, and his sons, John and Andrew.

Notable Spiritual Writing of 1997

A. J. BACEVICH
"Memoirs of a Catholic Boyhood," *First Things,* December.

CHRISTOPHER BAMFORD
"Burnished Gold," *Parabola,* Summer.

KRISTIN BARENDSEN
"Pilgrimage to Plum Village," *Yoga Journal,* October.

STEPHEN BATCHELOR AND ROBERT A. F. THURMAN
"Reincarnation: A Debate," *Tricycle,* Summer.

JOHN BERGER
"Nudging the Rock," *DoubleTake,* Summer.

GEORGE BERNANOS
"Sermon of an Agnostic on the Feast of St. Thérèse" (translated by
    Pamela Morris and David Schindler, Jr.), *Communio,* Fall.

VARDA BRANFMAN
"Some Extra Mothering," *Wellsprings,* Spring.

ROSEMARY BRAY
"A Voice in the Wilderness," *The New York Times Magazine,* December 7.

RAFAEL CAMPO
"Like a Prayer," *DoubleTake,* Winter.

JOSEPH CARY
"Believing," *Parabola,* Winter.

EDWARD IDRIS CASSIDY
"That They May All Be One," *First Things,* January.

TRACY COCHRAN
"The Pentagon Meditation Club," *Tricycle,* Summer.

PETER CUNNINGHAM
"Bearing Witness," *Tricycle,* Spring.

Christopher de Vinck
"Zuzu's Petals," *The Convenant Companion*, December.

Gai Eaton
"The Earth's Complaint," *Sophia*, Summer.

Carolyn Foote Edelmann
"Mysteries of St. Nectan's Glen," *Fellowship in Prayer*, February.

Eileen M. Egan
"Blessed Are the Merciful," *America*, September 20.

Sam Fentress
"Signs of the Kingdom," *Image*, Summer.

Alison Granucci
"Shot into Life," *ReVision*, Fall.

Kristen Halverson
"It Is Well with My Soul," *Spiritual Life*, Fall.

Wayne Harrel
"Song of the Bow," *Image*, Fall.

Barbara Grizzuti Harrison
"Alone in a Lofty Place," *The New York Times Magazine*, December 7.

Richard J. Hauser
"Give Comfort to My People," *America*, November 29.

Bill Hayes
"Deaf Church," *DoubleTake*, Winter.

Richard B. Hays
"Salvation by Trust? Reading the Bible Faithfully," *Christian Century*,
    February 26.

W. Paul Jones
"Courage as the Heart of Faith," *Weavings*, May/June.

Biret Maret Kallio
"Noaidi: The One Who Sees," *ReVision*, Winter.

David Michael Kaplan
"Resurrection," *DoubleTake*, Summer.

Richard Lewis
"Living by Wonder," *Parabola*, Spring.

ROGER LIPSEY
"Just the Mind at Work," *Parabola*, Spring.

MARK MATOUSEK
"Sacred Blather," *Common Boundary*, March/April.

DANIEL PAWLEY
"The Diary of an Immigrant," *Books and Culture*, March/April.

WILLIAM REISER, S.J.
"It Is Good for Me to Be Here," *Praying*, January/February.

JONATHAN SACKS
"Love, Hate, and Jewish Identity," *First Things*, November.

SCOTT RUSSELL SANDERS
"Wildness," *Orion*, Summer.

TOM SLEIGH
"The Incurables," *DoubleTake*, Summer.

JOHN SUITER
"Desolation Revisited," *Shambhala Sun*, March.

DAN WAKEFIELD
"Spiritual Impact: Encounters with Henri Nouwen," *Christian Century*,
    March 19–26.

WALTER WANGERIN
"Getting God's Name Right," *Books and Culture*, January/February.

TIM WINTER
"The Saint with the Seven Tombs," *Parabola*, Fall.

PHILIP YANCEY
"The Reverend of Oz," *Books and Culture*, March/April.

MARK AND LOUISE ZWICK
"Dorothy Day and the Catholic Worker Movement," *Communio*, Fall.

Credits